Shakespeare's
Theater of Presence

Title page drawing, "Presence," by Hernán Vera.

Shakespeare's
Theater
of Presence

Language, Spectacle, and the Audience

Sidney Homan

Lewisburg
Bucknell University Press
London and Toronto: Associated University Presses

© 1986 by Associated University Presses, Inc.

Associated University Presses
440 Forsgate Drive
Cranbury, NJ 08512

Associated University Presses
25 Sicilian Avenue
London WC1A 2QH, England

Associated University Presses
2133 Royal Windsor Drive
Unit 1
Mississauga, Ontario
Canada L5J 1K5

Library of Congress Cataloging-in-Publication Data

Homan, Sidney, 1938–
  Shakespeare's theater of presence.

  Bibliography: p.
  Includes index.
  1. Shakespeare, William, 1564–1616—Dramatic production.   2. Shakespeare, William, 1564–1616—Criticism and interpretation.   I. Title.
  PR3091.H6   1986   822.3′3   85-48170
  ISBN 0-8387-5105-9 (alk. paper)

Printed in the United States of America

To my beloved Gertrude and Marvin,
and their precious niece Norma

Also by SIDNEY HOMAN:

Ed., *A Midsummer Night's Dream.* Blackfriars Shakespeare Series (1970)
Ed., *Shakespeare's "More Than Words Can Witness": Essays on Visual and Nonverbal Enactment in the Plays* (1980)
When the Theater Turns to Itself: The Aesthetic Metaphor in Shakespeare (1981)
Beckett's Theaters: Interpretations for Performance (1984)

Contents

Preface
On a Book's Title

i

In *Shakespeare's Theater of Presence: Language, Spectacle, and the Audience* I am concerned with what the theater is *about*, and I purposely wrench the grammar of this opening sentence to underscore that operative word *about*. I mean *about* in two ways. First, I use it in the sense we imply when we say, "Is your mother about the house?" or, when coming upon someone in the midst of a project, "What are you about?" That is, at issue here is what "happens" during a performance, what is *about* when onstage characters, impersonated by actors whose role it is to sustain the illusion, are joined by an offstage audience, the receptors, indeed those whose presence ratifies that same illusion. I also use *about* in the looser sense of *consisting of, made from.*

The main title anticipates the first usage, recognizing that the play takes place in space and time, that its "presence" is meant to be public and communal, that what it is *about* is determined by those complementary "presences" onstage and off. To be sure, the commentary in this book is after the fact, after that *fact* of those complementary presences; it cannot be otherwise, unless one would want to interrupt an ongoing performance with an analysis of the onstage happenings. Rather, my subsequent commentary "recreates" an ideal performance, ultimately *my* ideal performance, and thereby treats what *might* happen, not during a single performance but potentially during *any* performance of the play in question. In this way, the first use of *about* distinguishes my approach here—or what might be called "performance criticism"—from, say, thematic or psychological or historical approaches that would surely take *about* in a third sense, as implying the subject matter of the play, or the real-life men and women imitated by actors, or the contribution the play makes to our understanding of the prevailing philosophical assumptions of Shakespeare's day.

The subtitle looks back to the second meaning of *about*, the material from which and *on* which the dramatic presence is built. Onstage those "materials" are clearly language and spectacle, and by the latter I mean

9

the physical presence of actors, props, and sets, as well as the stage itself, and, in the largest sense, the interactions among all four. Offstage that material is the audience, those fellow humans watching and listening to fellow humans pretending to be other than they really are. We recognize, of course, that what distinguishes theater from other media is the co-presence of its language and spectacle, the verbal and visual dimensions of the production. Without its language, a play would only be a *spectacle* in the most limited sense of the word; robbed of that meaning conferred by language, such an experience would resemble that of standing behind a thick pane of glass blotting out all sound, let alone conversation, and watching, say, a crowd waiting for a train to arrive. Of course, we could elevate such spectacle to the level of a primitive theater, yet only by bestowing thoughts, even imaginary dialogue on the people we saw but could not hear. Conversely, without its spectacle, a play ceases to be a piece for the theater and is more akin to radio or poetry. While a public reading of a poem can be "dramatic," the poem thus delivered is clearly not "drama." We individually convert radio into something approaching the legitimate theater only by filling its language with a scenario "seen" by, but also confined to the listener. By definition, however, the theater is a public event and, again, one ratified by the co-presence of actor and audience. As I like to remind my own Theater majors, actors performing onstage to an empty house are not in a play but only in rehearsal; and a crowd in an auditorium watching an empty stage is only a crowd in an auditorium watching . . . and not a theatrical audience whose presence is justified by their reception and interpretation of the stage's language and spectacle.

The four terms as used above—presence, language, spectacle, and audience—are thus rooted in the actual, in what is present at a perform-ance, for even the playwright's language is dependent on the actor's voice and on the audience's ear. Nor is stage language ever totally abstract; it is, more properly, metaphysical, chained to, influencing, and influenced by the stage's ongoing visual tableaux. In radio the actors, metaphorically speaking, face away from us, yet, excluding exits and regroupings for the next stage of its blocking, a play in the theater demands that actors face the audience, even if only in profile. We demand that the speaking be *seen*.

My method, in part, is therefore performance criticism. In no less equal part it has a metadramatic orientation, since it is the play's or, more properly, the playwright's own consciousness of the medium, built as it is on language and spectacle, that justifies my concern with the stage's verbal and visual dimensions. My argument here, in this post-McLuhan age, is that this particular medium is inseparable from its message. The pervasive references in the text to speech and sight, language and

spectacle, the verbal and the visual, are thus at one with the fact that
actors both speak and move and are in turn heard and seen by the
audience. The "tools" of the playwright influence, determine, *are* the
message: metadramatics is thereby thematics seen initially from the
outside. We expect the speech of a sailor to be sprinkled with nautical
metaphors, or a weightlifter's occupation to affect the way he appears
physically. No less happens to the playwright: his or her world view, as
enacted onstage, is shaped by a profession based on a verbal-visual
illusion sustained by actor and audience.

I have used *about* in three ways; allow me to add a fourth, though it is
close to the first use of *about* (in the sense of a present happening).
Whatever a play's theme—what it is *about* in the third sense in which I
have used the word—it is also about itself, conscious of itself, even as an
audience, however enveloped in the stage illusion, never confuses the
theater with reality. In fact, half of the pleasure we take in a good
performance is precisely that: our awareness that it *is* a performance,
that we are seeing an illusory "life" enacted through a medium, an
artifice. Conversely, no actor ever loses himself or herself so deeply in a
character that the role is confused with reality: if this did happen the
character would forget an assigned part, the dialogue, and be forced to
improvise.

At the conclusion of Leoncavallo's opera *Pagliacci,* when Pagliacci playing a husband in the play-within-the-play uses his role as a guise to
murder his adulterous wife and her lover, who are also replaying their
"real-life" roles in that same inner play, we encounter a moment when
reality breaks the artifice. Still, this violent "reality" is itself only an
illusion. Nor—to extrapolate from the argument here—if we could find
a real-life triangle of lovers to play the three parts, would we expect the
husband to follow Pagliacci's example. If by some absurd chance he did,
thereby taking his cue from the character just as Pagliacci takes a cue
from the character he impersonates, we surely would not expect his
words, as he murders the couple, to duplicate those of the libretto.

From this metadramatic perspective the same play, built on language
and spectacle and requiring that an audience be present to hear and see
the stage illusion, is no less *about* language and spectacle and hence is also
about itself. Portraying life through the theater also involves "reading" or
seeing life as a play, and I invoke here the Renaissance's own equation: all
the world's a stage and the stage is a little world, or a little O, as
Shakespeare calls it. Metadramatic criticism is thus the theoretical or
aesthetic complement to its more practical cousin in performance criticism. When I speak in the following pages of our "experience" *with the
play,* I also speak complementarily of our experience *with play,* with the
theater. Allow me to "flesh out" this abstract in three ways: a brief history

of how, for me, this dualistic approach developed (and here I will ask the reader's indulgence as I speak of two earlier studies—poor, but my own); two plays of our century—safely removed from Shakespeare's more complex example—that self-reflexively and graphically demonstrate the four terms that constitute the book's main and subtitles; and, at last, a road map of the nine chapters following the preface.

ii

In a sense I have backed into the present position, moving from a more "theoretical" metadramatic to a more "practical" performance criticism. In my *When the Theater Turns to Itself* (Bucknell University Press, 1981) the overriding issue was the theater itself as a controlling metaphor in the "worlds" of Shakespeare's plays, a metaphor grounded in the text, in the sort of self-reflexive theatrical images that Anne Barton has charted in *Shakespeare and the Idea of the Play*.[1] With such a "ground," I devised a three-stage critical narrative. Its first stage treated the conversion of Sly from a drunkard into an aristocratic spectator and Kate from an unpromising shrew to a co-partner in Petruchio's scenario, Shakespeare's own wrestling with an appropriate language for the stage in *Love's Labor's Lost,* and the positive and then negative portraits of the playwright in *A Midsummer Night's Dream* and *Othello*. Stage two involved controlling figures, surrogates for the playwright and hence commentaries on his power to influence reality; here I examined Rosalind, Duke Vincentio, and Hamlet. In stage three I considered Shakespeare's own divided attitude toward the theater, first in the character of Cleopatra and then in Prospero. In addition, *The Tempest,* for me, involved the significance of our release from the stage's artifice, even as *The Taming of the Shrew* served as an induction to that theatrical experience.

This thematic study shared the stage with an attempt to understand the medium as practiced by Shakespeare, and here I was and continue to be influenced by the writings of scholars like James Calderwood, especially in his *Shakespearean Metadrama* and, more recently, in *To Be and Not To Be: Negation and Metadrama in "Hamlet."*[2] Thus, *When the Theater* also treated the interface between the world offstage and onstage, the ways in which the theater offers what Murray Krieger would call both a "window" to reality, illuminating even as it alters our perception of the world offstage, and a "mirror" world, operating on its own principles, to a degree autonomous, and—given my own emphasis—ultimately constructed of metaphors based not on some offstage reality but on the materials of the theater itself: the playwright's craft, the art of the actor, the theater as both a literal and a figurative entity, and the presence and function of the audience.[3] My argument in *When the Theater Turns to Itself*

was that such aesthetic, or theatrical metaphors—as when the boy playing Cleopatra fears a Roman stage spectacle in which some "squeaking
Cleopatra" will "boy" her greatness—are the ultimate vehicle by which
Shakespeare not only establishes his stage worlds but also comments on
his art and, by extension, on the relation between that artifice and the
macrocosm it is designed to mirror. Since the audience witnesses such
metaphors during production, even as it constitutes part of the basic
theatrical metaphor itself, this self-reflexive imagery, I maintained, was
also the most immediate, the most powerful, and—because it emerges
from that collaboration of author, actor, and audience—the most democratic. *When the Theater* thereby embodies a philosophy of the medium,
though I was not arguing that audiences would be aware of this metadramatic dimension. Quite the contrary; they are unaware, since they are
part of its larger metaphor. Thus the "worlds" that I defined in the nine
plays discussed in that first book are recognizable only after the fact, and
I must conclude that I had placed a theory in advance of that actual
experience which had served as its basis.

Between that book and the present one there intervened a long
involvement with the theater of Samuel Beckett. If *When the Theater* was
part of a conscious design, emerging from my early speculations in an
article of the same title and then from a series of "explorations" in
subsequent pieces that would be redone into the book,[4] my *Beckett's
Theaters: Interpretations for Performance* came almost by chance. The War-
den of Florida's State Prison, this state's maximum security prison, invited a company with which I had been associated to bring there a
production of *Waiting for Godot*. I did not know at the time of the
invitation that, after the first American production of *Godot* had failed
before tourists at the Coconut Grove Playhouse in Miami and then
before would-be intellectuals in New York, the Actor's Workshop produced the play, with great success, at San Quentin. Our entire company
was overwhelmed at the inmates' response; during our production, and
then at similar productions at Florida's nine other state prisons, they
insisted on breaking the barrier between the "world" onstage and the
audience. In so doing, they would productively interrupt the performance by talking to the actors onstage, questioning them as if they were
real people, commenting on dialogue just delivered, asking the actors
still in character to explain this point or to reconsider that point. It was
an exhilarating experience, clearly at one with the simple fact that men
waiting were watching a play about men waiting. It led to my putting
Shakespeare aside for a spell and, over the next six years, throwing
myself into Beckett, with the help of my students, who were acting in
and directing all of his plays.

Beckett's Theaters came from this involvement, and yet I thought, in my conscious mind, that I was here applying to a twentieth-century play-wright, perhaps *the* twentieth-century playwright, the same meta-dramatic principles I had used for Shakespeare. To a certain extent I *was*, seeing Hamm, for example, as Beckett's own portrait of the artist; or Vladimir and Estragon as mock artists trying to establish an artificial world as a defense against the possibility of an absurd, nonworld ruled by an absent divinity; or the single character of *Krapp's Last Tape* as attempting through the art of the tape recorder to place in a comic perspective his otherwise tragic history. Yet when I considered the fact that the Beckett book emerged from six years of performance, par-ticularly those prison performances, that in moving among the media of the legitimate theater, radio, television, and the cinema Beckett inevita-bly presents a shifting definition of "theater," and that his consciousness of the theater is all-pervasive precisely because its artificial world chal-lenges an external reality that the playwright discredits in a way that Shakespeare never does nor could do, then I began to think of my theoretical metadramatics as almost redundant. The interplay within the dualistic notion of the world as a stage and the stage as a world that informs Shakespeare was simply not there, since Beckett's "macrocosm" is not the public world, or the "nature" that Shakespeare would have mirrored, but our own idiosyncratic internal world, one constructed entirely of words and verbal pictures. Sensing the difference myself, and then courteously prodded by a reader for the Press, I changed my initial title—*Beckett's Theaters: A Metadramatic Approach*—to the present *Beckett's Theaters: Interpretations for Performance*.

I now understood that my concern was no less with the actual mate-rials, the language and spectacle, the sense of presence, that Beckett used to sustain the stage illusion as he penetrated an inner world that "exists" only with and for its owner but that nevertheless challenges the playwright to make it public. And the theater is always public. Hamlet's "Now I am alone" (2.2.549), spoken appropriately after the actor imper-sonating Hecuba has left the stage, is contradicted by the audience, which overhears not only that line but the monologue that follows.

For me, the theoretical or metaphoric dimensions of theater I had discussed in *When the Theater Turns to Itself* were now no less actual, literal, present. Hence in *Godot* the clowns try through stage dialogue to establish a world in the midst of the impoverished physical set. In Beckett's radio plays, such as *All That Fall*, the stage world is by definition bodiless; here in this "theater of twilight" Maddy Rooney moves toward an inner world, sustained only by language, after her disastrous interac-tion in the public world of the train station. In the television plays, such as *Ghost Trio*, a visual medium, symbolized by stylized camera move-ments, interacts with a mysterious world, a larger reality present only at the edges of the camera's range. In *Film* and in two mimes Beckett rejects the domination of language peculiar to the radio plays and attempts through visual tableaux to portray that same world. The playwright thus uses a public, half-visual medium such as the theater to depict a private and verbally imaginative inner world. Conversely, in a purely verbal medium such as radio, he charts the tension between what is public, physical, and visual and what is private, nonphysical, and verbal.

In a certain sense, *When the Theater* told an optimistic story of a playwright defining in his theatrical metaphors the Renaissance notion of the world as a stage and, at the same time, celebrating the theater as the purest enactment of that notion. *Beckett's Theaters* told, if not a pessimistic story, then one where the playwright consciously adopts media hostile to his notion that our own reality is internal and then uses them in a daring but, paradoxically, creative way to enact the very tension between our self existentially present in the world and that buried self which remains almost incommunicable to ourself, let alone to others. The clash between language and spectacle in Beckett's various theaters embodies this tension, and in our witness to the enactment we contribute our own presence to the presence of the stage. Or, as a director friend once told me, if Godot fails to appear for the characters onstage, he fails no less for the "characters" in the audience.

This dual presence is precisely what Robbe-Grillet speaks of in his pioneering article "Samuel Beckett, or 'Presence' in the Theatre,"[5] and the same article gives the present study its main title. Realizing that I had employed a more practical performance criticism with Beckett, and thereby complemented and yet qualified the theoretical metadramatic approach in *When the Theater Turns to Itself*, I put down my Beckett and returned to Shakespeare, now wanting to combine the two approaches. Before spelling out the specific issues of that approach, let me apply it to two fairly recent plays, and thereby add to this abstract and now historical preface a practical critical performance.

iii

The "anticipated" plot of Peter Shaffer's 1965 *Black Comedy*[6] involves the attempt by Brindsley Miller, an impoverished sculptor, and his fiancée, Carol Melkett, to gain her wealthy father's consent to their marriage. To this end they have stolen valuable furnishings from Brindsley's neighbor, Harold Corringe ("the camp owner of an antique-china shop"), and planned an evening where the couple, along with Colonel Melkett, will entertain Georg Bamberger, a millionaire art collector who is coming to look at Brindsley's work. However, when the lights fail in the apartment within minutes of the opening of the first act, the preplanned evening gives way to a farce in which the couple must contend with Harold when he arrives unexpectedly; a middle-aged spinster, Miss Furnival; Brindsley's ex-mistress, Clea; and one Schuppanzigh, an employee of the London Electricity Board, whom they confuse with Georg Bamberger. Ninety percent of both acts occurs in total darkness, and the fun consists of mistaken identities, Brindsley's efforts to return Harold's furniture to his apartment, later efforts to conceal Clea, and the problems created when Miss Furnival takes an alcoholic drink in place of lemonade. Schuppanzigh is mistaken for the millionaire and the millionaire himself arrives late and promptly falls through a trap door leading to the basement.

Shaffer's clever stage direction asks us to pretend that a dark stage—this is how the play starts, with the actors themselves pretending the lights are "on"—is a fully lighted living room, and then, when the lights fail, that a lit stage is one totally dark for the characters, who now must pretend that they are stumbling about. This "reverse" convention is dictated by the simple fact that the audience needs to see a world that the characters comically, perhaps almost tragically, cannot. With the unexpected arrivals of Harold and then Clea, the lovers now need the darkness to disguise both the stolen furniture and an ex-lover's presence; conversely, the Colonel and then Schuppanzigh try to restore the lights, with Brindsley and Carol doing everything they can to prevent them. Hence the title *Black Comedy*.

By denying light and yet allowing the audience to see what the characters cannot see or can see only imperfectly—various lighters and candles are brought onstage only to be extinguished by the increasingly desperate couple—Shaffer asserts the importance of the stage's visual dimension, but in reverse, or by what a stage direction terms "a progress through disintegration." Darkness is here akin to deception, but the deception becomes progressively harder to maintain as the cast of characters literally grows. The inner, unanticipated play is itself aborted when Schuppanzigh, in the role of God, restores light to the evening, though of course when he does, the stage lights, by Shaffer's convention, go off for the audience and the play ends for us in darkness, while the repairman onstage shouts "LIGHT." Since we all are given in moments of weakness to conscious deception, we can sympathize with Brindsley and Carol, or, later, with Brindsley when he falls back in love with his former mistress. Yet the unplanned failure of light forces the same "understandable" characters into a new, unplanned play, and one beyond their control.

In one way, *Black Comedy*, albeit conversely, celebrates vision, that "normal" condition in which we see characters who see and respond to the same, tangible, present set. Once the visual is impaired onstage,

however, the verbal, the dialogue, suffers profoundly: intimate comments are delivered to the wrong party, with comically disastrous results;
Clea, remaining silent in the dark, overhears characters speaking negatively but unawares about her; the normally discreet Miss Furnival, now
drunk, becomes a different person, with a racy and revealing new
vocabulary; the repairman, by chance a German as is the millionaire,
finds that what he says is misinterpreted, though in a laudatory sense, as
the hosts insist on recognizing him as a major art critic. When Bamberger does arrive, it is no small irony that he is almost totally deaf. In
the bedroom Clea speaks *sotto voce* to Brindsley, and it is only when
others recognize her voice as she tries to impersonate the maid that such
verbal confusion, aggravated by the absence of light, is dissolved.

This same reverse celebration of light allows the playwright to underscore the significance of what is physically present onstage. Appropriately, Brindsley is a sculptor, and when he tries to convince
Schuppanzigh, already mistaken for the millionaire, that a statue of
Buddha (stolen from Harold) is best appreciated in the dark, he labels
his work an example of "Factual Tactility." Angered at the slanders
delivered to her unawares by Harold, Carol, and, for a time, Brindsley
(who is now trying to convince both his fiancée and himself that he no
longer loves his ex-mistress), Clea punishes her taunters with a game
called "Guess the Hand," forcing them to identify each other by touch.
Portraying a world denied its sight, and yet asking the audience to
participate in the making of the illusion by thinking of a lighted stage as
dark, *Black Comedy* thus demonstrates the precarious relation between
spectacle and language: the impoverished spectacle robs language of its
referents, and a world physically present but unperceived is at best
farcical. This dilemma, initiated by the absence of the visual and then
infecting the language by which we name and control the physical world,
is expressed graphically when Brindsley becomes hopelessly tangled in a
light cord while trying to remove one of Harold's antique lamps from the
set, or when Clea, the victim of slanders delivered unintentionally to her
face, twists Brindsley's ear in retribution. The onstage confusion only
suggests the primacy of the visual, both in the theater and in life:
literally, we are all potential victims, comic or even tragic, of a blackout.

Mark Medoff's 1980 *Children of a Lesser God*[7] makes a similar assault
on—and, in its course, a similar celebration of the verbal, of stage
language. It is a love story whose central characters are James Leeds, a
teacher of the deaf and speech-impaired, and his student Sarah Norman, who is both deaf and incapable of speaking or, more precisely,
unwilling to learn to speak. The play offers a panorama of speech: from
Leeds himself, to his students who are partially deaf but can speak as well
as "sign," to Sarah, enclosed as she is in her own world of silence. The

tension is generated here by the collision between a speaking/hearing world and that of a student who "speaks" only visually in sign language, or, given the effect of even partial deafness on the voice, of students who speak imperfectly.

Leeds's faith in language demands that he see the students, and Sarah in particular, as "different," as anguished because they are not "normal" and yet as eager to rejoin his world. Sarah, both defensively and then philosophically, becomes the champion of her language of silence—of the *physical*, since that word embraces everything from her sexual relation with Leeds (the one activity, she informs him, that she can perform as well as any speaking person) to her conviction that her silent world, expressed in visual signing, is not abnormal, let alone inferior, but equal, perhaps even superior to, a world of speech. In the major speech of the play, when she defends her cause, Sarah holds that her "eyes are [her] ears," that her ability to communicate visually is potentially greater than that of speaking people, since she can "say" in "one image an idea more complex" than can be contained in fifty words. Still, this conviction is inseparable from her anguish, and the play finely balances competing claims. Speech and language, Leeds is convinced, can be learned, and he invokes both Joyce's *Finnegans Wake* and a Bach concerto as the linguistic and aural "reward" awaiting his students. Against these, Sarah places her self-defined world of "soundful" silence, and when she becomes Leeds's wife in the second act, she claims that she can respond to music itself through vibrations.

Children is a political play, overtly "serious" in a way that *Black Comedy* on the surface is not. The characters halfway between the two leads, those who, though physically impaired, can still speak as well as sign, demand equal rights for their fellows, even as they are attempting to rejoin the speaking world. Sarah maintains, instead, that her speechless world is not some abnormal variation, but integral, meaningful, communicative on its own terms. Audiences, as I have observed, tend to sympathize with Sarah at the expense of Leeds, and Leeds's own character is taken to an extreme in the practical, initially insensitive director of the school. Yet, given the fact that most members of the audience cannot read sign language, the play still requires dialogue, sound; and therefore, just as Shaffer solved the problem of darkness by equating light with darkness, Medoff solves a potential problem by having Leeds and other speaking characters translate into words for the audience the sign language used by the students. When the couple at the end agree that each world has valid claims, that James will have to accept Sarah's silence even as she will have to acknowledge the hurt she feels in being a minority, the child of a lesser god, the anticipated union of the onstage characters echoes the play's own metadramatic argument for a union between its language and its physical basis, that spectacle informed, defined, and controlled by speech.

Appropriately, Leeds's new role will be that of translator or, in the words of the play, a "brilliant bridger" between language and the physical "signs" of language. Without this compromise, Sarah, speechless except for a horrendous cry of pain as she attempts to speak late in the play, can be accepted only as a physical being, or as the sexual object that men have earlier considered her. Conversely, this play, treating the "difficulties of communication" in a way that dwarfs the normal meaning of that phrase, establishes the claim of both silence and that physical basis or "sign" without which language itself is only an abstraction. At the start of the play we see on the blackboard this sentence, written by Leeds in his role as teacher: "Speech is not a specious but a sacred sanction, secured by solemn sacrifice." As the play, essentially through Sarah, challenges this conservative definition of the word, that sentence gives way to "Ontogeny recapitulates phylogeny," which Leeds translates as "we make ourselves over in our own image." As it suggests a gamut for speech ranging from the spoken word to the sign to silence, *Children of a Lesser God* itself communicates or enacts a more catholic notion of speech, even as it argues that variations of speaking or silent speaking themselves create different worlds.

The optimistic ending, in which James and Sarah vow to "listen" to each other and not be afraid of speech *or* silence, itself enacts the two interactive worlds of the theater, this visual and verbal medium whose tension and corresponding potential for resolution lies precisely in the coexistence of language and spectacle. In similar fashion, the co-presence of actor and audience, two seemingly antithetical components, is cause both for division and, as I have called it in the opening section of the preface, for a present collaboration established at each performance only to be undone by the next.

iv

This interdependence of language and spectacle, as presently enacted on the stage and no less presently ratified by the audience offstage, informs both the immediate onstage "world" of the play, the encompassing world of the theater during performance, and, by extension, the larger world outside the confines of the theater itself. I approach this topic in four stages.

Part I (chapters 1 to 3) is very much of a gambit, wherein I take one play in which there is a cleavage between our perception and that of the characters of a single onstage spectacle; then a play in which the characters try with language to assess and thereby to find meaning in a historical world whose "facts" are equally clear to characters and audience; and a third play where, with time, an initially tragic gap between language and spectacle is resolved. In *The Comedy of Errors* (chapter 1) we see no more or no less than the characters, but their ignorance of the co-presence of twins separates them from us; hence our positive interpretation of the events, based on our knowing that there is a factual explanation for the onstage confusion, runs counter to their own ongoing misinterpretations. We "share" the same stage, the same spectacle, but read it in radically different fashions. This same visual cleavage in them admits a linguistic one. If the onstage action seems farcical to us, albeit tragic or absurd to the characters, their own search to find an identity, both individual and familial, is not unlike our own, offstage, where "what is"—experience itself—may be no less relative to the orientation of the perceiver. In learning to "play" with conflicting readings of what the audience sees unequivocally, in remaining in the field of play despite temptations to abandon Ephesus, in being granted, as Egeon is, a day in which to extricate oneself from an otherwise fatal, closed situation, the characters justify the concept of play, of the theater itself. At the end, their visual distortion resolved, they join us in a single reading of the events, and then, like us, are prepared to make an exit from the stage.

In *Troilus and Cressida* (chapter 2) there is no problem with visual perception; the play recreates undisputed facts of history. Rather, the issue is how to evaluate in language these same facts, or how to reconcile the abstractions of language with what irrevocably "is." Specifically, this is Troilus's problem when the "ideal Cressida" he has established earlier confronts what he sees in Act 5: the "false" Cressida embracing Diomedes, content to be his mistress, just as she had once been Troilus's. Here, in a tragic sense, each character must acknowledge the fact that language is relative to the speaker and, no less so, to the hearer; the play itself sacrificially enacts the failure of any given character to offer a consistent interpretation of the war or of the individual lives that it alters. If the Ephesians' and Syracusans' existential complexity in *The Comedy of Errors* seems for a time tragic or even absurd, in *Troilus and Cressida* that same relativity is linguistic, rather than visual.

In the final play of this first part, *The Winter's Tale* (chapter 3), I am initially concerned with our attempts to find some principle of order in the romance's sprawling world. I then turn to a parallel but self-imposed dilemma when Leontes misreads Hermione's innocent offer of her hand to Polixenes as a sign of adultery. The issue for the characters here is to arrive at a consensus through language of what they communally see, and I examine, along with Hermione's offer of her hand in Act 1, four other moments, increasingly comic, when the language of interpretation is at variance with the stage spectacle, specifically: Paulina's laying down the infant Perdita before Leontes; Hermione's entrance at her trial; Florizel's taking of Perdita's hand as a sign of marital contract during the sheep-shearing festival; and, at last, Leontes, now repentant and a willing trainee of Paulina, taking the hand of what he assumes is a statue of his wife now dead for seventeen years. In the largest sense, *The Winter's Tale* charts the reconciliation between art (language) and nature (spectacle, i.e., the physical), and is therefore at first a tragedy and then a comedy, with both halves resting on the interdependence of the theater's own verbal and visual dimensions.

In Part II (chapters 4 and 5) I examine two extreme examples of stage spectacle, *Julius Caesar* (chapter 4) and *Macbeth* (chapter 5), plays in which the central character has a visionary experience: the ghost of Caesar (combined with Brutus's own "evil spirit") and the apparition of Banquo, along with the apparitions of the witches. What becomes the spectre's "reality" for Brutus and Macbeth is mere delusion for the other onstage characters, and this very separation influences our reading of the central characters. The ghost in *Julius Caesar* appears near the end of a play overwhelmed by problems in visual objectivity, for the philosophical and practical success of the conspiracy depends on the characters' ability to read accurately both Caesar and, no less, themselves. Here, however, the facts of Roman history are compounded by the presence of the supernatural, even as all philosophical systems prove inadequate to account for the cynical, cyclical history mirrored by the play. Only the women, otherwise subordinate to the male vision dominating Rome, are capable of "play" and hence have an imaginative, more encompassing vision. Though each in his own way, Brutus, Cassius, and even Antony fail as playwrights attempting to order the events unleashed by Caesar's assassination. It is only near death, in particular at that moment just before the battle of Philippi when Brutus sees the ghost, that vision in *Julius Caesar* becomes sufficiently flexible to account for its larger world.

In *Macbeth* the confusion between what is seen and heard generates a mania for certainty affecting the characters who inhabit a Scotland that is no less "displaced," uncertain because of civil war. Macbeth himself would superimpose an anti-play on the play's own historical chronicle, a negative, inner world that stands as a terrifying parody of the public stage. The appearance of Banquo's ghost, along with Macbeth's encounters with the witches, signals at once Macbeth's unique, exhilarating countervision as well as the fatal loneliness of his achievement. Trying to arrest history, Macbeth thus gives a special meaninig to the term *theater of presence*. In Malcolm's return, the play reasserts the productive, public, "present" partnership of language and spectacle once appropriated by Macbeth for an individual but self-defeating end.

In Part III (chapters 6 and 7) I look at two complementary examples in which language is taken to the extreme. Richard III (chapter 6) uses language as a tool for supplanting a historical reality with his own perverse world of self-serving illusion, and here I examine the social, philosophical, and theological implications of his appropriation of language that, if unchecked, would descend into the chaotic and, at length, the demonic. Like Macbeth's, Richard's idiosyncratic theater resists the public demands of Shakespeare's medium, and yet Richard's most extraordinary linguistic accomplishments, such as his opening speech "Now is the winter of our discontent," also invoke that antithetical, public world which will prove his undoing. If Macbeth's challenge is to the visual boundaries of the stage, Richard's is to its verbal half. Only in his last major speech, "What do I fear?" (5.3.182–206), is he able to see both his negative self and, by implication, a reverse positive self that has always been with him. Only in this closing monologue is he able to grasp that counterplay reestablishing the public, even political role of Shakespeare's theater which will drive from the stage his nihilistic, yet fascinating theater of one.

In *Henry V* (chapter 7), that history which completes the second tetralogy just as *Richard III* completes the first, we experience Henry's—and Shakespeare's—successful effort to find a language for the public world, a language allowing for communal, positive action. Here language *is* history, and Henry the playwright of his nation's history. Both the Chorus, who would elevate Henry's accomplishments to the idealism of the epic, and the comic characters, vestiges of Falstaff's days in the *Henry IV* plays, must be sacrificed to this public concern. In Henry's person dramatic speech both defines and shapes what we see and what we experience in the real world. Yet Act 5, in reminding us of the subsequent tragic history of Henry's own "speech acts," also reminds us of how fragile both his verbal creation and verbal creation in general actually are.

In Part IV (chapters 8 and 9), my own final gambit, I take two plays, *The Merchant of Venice* and *King Lear*, that provide catholic and contrastive demonstrations of the difficult but necessary balance between language and spectacle, both onstage and in the world offstage. In *The Merchant of Venice* the linguistically self-indulgent, "soft" world of the Venetians is countered by the physical, reductive, "hard" mentality of Shylock. The potential tragedy in this comedy stems from this misalliance of the verbal and visual; in a curious sense, Antonio and Shylock complement each other, "need" each other. Through Portia, however, the play is rebalanced in the "trials" of Shylock in Act 4 and the husbands in Act 5. To the male world of Venice, at once hyperbolic and grimly realistic, she brings the prerequisite sense of serious physical and verbal play. With a pastoral setting more common in the middle section of comedies like *As You Like It* and *A Midsummer Night's Dream*, Act 5 portrays the final, secular "heaven" where words and vision are united, where the balance between the constituents of our dramatic experience is inseparable from the sane ethics that Portia herself brings to the play.

King Lear literally stretches to the breaking point the verbal and visual, our own ears and eyes, and, in the process, the theater itself. Here I first review the play's revealing critical history, and suggest that in more recent commentary, arguing from various perspectives, that the play points to a life just outside its confines—a reality that art struggles futilely to enact—we are returning to the eighteenth-century suspicion that *Lear* demonstrates that nature is above even Shakespeare's art. After examining the play's divided attitude toward language, spectacle, role-playing, and the theater generally, I suggest that in the final tableau, where Lear bends over his dead Cordelia asking us to "look," we see at once a tragedy so open-ended that it metadramatically gives way to that real life offstage and, at the same time, a celebration of Shakespeare's theater for allowing us to see anew that same reality beyond the stage. *Lear* is at length art for life's sake, for a life that can only be imperfectly understood even as it must be endured. Here the illusory language and spectacle of the stage world admit their superior counterparts offstage as we respond to *Lear*'s own challenge to its medium, particularly in its final moments, and then take the play home, into our own hearts. We ourselves are *Lear*'s final theater of presence, and Shakespeare's tragedy sacrifices itself to underscore this "fact." If *The Comedy of Errors* represents our voyage, no less than that of its characters, into the field of play, *King Lear*, equally so, at once defines art's relation to life and releases us to that larger presence which the stage imitates and into which the play, its last line delivered, rightly dissolves.

My colleagues and graduate students who have seen these chapters in rough drafts, and whose commentary on them proves valuable as always, make fun of me for my lengthy notes. I have, they claim, still a graduate student's mentality, one that insists on documenting everything, and that plays out in the notes all the ramifications and alternative readings to everything I say in the main text. The argument goes: at this stage in his or her career shouldn't one unshackle such "subtextual" scholarship? I can only claim in my defense that by such copiousness I allow, or try to allow, an audience beyond my idiosyncratic self to be present. For if my combination of performance and metadramatic criticism depends on a sense of the play as happening, as something taking place through that collaboration of author, actor, and audience, then this articulate "audience" that has wrestled with these same plays now for more than four hundred years is a very special audience of presence, or, more properly, presences. And I am indebted to them.

Acknowledgments

Quotations from Mark Medoff's *Children of a Lesser God* are through the permission of the William Morris Agency, Inc. Quotations from Peter Shaffer's *Black Comedy* are through the permission of Stein and Day Publishers. The chapter on *The Comedy of Errors* originally appeared as "*The Comedy of Errors* and Its Audience: "'And Here We Wander in Illusions'" in the *CEA Critic* 47 (Fall-Winter 1984): 17–30.

For some very, *very* good reasons I have a special place in my heart reserved for Bucknell University. Once again I am grateful for the many kindnesses of the Director of the Bucknell University Press, Professor Mills Edgerton. And it has been a pleasure, once again, to work with Julien Yoseloff, the Director of Associated University Presses, and Katharine Turok, that press's Managing Editor.

Almost everything I say about the theater these days reflects my association with the two professional companies I serve as stage director. My fellow directors, actors, crew, and staff at the Hippodrome State Theater of Florida and at the Fable Factory know, of course, that my feelings for them are more than words can witness.

I am also blessed at the University of Florida in being a member of a splendid English Department, and for having a chairman, colleagues, and students willing to endure this rough fellow from south Philadelphia who, for better or for worse, is always "onstage."

Dr. Barbara Stephenson, my former graduate assistant and now a member of the United States Consulate in Panama, served as my in-house editor here, but as always, such mistakes as remain, large and small, are entirely my own.

Shakespeare's
Theater of Presence

PART I

*Language,
Spectacle, Audience:
An Opening Gambit*

1

The Comedy of Errors:
"And here we wander in illusions"

WHAT we hear and see at the present moment constitutes an experience unique to the theater, one not shared by nondramatic works that, operating by their own unique principles, must perforce have their own definitions of "experience."[1] This theatrical "presence" is especially ironic in *The Comedy of Errors*, given the significance of its past, that "history" extending from the birth of the twins, and from the coincidental birth of twin servants, to the accident at sea separating the family, to the separate lives led in Ephesus and Syracuse, with roughly seventeen years intervening before the Syracusan son and Egeon began the search for their family. No less ironic in terms of theatrical presence is the significance of the future, for there would be no play at all if the Duke had not extended Egeon's life until five that evening.

Given the improbabilities of its plot, what engages us in *Errors*, I believe, is not so much its mirror image of normal life but rather the gap in Shakespeare's theater of presence between our sense of the play's purpose and the perceptions of its characters who, until the very end, have no sense of their own play on that same stage we witness both aurally and visually. In seeing, at length, their whole play, they can be extricated not only from a comic dilemma but from the larger comedy itself, life's own comedy of errors. We are fixed; they are in error and are erring, in the older sense of "wandering." Our exit from the theater is therefore dependent on theirs.

i

As the "outside" audience our first requirement, then, is that we all see the same thing: however confusing they may be to the "onstage" audience, we recognize the two Antipholi as just that—as two. Conversely, the characters' inability to distinguish each other even finds precedent in the play's own prehistory: through Egeon's opening narrative one can

31

imagine the scene where, their mast split in two, the divided family sees its other half in a progressively diminished perspective until even vision itself went blank. Egeon comments that the "sight" of the three being rescued by the fishermen of Corinth was only "as we thought" (1.1.110–11). We, however, see precisely what we need to see, and thus the implied stage set of Syracuse, actually inhabited for seven years by father, son, and servant, need not exist for us.

For "them" even the most basic object, a prop like the rope or chain so solid it can be seen and touched, cannot be seen for what it is. The Ephesian Antipholus requests money and is brought a rope by his "servant"; Syracusan Antipholus finds his Dromio bringing not a rope as requested but gold, just as earlier he had received a chain without asking for one. For doing what one was told to do, as well as for not doing what one was told to do, a servant gets a beating. As several commentators have observed, Shakespeare quadruples the number of servant beatings from Plautus, yet to the servants so consistently beaten they are literally receiving "something" for "nothing" (2.2.51–52).[2] The characters, of course, devise numerous interpretations of these strange events, even though all miss the mark.

When we attach a meaning to such objects, if we see, as some critics have seen, a social or symbolic meaning to the chain, if we find in the composite gold-chain-rope an emblem of the play's dramatization of the tragicomedy of perception,[3] do we do anything less, however more consciously, than the stage's confused characters? We ourselves thus "confuse" or exchange an object so that we can avoid mere spectacle, and thereby we sustain that delicate balance of the visual and the verbal essential to the theater. Like the primitive *or* the sophisticate with his fetishes, the characters also sense in this transformation of gold to rope or of nothing to a chain a mysterious force that denies the literal, that alternately explains or reduces what was assumed, literally, to be only itself. Consciousness of this force, of the playwright whose craft invites our own more productive interpretation, alone separates us from them; as long as they remain unconscious of the source of their confusion they can see only conflicting purposes, or tragedies of adultery, or comedies of enchantment and of windfalls.

Indeed, the visual without the signifying power of language risks losing even its own physical base; at one point the characters onstage can only "witness" that Antipholus has vanished from the priory and been "borne about invisible" (5.1.187). There is no magic here, however, no occult force performing vanishing acts. If Ephesus in Saint Paul's letters has associations with witchcraft and sorcery, we see no such city here, despite the suppositions of the characters. The play is based on reality, a fact: the co-presence of twins.

This bare fact itself is paralleled by the single stage set, its unchanging presence in contrast to, say, the sweeping panorama—to use the movies' cliché—of *Antony and Cleopatra* or the spatial movement in *King Lear* from court to heath and back to court. In fact, while there is some debate as to the exact set,[4] we know that the bare stage itself served as the street or playing area, with three upstage exits signifying the house of Antipholus, Aemilia's abbey, and the Porpentine where the Courtesan lives. What appears to us, therefore, as a clear, contiguous playing area is not so for the characters, who see it as an arena of "tricks," where people exit only to reappear suddenly with changed identities, where, as the Syracusan Dromio believes, the secular earth has been transformed to a "fairy land" (2.2.189).

ii

Our identification with Shakespeare's characters through this need to interpret—and also, I might add here, through our ignorance of Aemilia's presence—is only a prelude to our larger identification when we acknowledge that their confusion both is and is not of their own making, and that this gamut thereby effectively covers possibilities of disorder in our own world. In his first discourse on the interrelation between time and baldness, Dromio rejects the Syracusan Antipholus's attempt to find something "sound" or "sure" or "certain" in time's assault on human existence (2.2.91–95). Still, in the face of this same relative time the characters persist in trying to establish something certain, a source for or a way out of their confusion, whether it take the form of a psychological explanation of marriage problems or the practical strategy of adopting as a reality a role that everyone but the recipient thinks of as his own.

As we acknowledge the play's illusionary status, its being about "nothing," that concession is then undercut by the simple fact that both during and after the performance we share the same world with the characters. In a sense the ending or resolution is secondary, for *Errors*, as a piece for the theater, concerns more than the onstage family reunion. The title itself tells us, despite the somber opening, that this reunion is a foregone conclusion. Their piecing together of what were otherwise disparate yet autonomous, integral narratives is itself a sign of what we must do. We cannot help being involved.

The theater is thus a community's attack on the obvious, no less than on narrowed vision; it insists on meaning because, at its core, it refuses to take the world, *any* world, as it is. What we see must admit a discourse, and like the characters themselves we too must "entertain the offer'd fallacy" (2.2.186). Adriana, among others, demands to "know the truth hereof at large" (4.4.143). In searching for a truth (if not "the" truth) or in seeking an interpretation, we, as the united community of its audience, also *charge* the stage world with meaning, an action highly significant in a play that presents a fractured community, in terms of both its history and its present lack of a common understanding.

The literal play thus becomes a play of charged presence, and this succession in which an object is enhanced informs the conversation between the Ephesian Antipholus and Balthazar as they debate what determines good entertainment: the fare or the host—in effect, the dinner itself or the context of courtesy (3.1.19–30). Clearly, in terms of the play, both are wrong individually and yet right collectively, and that the play at this point for those onstage cannot sustain such a union of existence and essence, if you will, is underscored when both would-be host and would-be guest are barred from the door. Those inside must come forth and join those outside so that outside/inside distinctions, a metaphor itself for the larger cleavage threatening the theater's community, can be dissolved. In terms of the play's visual core, the extremes to be avoided are what we might call the "reductively" physical (just before the Act 5 reunions, rapiers are drawn as the visitors threaten their hosts) and the "illusory" physical (Luciana is not a magician and, despite its reputation, there are no charlatans in Ephesus).

In point of fact, if the characters are not three-dimensional—and the mathematics of that phrase seems closer to the jargon of conventional theater reviewers—they are not without psychological traces of a malaise frustrating such unified vision.[5] We learn that the Ephesian Antipholus "hath been heavy, sour, sad" for a week before the day's actions, though Adriana herself cannot find the link between that condition and what appears to be his present "extremity of rage" (5.1.45–48). Egeon would gladly have embraced even "a doubtful warrant of immediate death" (1.1.168) if it had not been for the "incessant weepings" of his wife; significantly, he forgoes a death-wish for the sake of his mate and thereby allows the tragedy at sea to become a tragicomedy. Upon his entrances in Ephesus, Antipholus is in a state that can only be described as depressed: anyone commending him to his "own content" commends him to "the thing [he] cannot get". "Unhappy" because of his separation from his family, he will efface himself, going about the town "unseen," albeit "inquisitive" (1.2.33–40). Adriana is a creature of unfounded jealousy[6] and Luciana, otherwise clear-sighted, refrains from marriage even as she counsels Antipholus to conceal his adultery. Aemilia has withdrawn from the world into her convent, and the would-be nun in Shakespeare—witness Isabella—*must* be converted from such celibacy to marriage. In each case there is evidence of retreat, regression, withdrawal, and such action goes against the play's own insistence, and that of Shakespeare's theater generally, on a community of unified vision as a defense against the randomness of fate.

The central characters are therefore incomplete, lacking wholeness, not the "formal" man (5.5.105) of which Aemilia speaks. This exile from their complete selves is echoed in the various images of division: a ship split on the rocks, with even its auxiliary mast, which for a time serves to unite the family, split in turn; the two towns of Ephesus and Syracuse now "adverse" (1.1.15) over an act of cruelty in which Ephesians lost their lives for the very same reason now threatening Egeon; and—again—3.1, dividing the characters into those inside and outside the home. If the play lacks "real" characters, the fact is that until the very end the real characters themselves are fractured, elsewhere.

iii

Despite the duplication of the twins' first names, for the audience the play's verbal clarity is at one with its visual clarity; we can hear as ironic what the characters take as literal, and as untrue what they themselves take for the truth: Antipholus's confession of love for Luciana, for instance, is just that, and not the evidence of adulterous passion that she imagines. We know whether a command given a servant can be fulfilled, and in a play where everyone accuses everyone else of lying, we know that no one lies. For us, then, words fix on their proper referents, and even when the characters consciously play with language, as in Dromio's punning, we can detect an irony behind the smaller irony intended by the punster. However, given the characters' visual confusion, their verbal confusion follows hard upon.

Egeon ironically opens the play with a request that the Duke speak, that he "proceed" to "procure [his] fall."[7] What proceeds, of course, is not his immediate fall, since that is deferred until sundown, but rather Egeon's own narrative. Though the Duke orders him to "plead no more" (3), Egeon proceeds to do precisely that, his argument being that accident and not human design has cast him on these hostile shores. Egeon's speech, as many commentators have observed and as I have learned from directing *Errors*, is the most sustained and eloquent piece of poetry in the play. Yet it is delivered against a political context in which language has become rigid, inflexible, unplayful. The Duke speaks of his countrymen as having "seal'd" the "rigorous statues" of Syracuse with "their blood" (9), and of Ephesus's counterlaw as being "decreed" in "solemn synods" (13). Egeon will die when the Duke's "words are done" (28), and in this fact he takes a certain morbid comfort. Without the inner play to follow, the narrative itself would be irrelevant, nothing but a dead man's ineffectual, albeit moving account of a family's history. Hearing Egeon's words, even acknowledging that his presence here in Ephesus is not a sin of commission, the Duke is still powerless to change his nation's decree. In terms of the reality assumed by the characters in the play's thematic world, the lengthy narrative, while it provides coherence to Egeon's own life, can therefore at best be gossip, at worst, a waste of speech itself. For his listeners in this opening scene, onstage as well as off, Egeon is indeed silenced until that final appearance where execution rather than explication will or should be the order of the day.

Only when our own view expands into the second scene can we admit some alleviation from the verbally moribund world of that opening scene. In his edition, R. A. Foakes observes that Egeon's poetry continues into this second scene,[8] and that with the entrance of the Syracusan Antipholus and the scenic link provided by the First Merchant when he refers to a "Syracusian merchant . . . not being able to buy out his life" (1.2.3–5), we know that the seemingly impossible, Egeon's ransom, is now within the bounds of possibility. If Egeon is ineffectively loquacious, his son vows to be effectively silent—and visually obscure. On the advice of the First Merchant, Antipholus will deny his identity and spend his time viewing the town, rather than talking about his history, "unseen," although "inquisitive." He promises to be as secondary as his father was central in the previous scene: "I to the world am like a drop of water, / That in the ocean seeks another drop" (35–36). We will realize later, of course, that Antipholus's desire for anonymity will be as unrealized as Egeon's commitment to death: the father will be granted life, and the moody son forced into dialogue against his will.

For the characters, though, once the visual certainty breaks down—and this occurs a mere forty-two lines into scene 2 when the Ephesian Dromio returns in place of his twin with a reminder that the Ephesian Antipholus, also mistaken for his twin, is late for dinner—then verbal certainty also collapses. Word is literally divorced from object. Puns are sometimes unintentional and are not always playful, as when the Ephesian Dromio, locked out of his master's house, frustrates Antipholus when he translates the requested crowbar to *crow* (3.1.80–84). Indeed, here for a time the pun almost threatens to run off with a scene whose pathos is as great for the participants, especially for the excluded husband, as it is comic from our perspective. At one point a character employs "wit" to scan "every word" of a dialogue, and yet he cannot understand a thing that is said (2.2.150–51), cannot fathom the "folded meaning of [the] word's deceit" (3.1.36). If the object so misunderstood threatens to lead to its extinction, then words here quickly degenerate to a glottal sound, then to wind itself, and, what is worse, wind as crude and as insignificant as a fart: "A man may break a word with you, sir, and words are but wind" (3.1.75).

In order to "speak" to a master who beats him without cause, the Ephesian Dromio resorts to a fantastic metaphor in which his skin becomes parchment and the blows from his master the ink (3.1.12–14). We will recall Hamlet's somber question to Horatio: "Is not parchment made of sheep-skins?" (5.1.114). In his melancholy, the Prince would trace even the paper used by the playwright to its source in the skin of a dead, or sacrificial animal. By the end of *Errors*, where the verbal confusion matches its ancestor in visual confusion, all dialogue is dismissed as "mad" (282). The Syracusan Antipholus would even stop his ears against the exquisite poetry of the women he loves. If one cannot close up the orifice of hearing, then the only alternative is taking the next ship out from Ephesus, removing oneself visually *and* aurally from this town where object and speech seem helplessly intertwined and contradictory.

iv

Such visual and verbal confusion, and the resulting disparity in perception between audience and characters, is inseparable from the problem of time in the play, both real time and theatrical time. As Gamini Salgado keenly observes, for the characters themselves the only sure time is that accounted for in Egeon's narrative; only the past, all that time antecedent to the actual events of the day spent in Ephesus, proves orderly.[9] The twins speak confidently of the Dromios as their "almanac" (1.2.41), the visible record of their birth date, and Dromio confirms the fact: from the "hour of [his] nativity to this instant" he has served Antipholus (4.4.30–31). Balthazar appeals to the Ephesian Antipholus's "long experience" of his wife's "wisdom" (3.1.89) in order to prevent him from being too hasty in censuring her when he is barred from the house. Adriana's reference to the previous week during which her husband's humor was "sour" later becomes part of Aemilia's diagnosis of the source of their marital conflict.

Still, this same past-tense order just barely manages to make its way from the "pre-play" or from Egeon's "induction" to the inner play. The Syracusan Antipholus is quite right when he designates his time spent in Ephesus as "two hours" (2.2.148), but this will be the last temporal certainty he will know—until the closing moments. We realize, also, that Antipholus's present problems have very little to do with Aemilia's diagnosis, and if his long-standing service to the state prejudices the Duke to his cause, it alone cannot excuse his seemingly insane actions in the final scene.

Other characters, not at the center of the controversy, have a surer sense of time. The "wind and tide" (4.1.46) do indeed wait for the Second Merchant, though not for the Syracusan Antipholus; and for

Angelo there is no confusion when he announces that he "gave [the chain to Antipholus] even now" (55). Yet as this recent, orderly past recedes even as the play itself moves toward the moment of disclosure that will in turn allow debts to be paid and ships to depart with their intended cargo, such temporal sanity vanishes. Thus the "now" of the play, while still orderly for us, cannot be so for the participants. The Messenger declares that he has "not breath'd almost" (5.1.181) since he last saw the Ephesian Antipholus, yet no one onstage can possibly believe him since before his entrance they have been audience to a raving Antipholus.

Soon "time's deformed hand" (5.1.299) violates all temporal probability, rendering irrational both sight, as in the Messenger's conflict with the onstage audience, and language, the latter anticipated when Dromio desperately wishes his master's "mouth" could be as accurate a clock as his own (1.1.66). The servant twin bears the bruises of such disordered time.

Indeed, the two discussions of time most relevant to the inner play come from Dromio: one, his paradox that time at once bestows hair on men even as in passing it renders them bald, both of hair and of wit (2.2.77–108); the other, equating time with a bankrout or thief (4.2.55–62). Even these two accounts of time, once collated, are right only in a negative sense, for in *Errors* there is, with time, not a diminishment of reason but its replenishment. Given the improbability of two sets of twins sharing the stage, there is, inevitably, a high probability that the coincidence will in time be disclosed. This latter chance, nourished by time, is anticipated by the hair-line coincidences in the play: consider the juxtaposition of the twins' exits and entrances within minutes and even lines of each other (for example, 1.2.18–40 or 4.2.66–4.3.11), and the previously discussed inside/outside scene (3.1). Linked to the play's visual and verbal "matings" (3.2.54; 5.1.282), time here stands as both the cause and the victim of their distortions. The audience, of course, accepts this arbitrary stage time, as well as the violation of the plot. For us, therefore, "presence" embraces the fictive, perfectly ordered stage world, its bizarre doppelgänger experienced by the characters (an absurd fiction born from a historical fact of birth), and our own parallel reality offstage. For the characters, however, such presence can only be a cruel caricature.

v

The image of the actor is inseparable from this trinity of theatrical vision, language, and presence. Here we have actors from Shakespeare's company playing characters either forced into new roles or deprived of a past role, consciously trusting in what we ourselves admit as an impossibility in physics: that two people can occupy the same space. In effect, the play gives a comic, albeit revealing twist to Iago's observation, at once simple, complex, and potentially revealing: "Were I the Moor, I would not be Iago" (1.1.57). A warning, however: if we would agree that the distorted onstage image of the audience is not without significance, then the same may apply, in reverse fashion, to the metadramatically confused actors onstage. To what degree are we, offstage, actors unconscious of that play which otherwise passes as life itself?

Again, for the Ephesian master and servant, Act 3, scene 1 marks the death of roles they thought were their own. In a parody of the Greek ideal of our own double identity, as private person at home and public person in the *polis*, they are unwillingly forced into a public sphere offering them a role at variance with, rather than complementary to that assumed indoors. The stage itself, with its public playing area downstage and three upstage doors leading to residences, silently underscores this double plot. Luciana maintains that once outside his home, man is allowed a liberty—a field of play—that would be inappropriate indoors (2.1.1–43). Seeking to find his brother's home and, at the same time, to reestablish their common home, the Syracusan Antipholus unintentionally forces his brother to leave that house and "wander unknown fields" (3.2.38). Conversely, the women remain indoors and yet are responsible, in a sense, for the expulsion of the men, whether that expulsion take the form of Luciana's argument for masculine liberty, Adriana's confusion between husbands, or Aemilia's understandable but fatal choice in accompanying her husband on the sea voyage. Thus all three women serve not only as the home to which the men must return but also as their source of expulsion and thereby inspiration, offering each man a new identity, allowing the otherwise secure Ephesian Antipholus to play the role of his wandering brother, and the wanderer, the stranger, to fill the vacuum by becoming the domesticated spouse. As has been observed, the inner play is something of a dream world where one takes on—though here without much choice—a role either feared (the wanderer) or desired (the husband, complete with adoring wife, and with servants).[10] The twinship is thus both a fact and the grounds for translation to another identity.

Such playing, whether enforced or wished-for, is often terrifying, a displacement of reality—or of what was assumed to be reality—by relativity. The Syracusan Antipholus cries out, "Am I in earth, in heaven, or in hell? / Sleeping or waking, mad or well-advised" (2.2.212–213), while his servant wonders, "Am I Dromio? . . . Am I myself?" (3.2.74). At one point his twin compares himself to a football thrown about by the winds of volition (2.1.83). Like that of Sly's when he is transformed from drunken tinker to aristocrat, the change is equally exhilarating: both "man and master" seem "possess'd" (4.4.92), their new roles assigned by "inspiration" (2.2.166–67), and they themselves "transformed" (2.2.195). For them, ultimately, the metamorphosis of roles constitutes a downward spiral, from secure man to ape to ass (2.2.198–99).

The actor's own conscious playing of a role is here distorted, for we are doubly aware that the "man" onstage has both consciously and unconsciously assumed a part. The Syracusan Antipholus thus says more than he knows when he wishes to "lose" himself in Ephesus, or on that stage before us. Perhaps, as has been suggested, this loss of the normal self and the subsequent assumption of a new role shows man as a divided being, *homo sapiens* turning here, unconsciously, into *homo ludens*— Huizinga with a twist. The two Antipholi and Egeon are like old Adam, the man before revelation whom Dromio purposely confuses with the sergeant (4.3.13–33): arrested, unable to function in a new role, no longer able to play an accustomed role, or, like Egeon and Aemilia, held in abeyance, hidden until the final scene. Given the play-time allowed by Shakespeare through the Duke, though, that working day otherwise so confused here, Egeon emerges at length not as victim but as restored and restoring husband. Likewise, the enforced playing time allows the sons, discomforts notwithstanding, time to "dally" (1.2.59), to abandon oneself but also to search for one's other half.

The characters themselves also seem to call for such playing, such stepping outside of an assumed role. The Syracusan Antipholus asks Luciana to "teach" him "how to think and speak" (2.2.3), and the first advice he is given, we will recall, is to "give out" (1.2.1) that he is from Epidamium, in effect to counterfeit himself. In another sense, this "fairy land" (2.2.189) or "dream" (182) of multiple roles may be unconsciously wished for by the characters, and hence opposes the self-effacing mania of the Syracusan visitors. Or it may stem from an otherwise unfathomable discontent, such as the sour disposition of the Ephesian brother.

If playing a role has its ultimate source in the play's own master-plotter, that providential Shakespeare behind the scenery, its value is to be found in the play's playful servants, not free men but men already assigned a burdensome role, a "gentleman's gentleman" as the English would have it. Men suffering from often arbitrary masters, made even more arbitrary by the day's confusions, the Dromios are thus forced to adopt a sense of play for survival itself. The servants' humor is "merry" (1.2.21), and their ability to jest or play militates against the determinism otherwise implicit in the age's medical/psychological term *humor*. Even the Ephesian Antipholus, though normally conservative or unplayful, vows to "jest" (3.1.123) in spite of the "expense" to himself. Adriana is starving for a "merry look" (2.1.88) from her husband, and though he is in anything but a sportive humor, the Syracusan Antipholus chooses to adopt the fallacy offered by the strange events, to take part, in essence, in what he knows is a play, in something at variance with reality. If time is cruel here, that giver and taker as characterized by Dromio, there is still a "good time" in which to "jest" and hence a "time for all things" (2.2.64–65). Aemilia diagnoses the marital problems as caused by Adriana's inhibiting her husband's "sports" (5.1.77), while the Ephesian Antipholus "entertains" the arrest, despite his knowledge of his innocence, as a "sport" (4.1.81). In general, the play makes a clear distinction between an "ape" (one who consciously plays by imitation) and an "ass" (the helpless butt of humor, playful or cruel as the case may be).

Against the imposed plot, the cruel "mishaps" (1.1.120) that have separated the family, the terror in losing an identity or gaining one unsought, there stands this sense of playfulness that would wrest some of the power from time. Adriana asks the Syracusan Dromio to "play the porter" (2.2.211) and he does, violating his conscious knowledge of his role in a way that distinguishes him from *The Shrew*'s Sly. The otherwise sober Luciana calls on the Syracusan Antipholus to "muffle [his] false love with some show of blindness" (3.2.8) so as to prevent her sister from—appropriately—reading in his "eyes" and "tongue" (9–10) his reality as an adulterer. To divert the tragedy that will itself be diverted once disclosures are made, he can, with her instruction, "apparel vice like virtue's harbinger" (3.2.12), playing "secret-false" (15). Even the sober Ephesian Antipholus will "play" the faithless husband, choosing the courtesan because she is "witty" and "wild" (3.1.140), the playful opposite of the stereotypical Elizabethan matron, Adriana. Antipholus, in fact, will play that role "be it for nothing but in spite of my wife" (118). In a larger sense, each twin plays the other, and this, of course, applies to servants and masters. The Ephesian Dromio speaks to the issue when he asks his Syracusan counterpart, who is concealed indoors, to consider what it would be like "if thou hast been Dromio to-day in my place" (3.1.46).

Whatever the source of such playing—enforced, willed, chosen, or advised—it establishes a counterpoint to what the play itself had established in the opening scene, that moribund world, as I have called it, a scene caught in the past and promising nothing beyond a repetition with Egeon's death of a former act of political cruelty. Yet once these varied concepts of playing are established in the inner plot, the characters *stick* to the stage, the play's field of play, rather than fleeing, though the Syracusan Antipholus attempts to flee. Nor do they go mad beyond recovery, however sorely tempted, nor retreat to the abbey, as if such retreat were possible in a play forcing its characters together. The very essence of comedy, that coming together after a breach in station or personality has been healed, is at one with the Plautine plot that Shakespeare complicates only to uncomplicate.

vi

For us the issue, comically tested in *Errors*, is how to see the world as it *is*, how by "computation" (2.2.4) of its various ingredients to come to some assessment of what it is to be human in the context of a world that at any moment can overwhelm the individual, or how, in Dennis Huston's words, to live with the "potentially tragic problem of discontinuity in human experience."[11] Adriana claims to be "press'd down with conceit— / Conceit, my comfort and my injury" (4.2.65–66). She uses "conceit" here in two senses, as "understanding" and as "imagination," the latter alluding both to Shakespeare's talent and that art for which a taste must be acquired by the onstage participants. Though it would be absurd to imagine the characters coming to any other conclusion in Act 5, the final scene does represent the application of conceit as *understanding* to a five-act play that has been sustained, consciously and unconsciously, by the characters' willingness to play. If fate or Shakespeare creates the play, the character-actors sustain that creation by remaining in Ephesus, even if forced to do so, here in the legendary home of illusions and illusion-makers. At length they are able to see what is, what we as audience see. Once this happens, then language, so deficient until that moment, blossoms in their own long speeches splicing together the earlier disjointed narratives of their one-day mating. If these final long speeches are dull, they are so only because the characters now tell us what we have known, and in language, now functioning as a mere recorder and at one with its object, that no longer needs to be playful. Like the four lovers of *A Midsummer Night's Dream*, they speak of events "strange" if not "admirable" (5.1.27), but again, no magic is involved and here the doubting Theseus is replaced by a Duke who believes their common story precisely because "what is" has not been challenged but rather affirmed. There is no forest here, no separate world in contradistinction to reality or Athens. In Shakespeare's later comedy, the woman alone, Hippolyta, maintained the imaginative sympathy for the lovers in the face of Theseus's disclaimers; here in *Errors*—if I may borrow Hippolyta's line from *A Midsummer Night's Dream*—both men and women find the narrations growing to "something of great constancy."[12]

With this enforced play leading to the harmonious community of the final scene, the characters, without retreating to a forest, can also avoid worlds that have or should have no real existence. Persia (4.1.4)—any-where but here and now—remains only a theoretical destination for the Second Merchant. Nor does Aemilia remain locked eternally in the abbey; nor does her Syracusan son stay forever the wanderer or her Ephesian son the smug husband. The equitable but cruel state law applied to Egeon never materializes. Like that opening scene of *A Midsummer Night's Dream* that promises a tragedy on the lines of *Romeo and Juliet*, the opening scene here shows what can happen *without* play. But the stage, the arena of play, must "admit traffic" (1.1.15), and even as theater itself plays between the visual and verbal, *Errors* plays on its own seemingly inflexible opening situation. The family reunion in turn frees both the state and those characters who are not part of the original accident yet are affected by the family's separation. Without the "conceit" of Act 5 and of the play generally, Angelo would face imprisonment and the Second Merchant, going unpaid, would have to change travel plans. Unjust or light penalties, to be sure, but they indicate the potential replication when the eyes and ears of those most affected are not functioning properly.

Reality is thus not a constant in this play but rather a compromise between what is and how we perceive that "is." Again, the debate between Balthazar and Antipholus on what constitutes a good meal, the fare itself or the quality of the hosting, underlines this duality. Not to make dinner on time is both a temporal and a spatial fact, and yet at the same time a commentary on the mind-set of the "nonparticipant."

If man on the stage of both the theater and the encompassing world is at once actor and audience, he also must play both roles constantly, given the nature of dialogue and of the human community. The challenge then becomes: with this definition of reality as an ongoing compromise, can we agree on *one* counterfeit, with some room for difference, to be sure, but also with boundaries for difference? Can we see the *same thing*, albeit illusory in being not one thing but the product of a collective vision? Can the characters onstage and, by extension, on the world's stage do what those "characters" in Shakespeare's audience are assisted in doing by an onstage fiction balancing language and spectacle, all within the time scheme of probability? Dromio cannot valorize such absolute words as *sound*, *sure*, and *certain*, despite his master's insistence; those onstage and off, therefore, must learn to see as one "this sure uncertainty" (2.2.185). To rework Adriana's marriage metaphor, if we are all "undividable incorporate" (2.2.122), individual drops that cannot be isolated from the sea of life, and if the audience offstage can identify with those onstage, then, being doubly "undividable incorporate," can we still see and hear *roughly* the same thing?

vii

"Here we wander in illusions" (4.3.43), and the cry goes up for "some blessed power [to] deliver us from hence" (44). Our human goal is to decipher the source, albeit manifold, of such illusions. Bottom's *Pyramus and Thisby* also rests on such illusions; for example, Pyramus takes the sight of Thisby's blood-stained mantle as proof that she has been devoured by a lion, yet the results are doubly tragic precisely because the community so affected, the children and their parents, never comes together, as do their prototypes in *Romeo and Juliet*. That aristocratic Athenian audience, who fail to comprehend the parallel between Bottom's comic tragedy and what *A Midsummer Night's Dream* promises if Oberon and Puck had not intervened, is in *Errors* an all-knowing and harmonized audience. While *Errors* is not blessed with strong, sentient characters—a Rosalind or a Prospero—it does show characters moving away from isolation, out of such "adversity" (4.4.20) whether imposed or self-imposed, whether it be Egeon's mishaps or Adriana's "Self-harming jealousy" (2.1.102). Forced to play, forced to confront a world of illusions, the stage itself taken to an extreme, they make such a movement. Now, acting out of love, Adriana will ransom her husband, even while acknowledging that her "heart prays for him, though [her] tongue do curse" (4.2.28); she will pay his debt no matter how it "grows" (4.4.121) or seems to grow. Similarly, the Duke, while at first upholding the barrier between the two cities, releases Egeon from the ransom. The play's imposed *Measure for Measure* is dissolved just as the play of that name, through the wisdom of its own Duke, dissolves judgment, with the exception of the penalty placed on Lucio. Here, even a son is eager to pay the ransom for a father whom he has not seen since his nativity.

In the final scene the characters, like us, see the events of the day *as* illusions, as *theater*, as comic errors in a comedy of errors. Having been forced to play actors and audience in that illusion, they are now at "liberty" (2.1.7) from illusions as well as from their otherwise incomplete selves. Similarly, the actor's own impersonation completes our selves, bridging the existential gap between what we do and our perception of ourselves as doers or actors. The world is no different from what it was at the start; the facts remain the same: on this given day are present four members plus servants of the same fractured family. Only the perception, the *naming* has been altered. Players on both sides of the stage now share the common emotion generated by such liberty, relief, and release. Everyone becomes a "formal" man again (5.1.105), discovering the self through playing (or seeing and hearing, in our case) its opposite, and then rediscovering the self as it is defined in the context of the family.

Allowing ourselves to be transformed from actor to audience, we too are complete, having achieved that completion by journeying into the play, hazarding our everyday concept of reality for this fictive, shamanlike journey, a journey taken both for the profit at its end and for the pleasure when its parabolic curve returns us home. We can all go home now, for as we "came into the world" of the theater, we go out "hand in hand" (5.1.425–26), although the characters onstage and those characters offstage leave through opposing exits.

2

Troilus and Cressida:
"What's aught but as 'tis valued?"

C OLERIDGE thought that "there is none of Shakespeare's plays harder to characterize" than *Troilus and Cressida*,[1] and, indeed, many subsequent commentators have argued that it is not a play at all, and, if it is, that it is a bad play, or one not meant for the stage. Hence *Troilus* has been dismissed as proper for the reader's study but impossible for the theater,[2] an instance where Shakespeare was skeptical of any meaningful dramatic structure,[3] an interesting failure,[4] or one that overshoots the mark of satire,[5] a moment when Shakespeare, however secure in his craft, was given to experimentation,[6] producing a strange contribution to the age's dramatic production,[7] neither tragedy nor comedy but a farce,[8] a one-time attempt to write Jonsonian satirical comedy,[9] or satire so biting that we reject it since it punctures our own vital myths about Trojans and Greeks,[10] a play flawed, specifically, by the character of Troilus, who bears too many contradictions even as he is surrounded by thin characters who are little more than types.[11] For George Bernard Shaw, Shakespeare here "made exactly one attempt . . . to hold the mirror up to nature; and he probably nearly ruined himself by it. . . . At all events he never did it again."[12]

A second group of commentators—nicely summarized by Robert Kimbrough[13]—assumed that the play was a philosophical debate, and, accordingly, sides were taken: Troilus the romantic in a crass world/ Troilus the degraded sensualist; Cressida the naive young girl ruined by the power-hungry men of the play/ Cressida the scheming harlot; the Trojans elevated by their imagination, their intuition, their sense of honor[14] / the Trojans as materialists, rationalizing their acquisitiveness through high-flown poetry; the Greeks as practical men making do in an imperfect world, cognizant of themselves and of their limitations/ the Greeks as harbingers of that unromantic world of realpolitik to be ushered in with Elizabeth's death. Through such readings, the play becomes a treatise on honor,[15] or dishonor,[16] on idealism even if such

46

idealism can only be implied through the reverse image grounded in one immoral camp, or both.[17] The controlling issue becomes faith in an ideal or, conversely, adherence to the principles of order and political stability.[18] Various spokespersons for Shakespeare have been found in Troilus, Hector, Ulysses, Achilles, Cressida, Thersites, and even in Diomedes.

In time even these more partisan positions gave way to readings that argued against antithetical Trojan and Greek poles in the play. Parallels were found between the private love story and the war plot,[19] and between individual Trojans and Greeks[20]—a sense of dramatic balance in which the apparent differences between the two camps served to conceal Shakespeare's own condemnation of both sides, or gave evidence of his own impartial perspective.[21] Mars melds with Venus,[22] and if a "dialectic"[23] exists, it is not between opposing camps but within the individual characters, or in terms of issues (reason, honor, imagination, time, the relation of private to public life) common to all the play's inhabitants, whatever their affiliation.[24]

A third group of commentators has followed the example of Una Ellis-Fermor,[25] finding in our own indecision with the play a controlling principle of nonresolution, where debate gives way to a world so paradoxical[26] that no values can emerge, no authentic standard by which we might order the tragedy or comedy or satire,[27] a fallen world,[28] lacking a single topology,[29] a play whose own anti-art, or formlessness, is the perfect correlative for its picture of human inconstancy.[30] Shakespeare himself is here detached or impartial,[31] offering us his own disenchanted vision of mankind,[32] making our own uncertainty part of the play[33] and thus demanding a multiconsciousness from his audience.[34] Unlike *Hamlet*, *Troilus* is consistently anti-heroic,[35] full of anticlimaxes,[36] offering a negative utopia,[37] one whose only consistency is that principle of reductive substitution in which all characters and all ideals are leveled by a down-spiraling repetition.[38] For Clifford Leech this discordant universe only implies its opposite, and *Troilus* thus demonstrates how we "must make what we have as harmonious as we can."[39]

In *The Comedy of Errors* we see clearly what is happening, in direct contrast to the muddied vision of the onstage characters. For us the stage spectacle is certain—with the single exception that Aemilia is hidden from us until the final scene—and if there are problems in language, such problems are confined to those onstage. This very disparity between the visual and the verbal is reversed and yet also qualified in *Troilus*. What happens has already happened, and the Jacobeans, tracing their own history to the legendary Brutus who fled Troy and later established London, were surely familiar with the story and its outcome, here a grafted outcome in which Troy goes on to defeat and Cressida goes on to Diomedes before expiring, riddled with disease.[40] What "is" is: nothing is uncertain, and Shakespeare confirms the audience's own historical knowledge at the close of Act 3, scene 2 when Troilus, Cressida, and Pandarus step out of the present stage characters and, albeit ironically, anticipate their place in history: "Let all constant men be Troiluses, all false women Cressids, and all brokers-between Pandars" (202–4). Or when Agamemnon pronounces "Great Troy is ours, and our sharp wars are ended" (5.9.10), long before his country has hit on an equestrian stratagem.

These same three complex, seemingly contradictory critical responses just outlined suggest that if we as audience are sure of what we see, we lack a corresponding certainty with the language of *Troilus* itself, or with our own text as we apply it to the play. For us, no less than for Troilus, the issue is one of valorizing in language what we experience and, at the same time, reaching some consensus about that value. Actually, Shakespeare's audience, despite the prominence of the pro-Trojan Lydgate version of the wars, may have had something approaching a divided response to the two sides of the conflict, this even in the face of their pseudohistorical link with Brutus of Troy.[41] D. W. Robertson would have a similarly divided response to what had once seemed Chaucer's own singular romantic portrait of the lovers.[42] If, through the prophecies of Pandarus and Agamemnon, Shakespeare sustains the audiences'—both Renaissance and modern—certainty about the story, about what we see, he also enacts the split between such visual certainty and linguistic uncertainty most graphically in Act 5, scene 2, where Troilus, spying Cressida toying with her Greek captor, Diomedes, similarly bifurcates vision and language, what is and how "'tis valued" (2.2.52): "This is, and is not, Cressid" (5.2.146). He would let "stubborn critics, apt with a theme . . . square" what they also see onstage, the actress impersonating a faithless Cressida, with the general notion of womankind as it is abstracted through language (131–32). For the present chapter that eavesdropping scene will be my final concern because I think it embodies the play's own larger cleavage between spectacle and language.

That we have problems squaring our own idiosyncratic language with what is physically present onstage is generated, I believe, by Shakespeare's conscious choice—I do not think the play represents a failure— in devising a play in which that prerequisite metadramatic balance fails for us even as, say, it succeeded for us and, at length, for the characters themselves in *The Comedy of Errors*. Shakespeare is, in short, successful here with a pervasive image of dramatic failure. I approach the play in this fashion not in isolation but in the context of other critics, not all of them recent and each in his or her own way, who have also alluded to this self-sacrificial dramatic core in *Troilus and Cressida*. Such "allusion" has most often taken the form of a thematic reading where the issue, for example, becomes fair without (the "visual" as I would translate it) and foul within (the essence, as conveyed by language, of the otherwise appealing object). For one commentator this cleavage is enacted in the "putrefied core" or body from which Hector robs its "goodly armor" (5.8.1–2).[43] Because of this division, human will, as conveyed through language, can only be imperfectly represented in action.[44] The gap exists between what *is*, physical reality, and the "world of the individual . . . in part created by the nonrational structure of attitudes and feelings that are inseparable from perception."[45] Spirit or essence as manifest in language opposes the flesh, or the mechanical historical facts of the Troy story.[46] In a most provocative article Carolyn Asp defines a break between art, by which we gain immortality and transcendence, and life, which without the collaboration of art can only be transient and degenerate.[47] Arnold Stein speaks of Shakespeare's "negative dramatization" here, "as if the dramatic imagination were trying to oppose itself at every turn."[48]

My interest is not to forsake the readings of the first three groups of commentators, nor to confirm, if I could, the paradoxical readings of the fourth. Surely, we each go away with the text we ourselves have fashioned,[49] and such fashioning is justified as long as it interacts productively with Shakespeare's literal text and, in that same interaction, is alert to just what is obtained and at what cost.[50] My concern, rather, is to offer a reading of the play *as a play*, finding its organizing principle in what one critic, speaking not of Shakespeare but of Samuel Beckett, has called the "aesthetics of failure."[51] Here, again, there is no ultimate failure on Shakespeare's part, but only his use of a device. In a similar fashion, we recognize in *A Midsummer Night's Dream* that Bottom's wretched *Pyramus and Thisby* is rescued from total failure by its place in Shakespeare's larger design.

Again, the eavesdropping scene is the culmination of three successive stages in the play, with the first two given to language, and the third to the translation of such language into spectacle. To recycle the words of Richard Fly, Act 5, scene 3 stands as the "cataclysmic termination" of the gap between "verbal texture, spectacle, and action,"[52] and it is to this scene that these earlier stages inexorably move.

i

The first stage (1.1–2.1) finds its motto in Cressida's own "there's no comparison" (1.2.62) when Pandarus proposes Troilus as a "better man" than Hector. If Shakespeare's dramatic poetry is built on simile and metaphor, the "like" or "as" of grammar itself, the issue becomes, for characters and playwright as well: how does one use language imaginatively and comparatively so as to assign value to objects? The impossibility of such valuation's finding permanence in the world of *Troilus and Cressida* is underscored as Cressida's own "motto" is recast one scene later when Nestor sees Thersites as a perverse artist or manipulator "whose gall coins slanders like a mind, / To match us in comparison with dirt" (1.3.193–94).

Troilus's initial attempt to give words to his conception of Cressida is itself aborted, for by his own confession he "was about" to respond to Pandarus's observation that "she look'd yesternight fairer than ever [he] saw her look, or any woman else" (1.1.32–34) when his heart was "rive in twain" (35) by an otherwise inarticulate "sigh." A prelude to romantic speech, to be sure, this sigh still must give way to language itself, and Troilus announces his dilemma and, I think, the larger dilemma of the play when he confesses the impossibility of disposing of that sign by burying it beneath or in the "wrinkle of a smile" (38–40). When the same sigh does turn into language, his initial "comparison" of Cressida seems forced, too dependent on a negative extreme provided by others: her hand is more white than all other whites, which are but "ink / Writing their own reproach," and the "spirit of sense" in that hand stands in beautiful contradistinction to the rough "palm of ploughman" (55–59). Pandarus thereupon diffuses even these comparisons when he attempts to match Cressida with Helen, first confessing that his partiality as Cressida's uncle prejudices him and then dismissing the task of comparison itself, prejudices notwithstanding, with "But what care I? I care not and she were a blackamore, 'tis all one to me" (77–78). These prelusive attempts at language through comparison are themselves dispersed by the "ungracious clamors" and "rude sounds" (89) of an offstage alarum, and when Troilus, alone, tries to rekindle the comparison, his language, as several commentators have noted, sinks to a rather crass and revealing economic metaphor: she is a pearl, and he is the "merchant" who searches for it in the ship named Pandar (100–104).

Scene two complements this pattern of forced and then rejected comparisons as Pandarus and Cressida try to compare Troilus and Hector, with that effort itself abandoned when they separate the two men: "*Pan.*: Well, I say Troilus is Troilus. / *Cres.* [insincere, of course, since we know she prefers Troilus to all other Trojans]: Then you say as I say, for I am sure he is not Hector" (1.2.66–68). The scene opens with an unflattering comparison of Ajax to various animals, the point being that if he shares some of the respective virtues of the bear, lion, and elephant, the composite fails to hold together: he has "joints of everything, but every thing . . . out of joint" (19–30). Appropriately in this play, where the issue is one of matching language to vision, Ajax has as many eyes as "purblind Argus, all eyes and no sight" (29–30). The scene ends with two instances in which the physical outweighs the spiritual or, rather, in which courtly language is the veneer playing just above the lust of the observers. Cressida and Pandarus first review Helen's stroking Troilus's "cloven chin" with her own "white hand" (149) and then Troilus's witty equation of the hairs on his chin with his father and brothers, the one white hair standing for Paris, the "forked one." The implication is that Helen, the "merry Greek" (109), might play false with Paris as she has done with Menelaus. By transference, Cressida herself will play false with Troilus. The language that Pandarus and Cressida, like presenters, later apply to the parade of Trojan soldiers passing over the stage provides no more elevation than that of buyers appraising wares in a market. On Pandarus's exit, Cressida herself rejects language for the actual body of Troilus, which she has just observed: "Words, vows, gifts, tears, and love's full sacrifice / He offers in another's enterprise, / But more in Troilus thousandfold I see / Than in the glass of Pandar's praise may be" (282–85).

These opening scenes provided the context for Ulysses' "degree" speech in Act 1, scene 3. We no longer see that speech as an unqualified Elizabethan touchstone, and several commentators have suggested that what Ulysses really calls for is the orderly prosecution of a war whose justification is itself suspect, that he advocates no less than unquestioning allegiance to absolute authority. Besides, the speech is irrelevant in terms of the play's subsequent action—in two senses. Like Hector reversing his position in the Trojan war council, Ulysses will bring Achilles into the conflict not by what he says in formal language but by a theatrical stratagem, the first stages of which he outlines in the conversation with Nestor that closes the present scene. Here he conforms to the "crafty" Ulysses of legend and of Renaissance prejudice. In addition, what finally rouses Achilles to action is not even Ulysses' projected play, in which the generals loudly praise Ajax as their representative in the fight with Hector, but rather Achilles' own rage over the death of his companion Patroclus.

One relevant point in the degree speech, however, is that the violation of hierarchy is expressed as a conflict between those who draw up the plans for battle and those who do the actual fighting, a split between "the still and mental parts" and the "many hands [that] strike" (200–201) sustaining the argument, exhibited in the first two scenes, that design (or language) without a correlative and subsequent execution becomes little more than useless theory ("mapp'ry, closet-war" [205]). Conversely, enactment without a collaborating design leads to the present unproductive conflict in which both Greeks and Trojans languish.

The fissure here between language and spectacle, desire and performance, theory and enactment leads to two theatrical failures. One is
Ulysses' own playwright's scheme in which, theoretically, Achilles and
Ajax will play actors unawares. The other is Patroclus's own reported (we
shall see it staged in Act 2, scene 3) "pageants" (151) in which, "like a
strutting player, whose conceit / Lies in his hamstring," he impersonates
and parodies the Greek generals to the "loud applause" (163) of his own
jaded audience of one. Thus, what I have called Shakespeare's own
"theater of failure" in the larger play is here a miniature theater of
"paradoxes" (184) or—in our sense of the word—"absurdities."
    This first stage (1.1–2.1), then, is something of a metadramatic bell
curve, beginning as it does with two scenes given to failed comparisons,
progressing through language that is suspect and two theaters that are
either serviceable or low, and ending, in Act 2, scene 1, with an almost
allegorical confrontation between the physical extreme represented by
Ajax (or as Thersites says of him, "I think thy horse will sooner con an
oration than thou learn a prayer without a book" [2.1.17–18]) and the
wickedly verbal Thersites. With language thus having proved inadequate
in several senses, it is dramatically right that this first stage ends with
Ajax unable to "learn . . . [Thersites'] proclamation" (21). Once that
sought-after proclamation, the language preceding the actual battle, is
"learned" or announced by Achilles, it is dismissed as "trash" (126). This
same breakdown in language is repeated in Achilles' reply "I know not,
'tis put to lott'ry. Otherwise / He knew his man" to Ajax's compulsive
question, "Who shall answer him?" (127–129). Ajax is left with only
speculation as to its real meaning—"O, meaning you?"—since Achilles
exits without proffering an answer. We ourselves are left with the physical, nonverbal Ajax promising to "go learn more of it," but we might
ask: how can we know ("learn") in a world that so sullies the correspondence between language and object?

ii

    The play's second stage, Act 2, scenes 2 and 3, offers a variation on the
metadramatics of failed language that I have posited in 1.1–2.1. For in the
Trojan council scene the split is between "essentialists" like Troilus and
Paris,[53] who argue that the object, here Helen, is an empty vessel into
which meaning is conveyed by the beholder, and Hector who contends,
unsuccessfully, that there must be some trade-off between such external
linguistic valuation and the object's own inherent worth, which, if it does
exist, should serve as the proper stimulus for language. Actually,
Troilus's position is more complicated than such antitheses suggest, for
his point about making the quarrel "gracious" by reading Helen as "a

theme of honor and renown, / A spur to valiant and magnanimous deeds" (125, 199–200) is not his whole argument. He is also concerned about consistency with a principle, however flawed it might be in truth, just as Ulysses has ultimately no clear ethical basis for his insistence on observing degree during a suspect war. As Alice Shavli observes, Troilus's sense of honor is closer to a concern for reputation ("What will the world think of us if we abandon Helen?") than the true Renaissance concept of honor.[54] Thus his notion of "What's aught but as 'tis valued?" (54) has an ambiguous application to the problem of the play itself: does Shakespeare have a choice other than to corroborate a world, whose language is already corrupt, by a play in which dialogue and action—the "test" the onstage characters apply to the plot—do not synthesize? With no sure surrogate for the author on the stage—as there is to some degree, say, in Rosalind—we must reread the proffered text, just as we must, albeit comically, that of the courtiers in *Love's Labor's Lost*. I would observe that the earlier play, like the present one, is also strewn with theatrical failures, in the form of the Russian masque and the interlude of the Nine Worthies.

Like his earlier attempt to define Cressida, Troilus's description of Helen as "the life of our design" (194) is stillborn, a paradox: the object, as we shall see in Act 3, scene 1, bears little relation to that description. Stage one ended with Ulysses offering a rough draft, if you will, of the play to be perpetrated on Achilles through Ajax. Stage two ends with what can only be described as a botched performance, or a dress rehearsal with the central figure absent. Actually, one-half of that play succeeds, as Ajax, like Christopher Sly of *The Taming of the Shrew*, is duped into believing himself something other than he really is, for he takes Ulysses' sarcasm for Gospel truth, as confirmation of a noble character: a lord of "sweet composure" (2.3.240), the modern Mars, more eminent than Nestor himself. Even the miniature play's second half, focused on Achilles, may not fail entirely, for Diomedes observes that in "his silence" Achilles "drinks up" the "applause" lavished on his rival (201). Unlike Act 3, scene 1 in *The Comedy of Errors*, however, where we see both those inside and outside Antipholus's house, here we are confined to the characters outside Achilles' tent and have only a messenger's reports of his reaction or nonreaction to Ulysses' stratagems. Surely Ulysses' theater is used superficially for purposes of manipulation, like Hamlet's *Murder of Gonzago* or Claudius's staged duel in the final act of *Hamlet*, rather than as a mirror held up to the complex nature of these warring factions. Concerned with the possibilities of language both as a mirror and a shaper of reality and, by extension, of the theater's containing within itself the gamut spanning the physical and the metaphysical, these two initial stages are linked by Thersites' speech that opens Act 2, scene 3, where, denying any ethical significance in Ajax, Achilles, and Ulysses, Thersites draws language itself down to the level of a curse: a vengeance "on the whole camp" in the form of the "Neopolitan bone-ache" (1:22).

iii

In the play's third stage (3.1–4.5) the first two scenes in Act 3 provide the enactment of Troilus's "language" of love, whether delivered in Pandarus's chamber or the council scene, and thus both his private and public speech, the linguistic parallel to Shakespeare's double plot, here take form. Both women fall short of expectation, and especially Helen; Act 3, scene 1 is her only scene, whereas we shall see Cressida both before and after consummation with Troilus and then again, before and after, with Diomedes in the Greek camp. Responses to Helen vary: she is alternately seen as shallow, witty, the accomplished court lady, a sensualist, vulgar, repulsive. Clearly she is an inadequate correlative for Troilus's earlier grand "theme" or "life or our design." Her "failure" in dramatic realization—and, conversely, Shakespeare's success in being true to his own grand design—is expressed in her own appealing, but ultimately cloying verbal self-indulgence as she and Pandarus in their punning threaten to run the words *fair* and *queen* into the ground. The scene itself opens with music, a harmony ironically juxtaposed with the dialogue between Pandarus and the Servant, in which the "too courtly" Pandarus cannot "understand" his "too cunning" verbal partner (27–28). The scene is framed near the end by Pandarus's love song, in which "love" and its language sink to the groans of intercourse, the phatic "ha's" and "ho's," with an Amen reexpressed as "Heigh ho" (125–26).

The following scene (3.2) plays off its predecessor, even as Helen has comically characterized Cressida as her own "disposer" (3.1.87). Troilus's initial attempt to characterize Cressida—he first sees Pandarus as both a surrogate Cupid and Charon, and then the pun on death makes its way into Cressida's own "lily beds" (3.2.8–15)—soon verges on the inarticulate as the "imaginary relish" (19) of the sexual event threatens both his verbal ("I shall lose distinction in my joys") and—curiously—his physical powers (the euphemism contained in "my ruder power" [25]). Even this linguistic euphoria is lanced by Pandarus's lawyer's language ("In witness whereof the parties interchangeably") as well as by his suggestion that since "words pay no debts, give her deeds" (55–58). In contrast to the verbal, albeit shallow scene with Helen, here the visual—actions, deeds, the body—overwhelms the verbal. Cressida herself enters veiled, and is silent for some sixty lines, her first words being the rather prosaic "Will you walk in, my lord?" (60). Pandarus alternately must urge Troilus to "speak to her" rather than to the image of her, or to "draw" her "curtain" and "see" her "picture" (46–47). Ulysses' own concern about the abyss between the Greek's will for victory and the present stalemate is rephrased in Troilus's neurotic fear that the parallel "monstruosity in love" is the gap between "infinite" will and "confined" execution, between desire and act (82–85). Cressida complements him by observing that lovers have "the voice of lions and the acts of hares" and are therefore no less "monsters" than Troilus's abstraction of love itself (88–89). That negative image of the theater which we have already seen in Ulysses' stratagems and Patroclus's imitations is here sustained in Troilus's reference to "Cupid's pageant" (15), which, he insists wrongly, offers no emblematic figure such as Fear.

In this third stage of the play language gives way to execution, yet does not accompany it; Pandarus appropriately urges the incipient couple, "Have you not done talking yet?" (100–101). Playing the coy maiden who most immodestly anticipates the consummation, Cressida, as she confesses, is confined to her "tongue" (129–31). Her inability to find a more precise speech, though, is nothing but an invitation to Troilus to "stop [her] mouth" with a kiss, the orifice from which he now finds "sweet music" issuing (133). As I have observed earlier, the scene ends with those ironic vows exchanged among lovers and their go-between that have already been confirmed in the play's prehistory and will be confirmed again. Their mutual "Amen" will surely call up a similar Amen with which Thersites concluded his speech opening Act 2, scene 3.

These parallel flawed enactments in the Helen-Paris and Troilus-Cressida scenes, and the link between desire and performance both military and amatory, and hence between speech as both a public and a private medium, receive a "choral" commentary in the scene closing Act 3. Calchas presses his claim for an exchange of Cressida for Antenor, and Ulysses' play finally receives its staging when the generals, as instructed, play their roles in shunning the malcontent warrior. That play "works" in the sense that Achilles agrees "to see great Hector in his weeds of peace" (239). Yet it overshoots its mark with Ajax, who now takes so literally the role assigned him that he becomes the image incarnate of absurd pride, so much so that Patroclus, whose questionable gifts of imitation we already know, now effectively plays the suppliant to Thersites' "Ajax." In this play examining the nature of language, Thersites appropriately impersonates an Ajax given to monosyllables ("Hum" and "Ha!") or evasive speech ("*Patr.* Your answer, sir. *Ther.* Fare ye well, with all my heart" [298–99]).

The anticipation through language of the lovers' consummation, Troilus's linguistic "design" in elevating Helen to a "theme" of honor, and then the sorry enactment of such anticipation and design in the opening two scenes of Act 3 are themselves overwhelmed by time, by the play's acknowledged history, that "great-siz'd monster of ingratitude" (3.3.147) which Ulysses has described for Achilles. Troilus's own search for a metaphor for his lover that, like his vows, would outlast time itself is now transformed to the trinity of buyer (Diomedes), seller (Paris), and product (Cressida) in 4.1.76–80. The attempt to define by comparison is restated in Diomedes' cynical response to Paris's "Who, in your thoughts, deserves fair Helen best, / Myself, or Menelaus" (4.1.54–55). Cressida's own earlier enactment scene (3.2), where our response to her might still be divided, is replayed in the scene where this daughter "of the game" is passed among the Greek generals, with Ulysses redoing Troilus's "theme" as the "theme of all our scorns" (4.5.30), and with the balance between language and physicality conflated to "There's language in her eye, her cheek, her lip, / Nay, her foot speaks" (4.5.55–56). We hear a new, colder, more abstract language from Troilus, a prelude to his exercise in nonlogic in Act 5, scene 2: "How now, what's the matter?" and "Is it so concluded?" (4.2.58, 66). This sense of reduction and conflation extends to the double plot itself, as consanguinity prevents the anticipated match between Hector and Ajax, and the opposing armies put down their arms and play guest and host. Diomedes' initial sparring with Troilus is likewise diffused when, replying to the objection that he praises Cressida in his presence, he asserts his right "to be a speaker free" (4.4.121–23).

As the plot hastens to the eavesdropping scene, Troilus himself recognizes the destructive partnership between time and language. The exigency of the exchange of prisoners "strangles" the lovers' "dear vows" and "fumbles up" their goodbyes to "a loose adieu" (4.4.37, 46). The paradoxical vows of fidelity that closed Act 3, scene 2 are further qualified, for Troilus now recognizes that their renewed vows are subject to the corrosive "arts and exercise" of the Greeks in whose sweet "talk" there "lurks a still and dumb-discoursive devil / That tempts most cunningly" (4.4.86, 90–91). The phrase *Be thou true* is subjected to a rigorous scrutiny that almost leads to a quarrel between the departing lovers.

iv

Equated earlier with abuse and manipulation, its principle of imitation parodied by Patroclus's and later Thersites' impersonations, its otherwise complementary poles of language and spectacle divorced by the larger play itself, the image of the theater is now resurrected in the eavesdropping or what I. A. Richards calls the Betrayal Scene, Act 5, scene 2.[55] In a curious parallel to the final scene of *A Midsummer Night's Dream*, where we watch Oberon and Puck watch Theseus and his court watch Bottom's

Pyramus and Thisby, here we watch two audiences, Ulysses and Troilus and—to one side—Thersites, watch the tawdry, mechanical love-"play" between Diomedes and Cressida. Several commentators have observed that such levels of audiences are more akin to comedy than tragedy.[56] The device of a play within a play itself stresses self-consciousness and role-playing, and we think, say, of Berowne observing his fellow monks violate their vows with what they think are private confessions of love.[57] Whether Troilus's role as audience leads to such perception is an issue for debate, yet in this play where characters are more often types, where men only seem to play out predestined roles, here the fuller character of Troilus emerges precisely because his role as audience, his seeing his former self in Diomedes, enacts a split between the real and the imagined—a split in himself no less than in Cressida. Even this divided and hence three-dimensional character, in a play where Shakespeare's powers and his interest in characterization have been questioned, collapses at its end to a type, as lover becomes tyrant: Troilus will later pursue battle as single-mindedly as he has earlier pursued love in defiance of war. We will recall that he opens the play choosing to fight the "battle within" (1.1.3) rather than that without.

Here, too, the cleavage is resolved from our perspective as the "ultimate audience": we see a tableau of naughty lovers, there is no mistaking that. However mechanical, Diomedes' commentary is the proper correlative for what we see: he knows what Cressida is or has been forced to become and thus has no time for linguistic or amatory "fooling" (101). At last, we say with both relief and horror, a language worthy of the spectacle that Cressida now represents. This observation, to be sure, does not exclude sympathy for her, but rather only recognizes her passion, and that of Diomedes, for what it is.[58]

The one-scene "play" of betrayal has its own prelude, like the opening exchange between Bernardo and Francisco in *Hamlet*: Diomedes on duty as sentry, Calchas approaching him through the darkness. In this play playing so destructively with language, the sentry's command is "Speak!," a call for identification that, following Calchas's own request that the sentry first identify himself, is met with "*Diomed*. Calchas, I think," followed by the simple affirmation of the very family ties that have precipitated Troilus's loss, "Where's your daughter?" That line itself is a literal cue for Cressida's entrance one line later. This same positive link of person with name, between what one sees and the word assigned to the object, itself resolves a persistent motif of misidentification earlier in the play: Pandarus's assertion "Troilus is Troilus," which concludes his first attempt to define Troilus in terms of Hector (1.2.66); the identification of the Trojan heroes passing across the stage with their names and qualities (1.2); Aeneas's request that Agamemnon's "name" be assigned to one of the several Greeks he meets as he crosses enemy lines to bring Hector's challenge (1.3); Patroclus's "Who's there? Thersites?" at 2.3.23, and later Agamemnon's "Where is Achilles?" (2.3.76), spoken while Achilles himself keeps to his tent; the confusion of Helen and Cressida when the Servant refers too generally to "the mortal Venus" (3.1.32); Paris's "See ho!, Who is that there?" and, when the "who" is identified, Aeneas's complementary question "Is the Prince there in person?" (4.1.1–3); and Hector's question "Is this Achilles" (4.5.233) as the two antagonists identify each other as prelude to the fight following on the heels of the aborted fight between Hector and Ajax.

This same motif, in which ambiguous identification leads to renewed attempts to align name and form, receives a final variation moments before the present scene. As Greeks and Trojans enter the stage to Thersites' "Hey-day! sprites and fires!" (5.1.66), Agamemnon cries out "We go wrong, we go wrong," but is reassured by Ajax's pointing to the place "where [they] see the lights." Achilles then enters as a guide back to Troy and, seconds later, Ulysses instructs Troilus to "follow [Hector's] torch, he goes to Calchas's tent" (85), promising to keep Troilus company himself, the very act that establishes one of the two audiences in Act 5, scene 2. Thus, after the brief problem of identification in the prelude, all such problems of identification and identity vanish, only to be subsumed in turn by the larger philosophic issue of identity curiously couched in the past tense by Troilus: "Was Cressid here?" (125).

That question, explicated in the dialogue between Troilus and Ulysses upon Cressida's exit, is itself prefaced by what can only be described as a reprise of the issues of language and spectacle charted so far in the play. Diomedes insists that Cressida allow her "mind [to] be coupled with [her] words" (15), that she, in effect, know herself and the physical basis of her recent vows of love. Conversely, Cressida fears that this "sweet honey Greek" has tempted her to folly, that his passion, not hers, is the cause (18). He quickly challenges her with the charge that she is "forsworn" (22), and that charge replicates in the concern that oaths (26) and pledges (77), what one has "sworn," be true, that words promising consummation find their home in the physical act itself. Without such correspondence, language falls to the extreme of "palter" (48) that in turn only aggravates Diomedes: "One cannot speak a word / But it straight starts you" (100–101). Albeit from base motives, Diomedes insists that Cressida reverse her vow "not [to] keep [her] word" (98). If language in the play generally cannot enhance an object, if speech fails because its object cannot supply the corresponding essence, if it is not "precious of itself" (2.2.55), then Diomedes, for better or worse, argues for a simpler language as correlative for what Troilus now sees as the "withered truth" (46) of love: that it is carnal, that in the play's "generation of vipers" (3.1.133) it cannot be otherwise. The language of the play so far has had mythological matter incommensurate with its expression;[59] here is the "truth" displacing earlier attempts to "be true" to a loftier ideal.

In like manner articulate speech now falls to whispering as Shakespeare forces the actor playing Cressida to violate stage convention, which dictates that at least the offstage audience, if not the two present onstage surrogate audiences, hear everything, even if it be the inner voice of a character: the "words" she whispers to her "sweet guardian" fail to make the play proper. Beyond whispering, the scene threatens to fall farther into silence as twice Troilus vows—broken vows, at that—to "not speak a word" (44, 52). And if music represents the ultimate refinement of human speech, then here the "music sounding within" that alone graced Helen's one scene (3.1) is rescored as Thersites' double-entendre: "And any man may sing her, if he can take her cliff; she's noted' (10–11).

At the start of the passage involving Cressida and Diomedes, the ears and hence language dominates: Ulysses commands Troilus to "List!" (17), and even Cressida begs "a word in [Diomedes'] ear" (34). However, the lines conveying her exit stress the eye, the repository full of "turpitude" and given to the carnal vision portrayed in the love scene: "one eye yet looks on thee, / but with my heart the other eye doth see. / Ah, poor our sex! The fault in us I find, / The error of our eye directs our mind. / What error leads must err" (107–12).

The larger division between language, by which Troilus will shortly try to divide the ideal from the real Cressida, and spectacle, with that word here taking on its most pejorative overtone, is underscored by a series of dichotomies running through the passage: Ulysses' insistence that they go / Troilus's that they stay; Troilus's own division between his being "patient . . . outwardly" and tormented within (68); and the opposition of roles signified when Diomedes wears the favor of the lover whose identity Cressida will not disclose.

Thus, Act 5, scene 2 mirrors the larger play even as it provides a context for its own climactic moment when, with Cressida's departure, Troilus, a self-confessed artisan with language, must "make a recordation" to his soul (116), must define in words what he has just seen and about which there can be no mistake. The language he now employs is new to the play, an alternative to his own romantic vocabulary, the formal addresses of the council scenes, or the colorful, scurrilous talk of Thersites and Pandarus. Derick Marsh describes it as having a "clotted quality,"[60] and O. J. Campbell sees the speech as issuing from a "logical machine" forced to "perform feats of prestidigitation that make it creak ridiculously."[61] In this new language, and *with it*, Troilus now recognizes the division between his ideal and "th' attest of eyes and ears" (122), though the "negative" comparison takes a rather perverse (or inverse) form: only "if those organs had deceptious functions, / Created only to calumniate" could the visual/verbal impressions received from them square with his ideal, that "esperance so obstinately strong" (121–24).

That inverse form succeeds as the ambiguous question "Was Cressid here?" by which Cressida thereby bifurcates into existence (the woman who has just exited and who was therefore once here) and essence (that is, can the sullied creature who just departed be the same woman described and then enacted earlier in the play?). Ulysses, the man of rational language even if such rationality conceals political rationalizations, is pitted by that same question against Troilus, whose language now takes on a peculiarly litigious or scholastic quality. Ulysses' own "Cressid was here but now" (128) represents a thin attempt to bridge the gap between the pragmatic and the ideal. Troilus even provides an "out"—that can prove no out—to invalidate his self-proclaimed division between the ideal (language) and the real (the visual). Abstracting Cressida to "a theme / For depravation" (131–32), an image that can "square the general sex / By Cressid's rule" with the negative image of womanhood fashioned by "stubborn critics" (131–33), he is willing to deny that very abstraction on the one condition that Ulysses admit that the woman who has just exited was not Cressida. By logical extension, if Ulysses cannot do so—and of course he cannot—then the gap is thereby sustained between the ideal Cressida who existed in Troilus's earlier oratory and the present creature he has just witnessed. For a moment, therefore, three Cressidas threaten to flood the stage: the real, a positive, and a negative abstraction.

Language as rational discourse, as something logical and orderly, has thus doubled back on itself, and the only solution is for language, as now employed by Troilus, to divide rather than to synthesize. Separating the concept of myth into myth as story and the (true) myth behind the story, Douglas Cole suggests that as a mythmaker Troilus must now posit two Cressidas.[62] He thus works with "two language systems"[63] which, because they cannot be complementary, must destroy the very order that language otherwise provides us. This bifurcation thus constitutes Troilus's "new perspective on reality,"[64] but for this perspective to be enacted, for it to lead to action capable of sustaining a clear and single theme, one of its halves must be jettisoned. Inevitably, to square the ideal with the real, Troilus's former idealized love must be translated to idealized hate so that the perverse ideal heals the gap with the real: if Cressida is no longer his, she must be "Diomed's Cressida" (137), and he will pursue this newly formed hybrid with "prompted sword" to the death (175). The positive ideal now becomes an impossibility, announced by the series of nonfulfilling "ifs": "If beauty have a soul," "If souls guide vows," "if vows be sanctimonies," and so on (138–41). Only the negative nonideal is capable of translation into form. Between the two there is now a "spacious breadth" admitting "no orifex for a point as subtle / As Ariachne's broken woof to enter" (150–52).

In a brilliant essay on that image, J. Hillis Miller suggests that the inserted "i" in Ariachne is deliberate, admitting both Ariadne and Arachne: the former committing suicide after Theseus's abandonment of her; the latter, in some versions of the myth, taking her life after being humiliated when Athene tore her work to shreds.[65] Ariadne's thread through the labyrinth thus conflates with Arachne's woof, and this "bricolage" represents not a new system of truth, nor its alternative, but an image of the play's own divided world. For present purposes, the violent end reinforced by the conflated myths is inseparable from Troilus's own suicidal adherence—both literally and as confirmed by the historical defeat of Troy—to the very "bifold authority" (144) that can sustain the twin sides of the paradox of the ideal and the real only by converting the former to violent energy: "as much as I do Cressid love, / So much by weight hate I her Diomed" (167–68).

If Cressida exits with reference to the bifocal nature of the eyes (one eye focused on the present Diomedes, the other on the ideal, past-tense Troilus), Troilus summarizes his own resolve, just before Aeneas's entrance, with a horrendous imaged based on the ear, and one that holds his penultimate comparison in the play: the hurricane that "shall dizzy with more clamor Neptune's ear / In his descent" will be less forceful than his own "prompted sword / Falling on Diomed" (171–76). The comparison with Neptune's ear doubles back to the final comparison between Cressida and truth, besides recalling the vows that closed Act 3, scene 2: "Let all untruths stand by thy stained name, / And they'll seem glorious" (179–80). This movement itself, from vision to a reverse idealization of that vision, is capped with Ulysses' "Your passion draws ears hither" (181), literally a cover line for Aeneas's entrance, metadramatically a signal that Troilus's language at last matches Cressida's reality and, by extension, the reality of both love and war in the play.

Troilus's linguistic dexterity in trying to reconcile words to vision by positing, paradoxically, an absent Cressida as the ideal lasts no longer than the scene itself. With Act 5, scene 4 and until the play's final scene the cleavage between vision and language returns. The words of the prophet Cassandra, ratified by parallel predictions from Andromache and Priam, are dismissed by Hector as nothing more than "ill opinion" (5.4.17), while Troilus, earlier the artisan of language, is portrayed accurately by Hector as "savage" (5.3.49), a man now literally given to a "mad and fantastic execution" and driven by "careless force" (5.5.38–40).

Troilus himself enacts this cleavage when he tears apart Cressida's letter, separating its "words, words, mere words" from "matter from the heart' (5.3.108). Even Paris, the original cause of the conflict and Troilus's partner in the council debates, is reduced to the name for the bear-baiting garden west of the Globe (5.7.10–12). The division between existence and essence, language and spectacle, is itself made manifest on stage when Hector, marring his earlier reputation, unarms himself to cannibalize the "goodly armor" from the otherwise "putrefied core" before him (5.8.1–4). The power of language, and its relation to the external world, is recast as the screech owl singing the death of Hector to Priam and Hecuba and, in the process, turning them to stone (5.10–15–21).

Pandarus at length raises the issue posed by the larger play in three questions: "Why should our endeavor be so lov'd, and the performance so loath'd? What verse for it? What instance for it?" (5.10–38–40). His jingo about the honey bee who, "once subdu'd in armed tail," now fails to make both "sweet honey and sweet notes" (41–44) answers these questions raised by the world of *Troilus and Cressida*, whose center cannot hold once language separates from spectacle. On the other hand, Shakespeare's own skill as playwright is here directly proportionate to his ability to depict a situation in which human enactment, that delicate balance between the ideal and the real, language and spectacle, is itself violated.

v

This commentary on *Troilus and Cressida* was initiated by the pre-text or pretext of critical disagreement on the play: on its status as a play, as a member of Shakespeare's canon, as a play with a recognizable center or—with a bow to the third group of commentators—noncenter. My Ariadne's thread through this critical labyrinth has been to suggest that *Troilus and Cressida* itself rests upon a failed enactment, a conscious divorce on Shakespeare's part between language and spectacle—the theater's own prerequisite balance. Metadramatic criticism itself normally assumes that same successful balance irrespective of the play's own thematic direction. If, for example, in Hamlet's perspective the world violates the ideal—of father, mother, friendship, of certainty itself—the theater itself never fails him: its actors succeed as the brief chronicles of the times, be those times good or bad. The harsh historical judgment that Shakespeare's age made on Cleopatra does not invalidate, by one jot, her own dazzling theatrics as, in her final speech, she converts asps into lovers and then into babies sleeping at her breast, thereby establishing her positively imaginative world against the dull, historical inevitability of Octavius. Again, Bottom's *Pyramus and Thisby* fails for the aristocratic audience assembled on stage, yet in its otherwise inane conversion of tragedy into comedy the little play does, in parody, what Shakespeare himself does in converting a potential *Romeo and Juliet* into comedy.

With *Troilus and Cressida* perhaps the older critics were, in one sense, quite right: failed dramatic enactment is the exception in Shakespeare. It is thus easy to see why this combination of a carefully crafted negative metadrama and a historical disaster opens the way to charges ranging from the play's being the product of an author deep in some psychological depression to an experiment in a satiric medium with which the playwright so experimented only once. One critic suggests that its characters, faced with a world of grimy reality, with a conflict whose dubious justification may all too readily remind us of our own dubious engagement in Viet Nam, try to enter the world of the theater in order to transcend themselves,[66] to elevate themselves to a symbolic status, as if they were aware—Richard Fly makes a parallel observation[67]—of the parts they play in history outside the immediate theater. Granting the fact that the play, and the event itself, is not entirely devoid of materials for tragedy, one might extend this wish for transcendence to the audience itself, to our own notion of what theater does or should do. We assume a symbolic quota to the onstage happenings; otherwise, the onstage reality would be only life on the surface, and we little more than voyeurs. If both comedy and tragedy reconcile us to the real, we assume a distinction nevertheless: tragedy embodies the ideal, the proper course for a sensitive individual, that state of "readiness" (*Hamlet*, 5.2.222) or "ripeness" (*King Lear*, 5.2.11) which, while it cannot alter events, does elevate them beyond being merely random happenings.[68] Hamlet about to engage in that fatal duel with Laertes is very different from the unfortunate soul who boards an airplane little knowing of an impending mid-air collision. We grieve no less at the latter's death, but he hardly merits the appellation *tragic hero*. *Troilus and Cressida* thus may frustrate those demands for transcendence, for both character and audience, because of the gap between its actuality (the onstage spectacle) and the language that alone can provide the "O, altitudo" of which Longinus speaks when justifying art's fictive world that, precisely because of such elevation, is equal to reality, indeed is a vital complement to the reality outside its confines.

The critics whom I invoke in these final comments are those concerned primarily with the theatrical dimension of the play and who thereby provide another text to justify *Troilus and Cressida*, or Shakespeare's gamble in turning his theater against itself. If transcendence is here denied, then Harry Berger's observation is timely: since the present stage, as the prologue reminds us, exposes the author's and the actor's lack of confidence, and since the world thus presented is small, con-fining, without a "cosmic topology," then the emphasis must be on present performance and interpretation, on what we do have and on what may be "digested in a play."[69] The characters are merely actors strutting and fretting upon the stage for the actual and thus limiting two hours of the performance itself. Precisely because it lacks that transcen-dent ideal by which productive language escapes the vagaries of time (the very principle with which Shakespeare justifies his art in the Son-nets), we ourselves are thereby subjected to action that lends itself to a myriad of interpretations (the second wave of critical interpretation as described in the first section) that are ultimately not complementary but contradictory. Troilus, to be specific, is both romantic hero and jaded sensualist, and what he is like in Ulysses' account (4.5.96–112) is not what he is like in the council scenes, or what he becomes in the love scenes with Cressida, or—finally—what he is like after Act 5, scene 2.

In Berger's words, the conflict is between inadequate power in the character-actor and too much power or diffused power in the observers, those both on- and offstage.[70] If poetry holds implicit values in a way that facts or events themselves cannot—and I rephrase here the di-chotomy that Winifred Nowottny establishes between Troilus and Ulysses[71]—then the metamorphosis of Troilus from lover to butcher ("savage") signals the collapse of such values. If man is his language,[72] then it follows that man gets the kind of world—and the audience gets the kind of play—fashioned by that language. The otherwise transcen-dent Shakespeare is here absent in a way that opposes our sense of his presence, however qualified, in Prince Hal or Portia, or the Othello of "Then must you speak of one that lov'd" (5.2.343–56), or the Hamlet who, before dueling in the hall with Laertes, tells us "If it be now" (5.2.220–24), or Cordelia in her every moment onstage. Only Shake-speare's reverse image is here in the play's two wordsmiths, Thersites and, in a larger sense, Pandarus. But these are "showmen"[73] and not dramatists of a high order. As Thersites presses his metaphors of vene-real disease—and perhaps the older biographical scholars were as cor-rect metadramatically as they may have been unjustified biographically in suggesting that at the time Shakespeare himself was suffering from syphilis—the gross metaphor itself inhibits the satisfaction, the "good feeling" we get when the theater's metadramatic transcendence, the play's ability to complete its Aristotelian probability, counterbalances a negative thematic statement. My argument here grows from, say, our response to the final tableau of *King Lear*, where it is both horrible and yet *right* that Cordelia die.

Not only does the visual, the play's inadequate objective correlative for its language,[74] undercut the verbal, but the verbal does itself in: the language of elevation is properly and, thereby on Shakespeare's part, successfully canceled in Pandarus's curse ending the play. There has been speculation that the ending was an addition, perhaps for an Inns of Court performance or for the private theater.[75] This can, of course, be only speculation. I think it is more "probable" that the ending was part of the original play because this ending itself, given the play's metadramatic structure of failed enactment, is so probable. We will recall that the Restoration similarly found the ending of *King Lear* improbable, while for a century now, whatever the critical reading, be it A. C. Bradley's or Jan Kott's, we find *Lear's* ending wonderfully probable.

The eye has room "for only what it sees now,"[76] and it is therefore little wonder in this play, so lacking a reliable language to inform vision, that we are left eternally in the same "labyrinth of appearance"[77] that for the characters in *The Comedy of Errors* was only temporary and, for that matter, confined to the characters themselves. Aemilia's Christian imagery of baptism was as right for that play as Pandarus's syphilitic bequest is right for the present play. To put the distinction another way, Shakespeare's coupling in the early comedy of the metadramatics of language and spectacle after their severance is no more right than his metadramatic uncoupling of the two in *Troilus and Cressida*. That pattern of coupling, uncoupling, and comic recoupling—as I now conflate the otherwise separate patterns of *Errors* and this present piece "passing full of the palm comical," as its "Never Writer" informs "an Ever Reader"—is both reexpressed and reexamined in *The Winter's Tale* in the broad geography as defined by the movement between Sicilia and Bohemia.

3

The Winter's Tale:
"I am content to look on . . . to hear"

IN *The Comedy of Errors* the gap between language and spectacle stems from the characters' own comic misunderstanding of what they see in conjunction with the audience. In *Troilus and Cressida* our mutual certainty is undercut by the inadequate language employed by both Trojans and Greeks, and yet this same gap, this negative metadramatics, only sustains the definition of the theater as a present-tense union between language and spectacle witnessed and ratified by an audience. Like the early comedy, *The Winter's Tale* is based on a visual confusion, Leontes' misapprehension of his wife's innocent hand-holding with their friend Polixenes, with this confusion later echoed, though by accident rather than design, when Polixenes assumes that Perdita is a shepherdess and therefore a socially unfit mate for his son, Florizel. The ensuing violation of language, as opposed to the inadequacy of language in *Troilus and Cressida*, here admits its opposite, that exquisite poetry of the Romances, possible once the optical perspective of the erring males is cleared. Human design, in a sense, is more a factor here than in the farce or in the mature comedy whose events were already locked into place. The gap here is healed—no less—by human design, most clearly vested in Paulina, the surrogate playwright for Shakespeare. Because this is so, language and spectacle, once the resolution occurs, undergo an expansion rather than a reduction as in the two earlier plays. In its resolution *The Winter's Tale* at once works out the thematic implications of Leontes' initial error even as it justifies the play's, the theater's, allowing for such comic union from an initially tragic situation. Like and also very unlike its predecessors, this late romance offers a catholic engagement of the trinity of theatrical "prerequisites"—language, spectacle, and presence—that are the basis of my inquiries here.

These same three prerequisites further allow us to consider the several issues that have long been a concern to scholars and critics, not to mention directors. Once characterized by Ben Jonson as one of those musty plays that "make nature afraid,"[1] *The Winter's Tale*, precisely because of its scope, admits a search for its organizing principle.[2] With a plot superficially "loose" when matched with Shakespeare's bravura performance in *Errors*, with no clear historical context as in *Troilus and Cressida*, its sprawling organization also demands attention to Shakespeare's own craft. Indeed, given his use of what has been described as antiquated,[3] or perhaps self-conscious techniques, not to mention set pieces such as the debate between Polixenes and Perdita about art and nature, and the presence of playwright surrogates like Paulina and Camillo, *The Winter's Tale* begs consideration of the principles of art itself.[4] With the gap of sixteen years between its halves, along with the appearance of Time as a choral figure, the play also raises the issue of art's ability to create an illusory permanence in the face of the temporality of that real life offstage.[5]

For me, the play celebrates women as the embodiment of the physical, of life itself, as a force very distinct from the men who would impose a false, potentially tragic, imaginary "life" or world, one built upon lifeless abstraction as well as upon language that, because it is divorced from what is, can only prove destructive.[6] In the simplest sense, the gap between language and spectacle is of masculine origins;[7] the long-delayed union of these constituent parts of meaningful theatrical experience resides with the feminine, with the play's trinity of women: Hermione, Paulina, and Perdita. In this regard, the play, though it is hardly propaganda, is something of a feminist critique of the male world, of that same world which dominates *Troilus and Cressida*, and also dominates *Errors*, albeit comically, until the appearance of Aemilia in the final scene. The woman, therefore, as the embodiment of the productive relation between the physical (or spectacle) and language, is both a unifying principle and, no less, the principle of "theater" championed by the play. These two principles are made manifest in five very specific visual tableaux, three involving the joining of hands, two the presence of a persecuted woman: that moment in Act 1, scene 2 when Hermione gives her hand to Polixenes and thus unwittingly incites Leontes' jealousy ("Too hot, too hot! / To mingle friendship far is mingling bloods" [1.2.109–10]); Paulina's stratagem in Act 2, scene 3 as she lays down the infant Perdita before Leontes with "Here 'tis—["the good queen"] commends it to your blessing" (2.3.65–67); Hermione's appearance in Act 3, scene 2, signaled by the Officer's line "It is his Highness' pleasure that the Queen / Appear in person here in court," upon which she enters and stands silently while Leontes' indictment is read (3.2.9–10); the joining of hands in Act 4, scene 4, completing the marriage vows between Florizel and Perdita, minutes before Polixenes discovers himself and severs the union (4.4.362–91); and that exquisite moment in the final chapel scene

when Paulina asks Leontes to "present your hand. / When she was young,
you woo'd her; now, in age, / Is she become the suitor? (5.2.107–9).

i

As Hermione offers her hand to Polixenes, the gesture is linked with
her language on those two occasions when she spoke "to th' purpose"
(1.2.100) in winning over first a "royal husband" and now his "friend"
(1.2.106–8). Her sudden, seemingly effortless victories are in contrast to
the "three crabbed months" that, by his own confession, it took Leontes
to convince a younger Hermione—indeed, a Hermione of Perdita's age
in Act 4—to "open [her] white hand, / And clap [herself his] love." The
exchange of hands, ratifying both love and, now, friendship, is, of
course, suddenly twisted by an outburst of jealousy from Leontes that
has presented, for critics and directors, such problems of motivation.[8]
Leontes' perverse mirror, this distorted sight, now drives him to question the very image of his own once-innocent self, the child who serves to
reverse time's movement by providing a mirror of the father in his own
youth: "Mamilius, / Art thou my boy?" (119–20).[9] Sullied by Leontes'
vision of "paddling palms and pinching fingers" (115), the exchange of
hands will be dignified only near the end of Act 1 in Polixenes' cry to
Camillo, "Give me thy hand" (1.2.447), as he entrusts his safety to the
man who thus proves his friendship by an act whose deception of his
master is as real and positive as Leontes' reading of a similar sign has
been false and negative.

Ratified by marriage, then called into doubt by Leontes to the degree
that he would deny the parentage of Mamilius, the adult heterosexual
union is, undeservingly, set in opposition to that sexless, innocent, and
curiously nonverbal boyhood union where, in Polixenes' eloquent description, the friends "chang'd . . . innocence for innocence." If the boys
did speak, theirs was a language that was, properly, prelinguistic, a
"bleat[ing] the one at th' other" (1.2.67–69). Were they to speak at some
level beyond the harmless sounds of sheep, it would have been to declare
themselves "not guilty" to any divine charges of wrongdoing (74). More
than one scholar has pointed out that an issue central to the play is how
to move successfully from childhood, and its concomitant language, to
adulthood, and to that language demanded by and appropriate to maturity.[10] The "adult" language we do hear in the second scene, however, is
curiously legalistic, static, sterile, even contentious under the veneer of
courtly speech. The expressions of friendship have a strangely economic
ring: Polixenes speaks of his inability to repay Leontes' kindness as going
home "in debt" (3–6), and of "multiply[ing]" a single "we thank you" by
"many thousands moe," with his friend "pay[ing]" those same thank-

you's only when they "part" (7–10). On the principle of equity, one extra week visiting Sicilia will be matched by a "commission" enforcing Leontes to spend an equal "month" in Bohemia (40–41).

Four of the five visual tableaux by which I suggest the play may be organized involve men seeing adult women as they are, and then, after complementing such sight through language, taking the hand of a woman as a mark of friendship or of marriage or of remarriage. For Hermione, there is no conflict between the visual/feminine and the masculine/ verbal, nor in the movement from innocence to maturity. If adulthood brings with it the possibility of "fault," a slip from innocence, she playfully suggests that the sins are no sins if sexuality be contained within marriage (83–86). Indeed, Hermione, again playfully, manages to combine the physical and the verbal as she speaks of being "cram'[d] with praise," of being made by man's words "as fat as tame things" (91–92). Her only fear is that if "one good deed" dies "tongueless," it "slaughters a thousand waiting upon that" (92–93). She even rescues that cold economics of her husband's speech by lightly equating such "praises" with women's "wages" (94).

The masculine corruption of language leads to that of sight. Calling for servants to "bear eyes" to see his "honor" clearly (309–310), demanding that Camillo "see" the adultery as "plainly as heaven sees earth and earth sees heaven" (314–15), Leontes rhetorically and self-defensively asks if his own sight is "so muddy" that he might see what is not. Even Polixenes fears that he himself may be "sighted like the basilisk" (338). The comic disparity between our vision and that of the characters in *The Comedy of Errors* thereby darkens here, with the added irony that the disparity is now confined to a single onstage character, a "misvision" in which Leontes places such faith that he is willing to concede that if what he sees and hears, even at the level of inarticulate "whispering," is nothing—that is, if he is wrong—then the entire cosmos, "the world . . . The covering sky," is nothing (284–96).[11]

This distortion of vision and language infects the concept of theater itself. Leontes sarcastically links a child's play and his mother's sexual play with an immoral theatrical "play," seeing himself as performing "so disgrac'd a part" that the audience's response will be to "hiss" him to his grave, with contempt and clamor serving as his "knell"—a hostile audience reaction if there ever was one (1.2.187–90). Joan Hartwig observes that in becoming audience to his own stage actions, Leontes takes a suspect pleasure in demeaning himself as a mere actor directed by some force beyond human choice.[12] Characters here frequently function as audience to each other, but always in a negative way. Leontes sees his youthful self in Mamilius but the image becomes for him only a source of disgust. Polixenes finds in Camillo's "chang'd complexions" (381) an unfortunate "mirror" of the "alteration" he feels in himself, even as he enters concerned that he has just seen on Leontes' countenance eyes that avoided him and "a lip of much contempt" (368–73). Minutes before Polixenes' entrance, Camillo has advised his King to put on an actor's face, "a countenance as clear / As friendship wears at feasts" (343–44), as he himself feigns agreement with Leontes' plan to poison his friend.

A playwright making something out of nothing, Leontes is, however, partially counterbalanced near the end of Act 1 by Camillo as a playwright who here and later in Act 4 would redeem his master's black comedy with a theater spawning reunions and, in the reading of some commentators, redemption in and through time. The negative playwright who subjects the kingdom to "the fabric of his folly" (429), whose "gracious queen" now sinks to becoming "part of his theme" (459), is thus offset by Camillo as he offers his hand to Polixenes, becoming the "pilot" (448) who through time will lead the play from what presently seems irrevocable tragedy to comedy.

ii

Hermione's innocent offer of her hand to Polixenes is perversely echoed in Act 2 when Leontes grasps Antigonus's arm, equating the certainty of that rough physical contact with his own certainty as to his wife's adultery: "but I do see't, and feel't, / As you feel doing thus [*grasps his arm*]—and see withal / the instruments that feel" (2.1.152–54). Conversely Hermione's innocent, instinctive "stratagem" in giving her hand to keep Polixenes from leaving Sicilia finds a parallel here in Paulina's deliberate stratagem, her theatrical gesture performed before Leontes in "*laying down the child*" (2.3.67SD) as yet unnamed, and whose legitimacy the father denies. Paulina's "words [are] as medicinal as true," and to insure that Leontes does indeed see the child, she threatens to make "trifles of [anyone's] eyes" who would interrupt her (2.3.37,63).

The earlier misinterpretation of the holding of hands suggests *homo sapiens* taken to a perverse degree, for here such knowledge, embodied in Leontes as he cries out sarcastically, "Alack, for lesser knowledge! how accurs'd / In being so blest!" (2.1.38–39), is sterile, a dead end, reductive, *illusory*. "Play," on the other hand, suggests the power to grow and change, and is thereby productive. It is not without significance that *The Winter's Tale*'s own theatricality, its consciousness of its self, increases geometrically, culminating in Paulina's grandest play, the staged encounter in the final scene between the reunited family and the "statue" of Julio Romano.

This "true" theater, promising some relief from Leontes' constrictive, nonplayful world, is itself overwhelmed by the King's own pejorative sense of the theater: he finds "a plot against" his life where there is, of course, no plot; perversely defines that restorative power of illusions with his sarcastic "All's true that is mistrusted"; speaks of his own negative plot as "my design"; and sees himself as the wretched subject, the "pinch'd thing," of those who would "play" with him "at will" (47–52).[13] What Hermione takes as "sport" (or an absurd reading of the facts), her husband twists to the imagined adulterous "sport" that leads to the pregnancy, "with that she's big with" (58–61).

The second act is transitional not only because of this combination of positive and negative versions of play but also because of its increased emphasis on the visual, on that solid reality that Leontes' language can distort but cannot, ultimately, destroy. Hermione knows she holds "clearer knowledge" (97)—a reversal of Leontes' own unintentionally accurate phrase "lesser knowledge" (38)—even though such clarity of vision is presently overwhelmed by the increasingly destructive court language of her husband.[14] Paulina, the positive strategist or playwright of this second movement, is especially given to the visual. From the jail she announces her hope that Leontes "may soften at the sight o' th' child" (2.2.38), and argues that "the silence often of pure innocence / Persuades when speaking fails" (39–40). Speechlessness or visuality, anticipated in Paulina's lines, will now constitute an increasingly significant variation upon the tense dichotomy between language and sight. Antigonus wishes that Leontes had first "tried" Hermione in his "silent judgment" before speaking in public ("without more overture" [2.1.171–72]). Leontes' earlier "Look on her" here becomes Paulina's "Behold" (2.3.98). Minutes before her exit, that "Behold," delivered to all the lords assembled, changes to the more direct "Look to your babe" (126).

Conversely, the sterile, litigious language of the first movement now sinks to the inarticulate as Leontes neurotically and ironically finds the speeches of others nothing more than calumnious sounds, "these hums and ha's" below recognizable speech, interjected between assertions that Hermione is "goodly" and "honest" (2.1.74–76). He delivers what Coleridge calls "a soliloquy in the mask of dialogue."[15] While typecasting Hermione as an "adult'ress" (2.1.78), Leontes fears that her sexual violation will not only invalidate the social hierarchy separating aristocrats from barbarians but will also violate the "mannerly distinguishment" in the separate languages of the "prince and beggar" (2.1.82–87). She thus offended both his marriage bed and his courtly speech, and Leontes' sarcastic reference to the "vulgars" who would brand her act with "bold'st title" will echo ironically in Act 4 when the rustics' sheep-shearing festival provides the ground allowing for poetry and imaginative speech to be reborn (94).

If Paulina would "prove honey-mouth'd" (2.2.31) in Hermione's behalf, the husband despairs of all human speech and can now find linguistic security only in the gods. Antigonus's exit with the child coincides with Leontes' announcement that it has been some twenty-three days since Cleomines and Dion have been absent from the kingdom on their journey to Delphos and that they are now returned.

iii

At the center of the play's third movement is not so much an action, such as offering a hand or laying down a child but the simple stage direction, *"Enter* Hermione *as to her trial"* (3.2.10 SD). Hermione's silent presence supersedes, both literally and figuratively, Paulina's visual stratagem of the previous movement, even as it anticipates her "role" as statue in the play's final scene. Here, that presence underlines the association between the woman and the redemptive visual.[16] Assured that Leontes, at last, will adopt a Hermione-like "patience" in bearing and atoning for his failure to have faith in his wife, Paulina also promises to "say nothing" (3.2.231–32), whereas earlier she had been accused of being careless with her tongue in admonishing her King. In his excellent article on *The Winter's Tale*, William Matchett observes that, increasingly in this play, Shakespeare shows the "limitations of language as a medium" to the degree that, in the chapel scene, silence itself "becomes the final language."[17]

Opposed to such silent language, an oxymoron beyond Leontes' present comprehension, that language associated with the men threatens to destruct itself. The charge read by the Officer and sanctioned by the King stands as a cruel rephrasing of the Jailer's earlier "legalese": "Hermione, queen to the worthy Leontes, King of Sicilia, thou art here accused and arraigned of high treason," and so on (3.2.12–21). Against this crabbed prose, however, stands the biblical simplicity, and truth, of Apollo's pronouncement: "Hermione is chaste, Polixenes blameless, Camillo a true subject," culminating in the lyrical "that which is lost be not found" (132–36). Denying Leontes' "indictment" (11), Hermione quotes the two words that she knows are useless at present, "not guilty" (2); that phrase, of course, will recall the "not guilty" that Polixenes along with Leontes could have said to the "imposition" of original sin, had their youth "ne'er been higher rear'd / With stronger blood" (1.2.72–74).

It is also in this third movement that Leontes' sullied theater is taken to the extreme. Following the reading of the indictment, Hermione opposes her innocence, which presently only the audience of the gods can ratify, to Leontes' obscene "history" or play that has presently succeeded before a court audience, a plot "devis'd / And play'd to take spectators" (3.2.35–37).

Yet, as the play approaches the pivotal Act 3, scene 3, where the death of Antigonus is juxtaposed, almost comically, with the rustics' discovery of Perdita, the positive image of the theater returns. Antigonus, who earlier would have dismissed vision or "dreams" as "toys," the mere effusions of "slumber," is now willing to take seriously the "sight" of Hermione, to believe that the dead can return to us through a visionary experience (3.3.39–41).[18]

The restoration of the visual, of what *is*, and the rebirth of language as a means of giving permanence to the physical receive their fullest enactment so far in Act 3, scene 3, the first scene set in Bohemia, or at least set upon its shores. This visual renaissance, though, has a comic enactment. Antigonus's *"Exit pursued by a bear"* (3.3.58 SD) is at once tragic and comic, never failing to evoke laughter, embarrassed or not, from the audience.[19] The Shepherd and the Clown are, by definition, physical beings, workers whose place of labor is the field, not the court. Still, there is also a more refined "poetry" accompanying this restoration of the physical. The Shepherd knows that what they "see" before them is "a thing to talk on when [they] are dead and rotten" (80–81), a visual experience that might sustain one in old age, just as in the opening scene Camillo claims that the very presence of Mamilius "makes old hearts fresh" (1.1.39). In his exquisite pastoral prose the Clown offers an account of the sinking of the ship that ingeniously combines sight and sound: "but, first, how the poor souls roar'd, and the sea mock'd them; and how the poor gentleman roar'd, and the bear mock'd him, both roaring louder than the sea or weather" (88–102). As they turn from "things dying" to "things newborn," the references to sight flood their rustic speech: "but look thee here, boy"; "Here's a sight for thee; look thee"; "I'll go see"; "If thou mayest discern"; "fetch me to th' sight of him" (112–35).

This comic symphony between language and spectacle is anticipated by the opening scene set in Delphos. We "hear" about both the visual and the verbal dimensions of the scene: of the "fertile . . . isle, the temple much surpassing / The common praise it bears"; of the "ceremonious, solemn, and unearthly" sacrifice; and of "the ear-deaf'ning voice o' th' oracle, / Kin to Jove's thunder." Against such inspired description, Cleomines opposes Leontes' own "proclamations, / So forcing faults upon Hermione." For the messengers the experience strained their visual and verbal "sense[s]" to the degree that they were rendered as "nothing." Using a subtle birth metaphor, they assume that the language of the oracle, currently "seal'd up" by Apollo's command, will, when "discover[ed]," produce "something rare," its "issue" being "gracious."

This reported vision, along with Antigonus's account of Hermione's appearing to him in sleep, suggests that there is a reality, a world of being, existing beyond the consciousness of the audience, the one supposedly sure and ultimate reality present at performance. Yet the appearance of Time brings into enactment such moments otherwise beyond optical certainty. Time may be only an actor's impersonation, yet, as he contrasts his suprahuman dimension with the "reality" of Sicilia, or of Bohemia, we also recognize the relativity of such distinctions: all the constitutent parts of the play, no matter how earthly or how mystical their setting, are equally illusive. Appropriately, Time calls for a strengthened visual participation, much as the Chorus of *Henry V* does in asking that we use our "imaginary Forces" to enhance the otherwise meager vision provided by the stage set (prologue, l. 18), or that we "play with [our] fancies" in seeing Hal aboard the ship sailing for France (Chorus, Act 3, l. 7).[20] We see a suprahuman figure materialize, with apologies not for thus stretching our visual imagination but only for the playwright's violation in "slid[ing]/ O'er sixteen years" (56).[21] We are addressed here as "gentle spectators," not as "hearers," though "spectators" can encompass both seeing and hearing. Time itself is a fellow "witness" to what we are about to see, and, like a presenter, would control our vision, or make sure that we ourselves are sure of what we see: the setting is identified; he prepares us for Perdita's change from infant to young woman; and we are reminded that offstage Leontes continues his penance. This new, productive vision promised by Time is now linked with time itself. Against the constrictive, devouring time of those first three movements set in Sicilia, that compulsive "rush" of events in which a departing friend is transformed into a villain, and the term of pregnancy into proof of adultery, we now see time as comic, given to "growing" as much as it was given earlier to dying. The stress is no longer on the past but on "the glistering of this present" (14), on Shakespeare's own theater of presence. Our patience, linked to Hermione's own patience and the patience that Leontes now embraces, will now bear fruit in "th' freshest things now reigning."

iv

As he takes Perdita's hand to initiate the wedding contract, Florizel expands Leontes' earlier reference to Hermione's "white hand" (1.2.103) into a trinity of metaphors: "I take thy hand, this hand, / As soft as dove's down and as white as it, / Or Ethiopian's tooth, or the fann'd snow that's bolted / By th' northern blasts twice o'er" (4.4.362–65). Polixenes himself comments on such metaphoric extravangace, noting that his son "seems to wash / The hand [that] was fair before" (366–67). The hyperbolically lyrical occasion is then revised downward by Perdita's adoptive father's more pedestrian "Take hands, a bargain" (383). At length, Leontes' tragic misinterpretation of the hand-holding between wife and friend is revived as Polixenes discovers himself, severing the lovers' marriage, or what Perdita calls "this dream of mine" (448).[22]

This physical affirmation of the marriage vow is at one with a larger stress on the physical and visual pervading Act 4. Based not on abstractions but specifics such as "daffidills," "the white sheet bleaching on the hedge," "a quart of ale," and lovers who "lie tumbling in the hay" (4.3.1–22), Autolycus's poetry also announces the primacy of the present, that summer season providing the setting for both love and robbery. He is unconcerned with the past ("the winter's pale"), and careless of the future even as it stretches to eternity; for "the life to come" Autolycus would "sleep out the thought of it" (30).[23]

As she responds to Florizel's lightly sarcastic rejoinder that she seems to cover him with flowers as one would a corpse, Perdita's own sense of presence is conveyed through the portrait of lovers buried in flowers, her Florizel "quick and in [her] arms" (132). She shares here the essence of wholesome sexuality expressed sixteen years ago by her mother. Whatever qualifications Polixenes may make to the exclusive nature of her bouquet, the fact is that here the physical leads to the poetic and thus reverses the suppression of the physical by that diseased langauge and imagination of the opening scenes.

Paulina's earlier command that Leontes look to his son, that desperate attempt in the play's first three movements to give the visual parity with the verbal, is now reexpressed in Florizel's requests to "lift up your countenance" (49) and "lift up thy looks" (479) when Perdita wavers in questioning his fidelity after Polixenes' disclosure. A surrogate for Paulina, old Camillo makes a telling pun when he says that in the presence of Perdita he would be a sheep of her flock, leaving "grazing" for "gazing" (109–10). That pun returns in the Shepherd's "for never gaz'd the moon / Upon the water as he'll stand and read / As 'twere my daughter's eyes" (172–74).[24]

What was earlier Leontes' longing for the word here becomes a longing for the visual: Camillo would "purchase the sight again of dear Sicilia" (511) for he now "thirst[s] to see" his former master (513). Actual sight is transformed to the visionary when Camillo imagines that he can "see / Leontes opening his free arms, and weeping / His welcomes forth" (547–49), in effect anticipating the play's final two scenes. Part of the vision, I should note, includes Leontes' kissing "the hands" of Florizel's bride (550–51).

The complex transformation and elevation of the visual is accompanied by changes in the other elements involved in the theatrical enactment. The closed language of the initial scenes opens up here to a variety and richness in texture that we have not heard before. Perdita herself reintroduces her mother's word "gracious" (4.4.5, 8). Silence, a negligible factor earlier, now complements enhanced speech. Tiring of the dialogue between the rustic lovers Dorcas and Mopsa, the Clown silences them with "Not a word, a word," and calls for a dance instead (4.4.164–65). Upon the dissolution of the marriage the Shepherd confesses that he "cannot speak," that Polixenes' intervention has robbed him of his dream of filling "his grave in quiet" (4.4.452–54). These comic yet negative references to silence are subsumed into Florizel's positive description of Perdita as a living statue, as one who in her dancing is like a wave of the sea, constant yet also ever-changing (4.4.140–43).

The infusion of self-conscious poetry, extending from Autolycus's ballads and lyrics to Perdita's emblematic flowers, to the lovers' poetry, to the silence that "speaks" as it complements speech, admits music and dance, kindred arts that until now have been suppressed in the play. With the veracity of Autolycus's ballads confirmed by the judgment of "five justices' hands" (283–84), we hear the song in three parts sung by Autolycus, Dorcas, and Mopsa, whose subject, as John Armstrong suggestively argues in *The Paradise Myth*,[25] is the wish that "their days may somehow break into the unknown," the song itself pointing "to the Beyond": "Get you hence, for I must go / Where it fits not you to know. / Whither? O, whither? (197–308). If it points to the beyond, or to the play's own immediate comic future in Act 5, music here also allows a happier sense of the past to return: the Shepherd urges Perdita to emulate his "old wife" who "would sing her song" while entertaining guests (4.4.55–62), and, whatever quarrel exists now between father and son, Florizel remembers that it is his "father's music / To speak [Camillo's] deeds" (4.4.518–19).

The heightened dramatic poetry, even as it begets music and dance, is at one with the self-conscious theatrics of the scene, this fourth movement's own metadramatics. Anticipated earlier in Camillo's and Paulina's stratagems, the theater as the core metaphor blossoms here; disguises and role-playing—conscious or unconscious, positive and negative—are everywhere.[26]

Polixenes, curiously, initiates such theatrics in a negative way with "We must disguise ourselves" (4.2.54–55) as he sets off with Camillo for the "business" (51) of exposing his son. Autolycus, of course, is master of supposes, playing everything from an impoverished courtier, to the "victim" of himself, to an artist offering, for sale of course, ballads and lyrics of quality.[27] Florizel serves as presenter to Perdita, finding in her "unusual weeds" no mere shepherdess but Flora herself "peering in April's front" (4.4.1–3). She, in turn, fears that Florizel, a "noble" piece of "work," is humiliated by his own disguise because he is "so vildly bound up" (21–23), though his own justification for his disguise is that the gods themselves have not been above playing roles lower in the social hierarchy, taking upon themselves the "shapes of beasts." (25–27). Positive role-playing, "transformations," are justified by love: the gods' disguises were "never for a piece of beauty rarer, / Nor in a way so chaste" (32–33). Perdita, of course, unconsciously "plays" a shepherd's daughter. Robert Uphaus reminds us that in the play's larger scheme Polixenes, to some degree, plays Leontes of Act 1, while Florizel and Perdita play a youthful Leontes and Hermione.[28] Florizel's own productive playing is suggested when he exchanges clothes with Autolycus, and thus symbolically inherits some of the rogue's free spirit.

There is a practical side to such playing as well. Camillo plots how to "frame" Florizel's departure from Bohemia to "serve" both his "turn" and that of the play generally (4.4.509), and gives a playwright-director's instructions on how the lovers are to "present" themselves in Sicilia (544), thereby making the projected "scene [they will] play" his own handiwork (593). To this end he supplies a costume for Florizel (Autolycus's) and a male disguise for Perdita so that she can "disliken / The truth of [her own] seeming" (650–53). Perdita stresses such role-playing for the audience: "I see the play so lies / That I must bear a part" (655–66).

This productive stage-managing, however, receives its parody in Autolycus as he describes for the audience his own offstage cozenings (595–618) and then offers a bravura performance of such by impersonating a courtier in the king's employment. Role-playing is catching, and Autolycus allows the Shepherd and Clown to pretend not to be themselves so as to avoid those curses and tortures awaiting father and son if they bring Polixenes the sad news of his son's escape. Actually, however self-centered and mean Autolycus's earlier trickery has been, here, beyond his conscious intention, he at best aids Camillo in his plan and at worst impedes, but only slightly, the discoveries of Act 5, scene 2. In the "debate" between Polixenes and Florizel over the exclusion from her bouquet of flowers produced by grafting, the flowers so excluded are, I think, emblematic of lower art, the art of trickery, by which she could be "painted"—made other than she really is—so as to seduce a gullible lover (101–2).[29] She thereby refers, albeit indirectly, to Autolycus's art, which is fast dissolving as a force in the play. His charming but ultimately bastard talent serves for our entertainment but is itself the prelude to a finer art—manifest first in Camillo's scheme and then more magnificently so in Paulina's "statue."

Shakespeare's theater itself is moving from Leontes' black magic to the comic, transitional magic of Autolycus to—reversing here Polixenes' sarcasm—the productive "enchantment" (434) of Act 5, scenes 2 and 3. We are approaching an art that is inclusive, an art that is a part of life as determined both by human will and by forces beyond our control, an art that unites what man and time have "undone, undone" (4.4.460). Norman Rabkin calls the movement "a transformation of the art of tragedy into the life of comedy."[30] The contractual exchange of hands between lovers and then among the waiting society that approves the match is thus the visual onstage emblem of this high concept of the theater. If those hands are undone by Polixenes' temporary "return" to the Leontes mentality that sixteen years earlier misinterpreted his own innocent clasping of Hermione's hands, the Leontes we see in Act 5 will prove that his earlier self exists no longer.

v

An exchange of hands is at once a physical and symbolic expression of union, and such exchanges in *The Winter's Tale* suggest the very unions toward which the play itself moves.

As Hermione descends from her pedestal in the play's final scene, Paulina instructs Leontes to "present [his] hand" (107) to the living statue.[31] Indeed, if he fails to present that hand, and thus "shun[s] her," he would "kill her double"; the near-tragedy of the first half thus encroaches on the near-comedy of the second half. As a symbol, the hand dominates the chapel scene; even Romano's statue "excels what ever yet you look'd upon, / Or hand of man hath done" (16–17). If Leontes has the fortitude to stare further at the statue, rather than exiting under the profound emotions generated by the sight itself, Paulina promises to make "the statue move indeed, descend, / And take you by the hand" (87–89), though in thus doubling its already amazing proximity to life she risks being judged a witch, "assisted / by wicked powers' (90–91). So resolved, Leontes is rewarded not just with the exchange of hands but with an embrace, and this new emphasis on touch, coming on top of what is now a perfect blending of the play's linguistic and visual dimensions, absolves her in Leontes' view of any charges of practicing black magic: "If this be magic, let it be an art / Lawful as eating" (110–11).

The two scenes preceding this chapel scene function at once as overtures to it and counterpoints to each other. On the one hand, Paulina would, literally and figuratively, root Leontes in the past, extending a penance of already sixteen years' duration by insisting that he not remarry until a second wife "as like Hermione as is her picture, / Affront his eye" (70–75). Conversely, she gives the present, the imminent entrance of Perdita, a higher priority: "so must thy [Hermione's] grave / Give way to what's seen now!" (97–98). The Servant claims that Perdita surpasses the dead wife—"she [is] / The fairest [he has] yet beheld" (86–87)—and, echoing the movement from visual to verbal that informs the play's second half, contends that once she has "obtain'd your eye," she "will have your tongue too" (105–6). For Leontes, however, no such competition now exists between mother and son or son and father: "Your mother was most true to wedlock, Prince, / For she did print your royal father off, / Conceiving you" (124–26), lines that will recall his inability earlier to accept Perdita as visual evidence of her natural parents. Any tension between present and past visual signs is suddenly but ironically dissolved as Leontes sees in Perdita and Florizel the reincarnation of the couple he had accused of adultery: to him they are "gracious," "begetting wonder" (131–34).

Still, there is a somber, almost tragic tone just beneath the comedy. The sight of Hermione would "incense" Leontes to "murther" a second wife, and he expresses his resolve not to remarry by contrasting her eyes that are like "stars" with "all eyes [that are] else dead coals" (61–62, 67–69). If, like Camillo, thirsting to look on Sicilia while still in Bohemia, Leontes would now "desire [his] life / Once more to look on" Polixenes (137–38), he is also chided by Paulina for having an "eye [with] too much youth in't" as she compares Perdita unfavorably with the wife/mother: "Not a month / 'Fore your queen died, she was more worth such gazes / Than what you look on now" (225–27). Vision in this scene appears to fluctuate between the poles of life or presence and death or past. Leontes knows that if he had once seen Hermione as everyone else saw her, he might "even now / . . . have look'd upon [his] queen's full eyes" (52–53), and thus the sight of Perdita, however pleasing, only makes him think "of her / Even in those looks [he] made" (227–28). Paulina would bring that past sight into the present, playing the part of Hermione ("the ghost that walk'd") as well as the presenter bidding Leontes to "mark / Her eye" and filling his ears first with "shrick[s]" and then with the words "remember mine" (63–67).

This flux in the scene's visual dimensions is matched by one in its language. If Leontes' speech now has a gravity, indeed a poetry that we have not heard before, Polixenes, as reported by the Lord, has assumed Leontes' earlier role, assaulting both ears and eyes by making the "poor men in question . . . quake" beyond anything the Lord "saw," and closing his own "ears" to their pleas (197–202). Knowledgeable about Camillo's master plan, we know that such concerns will most probably prove groundless: as stage manager, Camillo so far has a perfect record. However, for the characters onstage the visual dimension of the scene and, to a lesser degree, its verbal half are in a state best described as being in suspension, at worst in a threatened dissolution.

This divided response toward vision and speech is reversed in Act 5, scene 2, with the irony that the scene is, properly, only a reported scene, an extended messenger's report, which, unless handled properly by the director, can fall flat onstage. Indeed, many productions of *The Winter's*

Tale delete the entire scene or compress its some one hundred and seventy lines. Why the various reunions, excluding that of Hermione and her family, are reported rather than being enacted may have to do with Shakespeare's decision not to detract from the ultimate reunion in the final scene, or to juxtapose a scene conveyed essentially by the language of the excited Gentlemen with the overwhelming physical presence of the statue in Paulina's chapel.[32] In terms of the ongoing tension between language and spectacle in the play, I might observe that here meaningful language, so long discredited in the play, or possible only in the "green world" of Bohemia, triumphs. In fact, properly done, the scene is not static: the messengers grasp each other in wonder, punctuating their narrative with animated hands and facial expressions.

As preparation for Leontes' redemptive taking of the statue's hand, we hear in this second scene of those now united "holding up [their] hands" in wonderment, and "casting up [their] eyes . . . with countenance of such distraction" that the observer could discern only their garments and not their faces (46–49). One likes to imagine that if the scene were enacted on the Globe stage, the spectators in the pit would indeed see only flowing garments uplifted by hands held heavenward in a gesture of amazement and would therefore be unable to link actor with character except by the difference in costumes. The Clown himself parodies the scene—perhaps even enacting the reported moment by grasping the hand of Autolycus or his father—when he proves his new status by informing us that "the King's son took me by the hand, and call'd me brother" (140–41), a union, if you will, of county and court, paralleling in comic fashion the growing unions between Bohemia and Sicilia.

Paulina's unsuccessful laying down of the child itself is reversed here. Grieved at the loss of her husband, Paulina, we are told, now "lifted the Princess from the earth, and so locks her in embracing, as if she would pin her to her heart, that she might no more be in danger of losing" (76–78). We will recall the Shepherd and Clown earlier picking up the child that Antigonus, following Leontes' orders, had cast down.

If language, rather than the theater's balanced visual/verbal enactment, is the focus here, that language in turn elevates the reported spectacle as the Gentlemen tell us what they have "perceiv'd" (10) offstage. The royal party "seem'd almost, with staring on one another, to tear the cases of their eyes" (11–13). Paulina herself "had one eye declin'd for the loss of her husband, another elevated that the oracle was fulfill'd" (74–76). The Third Gentleman cites the relating of Hermione's death as a moment that "angled for [his] eyes" (83), and the Clown's earlier claim that he had not "wink'd" since that time he saw the deaths on sea and on land and then reported them to the Shepherd is echoed in the First

Gentleman's observation that "every wink of an eye some new grace will be born" (110–11). What was seen even threatens to go beyond telling: the Third Gentleman informs his audience, "then have you lost a sight which was to be seen, cannot be spoken of" (42–43). The sight, if all the "world could have seen't," would become a scene of "universal" rather than specific amazement (91–92). Whatever Shakespeare's practical purposes in not showing the scene, what is told here suggests spectacle beyond stage enactment, a fabulous "old tale" beyond optical comprehension (61).

Language now merges effortlessly with vision, as well as with the physical. The participants, we are told, had "speech in their dumbness, language in their very gesture" (13–14). The "mating"—to borrow that word from *The Comedy of Errors*, admitting at once confusion and blending—superimposes eyes and ears, or rather commingles them no less than the scene's thematic mingling of joy and sorrow: "the wisest beholder, that knew no more but seeing, could not say if th' importance were joy or sorrow; but in the extremity of the one, it must needs be" (16–19). Even the present and effective narration—though we might still wish to see as well as hear about the multiple reunions—turns upon itself, for each successive report "lames" its follower; each new encounter "undoes" the previous "description" (57–58). Shakespeare seems to want the theater to work both ways here: to make effable the ineffable.

This physical "deficiency" in Act 5, scene 2 is, however, more than compensated for by the final scene, as we see the ultimate reunion—like that between parents and children in the final scene of *The Comedy of Errors*—enacted rather than narrated. It is an especially tactile one: Leontes would kiss the statue's lips, and must be warned by Paulina that he would both "mar" the still-wet "ruddiness" of those lips, and "stain [his] own / With oily painting" (80–83).

As Paulina leads the onlookers through the various stages or stations of revelation, the slightest movement seems significant, most especially that moment when the statue *"comes down"* (103 SD). Audiences, knowing that an actress impersonates a statue, generally strain their eyes to penetrate the charade, and I am reminded here of the vaudeville act that made its way into television during the infancy of that visual/verbal medium in which actors would specialize in so minimizing stage movement, including the blink of the eyes, that even though on live television they would seem frozen within the frame. Here, even deprived of stage movement, spectacle commands our attention. A silent, motionless emblem, Hermione reminds Leontes of when "first [he] woo'd her." And in her wonderment Perdita imitates the pose of her mother (34–42). Little wonder, therefore, that references to eyes and to seeing flood the scene: "To see"; "we saw not / That which my daughter came to look upon" (10–

13); "her dead likeness . . . / Excels what ever yet you look'd upon" (15–16); "Behold, and say 'tis well" (20); "the sight of my poor image" (57); "No longer shall you gaze on't" (60); "So long could I / Stand by, a looker-on" (84–85); "Mark a little while" (118). Hermione's first words are "You gods look down" (121). As befits a discovery scene—the most extensive one in all of Shakespeare—vision here precedes language. Paulina breaks through this immobility with the presenterlike line "you perceive she stirs," the prose here instantly becoming redundant as *Hermione comes down* (103).

The language that we do hear is at once simple and eloquent, with something of the biblical quality of Apollo's own proclamation. Earlier proclaiming in defiance of the gods' own judgment, and unwilling to endure Paulina's "chat," Leontes now is "content to hear" (93). Yet, as he clasps Hermione's hand, even the speech of this revitalized suitor becomes unnecessary. If the present scene were, like its predecessor, only reported, it would resemble "an old tale" that the hearers would have "hooted at" (116–17).

vi

As the characters kneel before the statue (44) or speak of new-found "faith" (95), of that which was "dead now awake[n]" (98), of life as a force that "redeems" (103) death, it is tempting to see the scene as somewhat unearthly, as a momentary infusion of paradise into a secular world otherwise caught between earth and heaven. Yet such an allegory of salvation, suggestive as it may be, must coexist with the patent fraud not only of Paulina's stratagem but of Shakespeare's as well. S. L. Bethell has argued that the antiquated dramatic techniques, used here and elsewhere in *The Winter's Tale*, force us to seek for mystical meanings,[33] and I have no quarrel with this observation. However, such "meanings" are housed within the confines of this world, dim reflection though it may be of the divine. The art thus employed, by Romano *and* by Shakespeare, is one whose aim is to present "life as lovely mock'd as ever" (19), an art that a penitent Leontes equates with such a mundane human activity as "eating" (111). The fusion of spectacle and language, after a sixteen-year divorce, is natural, mundane, and thereby no less a tribute to the "carver's excellence" (30).

At the end, however buoyed by the elevated language and spectacle of Paulina's chapel, Leontes assumes the practical function of a stage manager[34] as he orders Paulina to "lead us [characters both on- and offstage] from hence" (152). There will be conversation after the play in which "we [again, audience both on- and offstage] may leisurely / Each one demand, and answer to his part / Perform'd in this wide gap of time" (152–

54), but for us that conversation will take place in the secular atmosphere of the home, not the theater. What Leontes and his family discuss will be beyond stage enactment.

As a romantic undergraduate coming from the otherwise practical 1950s, I remember being caught between the daily experience of stage work and the philosophically transcendent view of Shakespeare espoused by a teacher who was also my surrogate father. When it came time to write my senior thesis on *King Lear*, I was, in effect, caught between Granville-Barker and G. Wilson Knight, and tried my best to compromise with a subtitle, "Art for the Sake of Life." I think in my maturity that that same compromise holds true for what happens here in *The Winter's Tale*.[35] The language and spectacle of this play, at length transformed from tragedy to comedy, now enact what we can say and what we can see in the only world we have, in that world which Leontes yearns for in his final command: "Hastily lead away."

PART II
The Frontiers of Spectacle

4

Julius Caesar:
"Night hangs upon mine eyes"

LATE in the play Brutus sees a hybrid ghost containing both Caesar's spirit and the specter of Brutus's own troubled conscience. This "optical bifurcation" disturbs a play that, on the surface, seems given to the secular, masculine world of realpolitik. Actually, the supernatural has been present much earlier in the portents seen near Caesar's assassination, but the men—though not the women in the play—have either not witnessed such portents or, if they have, have used them as confirmation for their own practical political ends. *Julius Caesar* itself is rooted in historical fact, *has happened*, but the presence here of the supernatural, of what challenges mortal vision, suggests a sphere of influence beyond the rationale of history. Commentators on *Julius Caesar* have also been divided not only as to the ghost's significance[1] but to that of the larger play.[2] These bifurcations—the hybrid ghost who in Plutarch is simply Brutus's evil spirit, as well as the co-presence of the secular and the supernatural, and of male and female vision—when added to *Julius Caesar*'s current status as a "problem play"[3] are at one, I think, with the issue of how we—both characters and audience—interpret what we see onstage, or what in modern criticism would be called the relation between the sign and the signifier.

I believe that in *Julius Caesar* we are confronted with two incompatible plays. One is exclusive, grounded in the facts, depicting a political world in which males confidently, for a time, "read" events in terms of their own prescriptive standards, a world in which what we see is what we *can* see. The other play, one that will prove dominant, includes but goes beyond this secular drama, enacting a mystical, timeless world to which the women, Portia and Calphurnia, prove especially sensitive, one mocking the conspirators' progressive, cause-and-effect mentality with its own cyclical, and therefore cynical "history." This second world demands a sense of visual play for which the playless conspirators prove inadequate, and is a world rendering invalid the Romans' attempt to read Caesar

87

accurately in life, not to mention that Caesar existing in death who visits Brutus on the eve of battle. For the rationalistic conspirators, interpretation is both the issue and their curse.

i

This issue of interpretation confronts us from the very start. Workmen, having put on holiday costumes to celebrate Caesar's return to Rome, are condemned by Flavius for misunderstanding the significance of the occasion, for confusing Caesar with Pompey, or rather not properly grasping the nature of Caesar's victory, a victory not over a foreign enemy but rather in civil war. From Flavius's perspective, therefore, the "certain Commoners" appear "upon a laboring day without the sign of [their] profession" (1.1.4–5).

The Tribunes' own interpretation of a misinterpretation spreads to the first meeting between Brutus and Cassius: Cassius has inferred that the absence of "gentleness" in Brutus's "eyes" is a sign of his friend's anger ("passions"), whereas to Brutus this apparent indifference is actually a sign that he is "with himself at war" (1.2.31–50). If Brutus, alarmed by Caesar's rise to power, finds himself painfully divided on the issue of assassination, then Cassius, whose mind is already made up, offers his friend the means to interpret that issue rightly, at least as Cassius sees the right: he would provide him "mirrors" that can "turn / [Brutus's] hidden worthiness" from those warring insides to a clear image before his "eye" (56–57). In seeing clearly his own present "hidden worthiness," Brutus will then be able to commit himself to action. Later, in the same scene, Brutus interprets Caesar's entrance, noting the "angry spot" on his brow, Calphurnia's "pale" cheek, Cicero's "fiery eyes," and the general demeanor of Caesar's followers, and concludes—wrongly, as it turns out— that Antony's attempted staged coronation has not gone well (1.2.182– 88). The same offstage event, not witnessed directly by Brutus, will later be described in great detail by Casca (1.2.218–94), but his prejudice against Caesar makes us question the accuracy of his report. Actually, Caesar's collapse and attendant humility (Casca describes him as leaving the stage "sad away") may be either literal or staged but, in either case, represents a distinct dramatic success with the offstage audience. Antony, whose abilities in manipulating events are confirmed by his "performance" during the funeral oration, later uses this same reluctance on Caesar's part to demonstrate his friend's concern for Rome. Only by reading the offstage event metadramatically can the truth of the event be grasped: Caesar and Antony either planned the incident, or it was a fortuitous event on which Antony will later capitalize.

Between Brutus's and Casca's interpretations lies Caesar's own: thin men, such as Cassius whom he sees near him, are in Caesar's judgment most given to conspiracy. When Antony differs with the general, making the perhaps superficially courteous observation that Cassius is a "noble Roman, and well given" (197), Caesar opposes this reinterpretation and then invites Antony to speak more "truly" by whispering in his right ear his true sentiments. Since Antony's revised interpretation, given to that "right" or good ear, is delivered offstage upon Caesar's exit, we have as little chance of knowing Antony's assessment of Cassius as we have clear evidence that Caesar's own interpretation is itself on target, coming as it does on the heels of Cassius's first attempt to lure Brutus into the conspiracy.

Throughout the play characters frequently act as surrogate audience to interpret the onstage events. Able to see but not to hear him, Brutus and Cassius, moments before the assassination, differ as to what Popilius Lena's animated but unheard conversation with Caesar signifies. Brutus's comforting interpretation, that Lena is not disclosing the imminent assassination, prevails, but is based only on such visual evidence as the fact that Lena "smiles, and Caesar doth not change" (3.1.18–24). For all we know, Caesar, the consummate politician, who may have faked a collapse at the would-be coronation, may be acting again, concealing his true response with a poker face. The assassination itself is provoked by the dramatic stratagem of having the conspirators oppose Caesar in his decision to banish Publius Cimber, forcing Caesar to insist on the singular and thereby exclusive nature of his interpretation: "Let me a little show it, even in this— / That I was constant Cimber should be banish'd, / And constant do remain to keep him so" (3.1.71–73). If interpretation is at best a process, pluralistic and existential, we, no less than Caesar, are faced here with the fatal nature of an interpretation that is inflexible, exclusive. The paradox of interpretation later seals the fate of the conspirators. Brutus's decision to attack Antony and Octavius—based on his assessment that "the people 'twixt Philippi and this ground / Do stand but in a forc'd affection" (203–12)—wins over Cassius's own more conservative plan; Brutus's decision, as we know either from the play or from history, is the wrong one.

Cassius's death is itself the result of Pindarus's misapprehension of defeat for victory, and it is Messala who properly characterizes the problem and the potential tragedy of interpretation: "O hateful error, melancholy's child, / Why dost thou show to the apt thoughts of me / The things that are not?" (5.3.67–69). Titinius uses the singular pronoun but we could properly substitute the plural in his "Alas, thou hast misconstrued every thing" (84). Shakespeare offers a telling emblem for the problem of understanding when Lucilius impersonates Brutus on the battlefield (5.4), while the enemy, predictably and symbolically, conclude that they have "ta'en" Brutus prisoner.

During the funeral orations Brutus's interpretation of Caesar's life is reinterpreted by Antony. This same formal clash is anticipated earlier when, after Brutus's symbolic reading of the assassination as a sacrifice rather than a butchery, Antony in a moment of exquisite daring asserts precisely what Brutus would deny as he asks each conspirator to "render [him] his bloody hand' (3.1.184), thereby reinstating the rejected reading of *butchery* as well as breaking up the conspiracy's integrity—Brutus had insisted that they act as one, that such unity obviated any need for oath-taking (2.1.114–40)—by asking that the conspirators, whom he calls by their separate names, shake hands with him individually. If anything, Antony's powers of interpretation, whether self-serving or motivated by honest passion—and even this dichotomy works against a single response—are greater than Brutus's: it is Antony's prediction of "civil strife" (3.1.263) rather than Brutus's promise of a new-found peace that prevails.

The range in such misinterpretation of visual evidence, this optical distortion, is suggested by two otherwise "minor" events. One is that seemingly irrelevant conversation among Decius, Casca, and Cinna, in the very center of the scene where the conspirators confront Brutus, as to the proximity of the rising sun and due east (2.1.101–11). Not simply covering time onstage while Brutus and Cassius whisper apart, that conversation, I think, also stands as a microcosm of the larger, less innocent, visual distortions in the play. Casca asserts confidently that the sun does not rise in the east, and when Cinna answers affirmatively to Decius's rhetorical question ("doth not the day break here?"), Casca resolves the problem, though in a complicated way: both men, Decius in his rhetorical question that implies a "yes" and Cinna in his complementary answer, are "deceiv'd." The sun actually rises "a great way growing on the south," given the "youthful season of the year"; two months from the present the same sun will rise "up higher toward the north"; and it is the Capitol itself, not the sun, that "stands" toward "the high east."[4]

Cinna will be "confused" again when, stirred up by Antony's oration, the mob confuses the poet Cinna with the conspirator. Visual confusion yields to semantic confusion arising from the coincidence of names. The poet first tries to "locate" himself by place: he is going to Caesar's funeral, and as a friend, and he comes from his home that—recalling Casca's linking of the east and the Capitol—is near the Capitol. Failing to convince them, he then argues in terms of his profession: he is a poet rather than a conspirator, a maker rather than a destroyer. Juliet's poignant and ultimately ironic question of what's in a name then receives a cruel enactment when the mob, indifferent to names, decides to murder Cinna anyway, whether he be poet or conspirator. Mistakes in naming the points on the compass have widened now to include a public indifference to the names by which we distinguish characters on- and offstage.[5]

These same problems of seeing clearly the physical, external world and the men who inhabit that world are compounded once the supernatural enters the play. The "blunt" Casca of Act 1, scene 2, offering his reductive analysis of Caesar's attempted coronation, becomes the "breathless" Casca of the following scene, terrified, awe-struck by the monstrous portents he has observed. He interprets the "tempest dropping fire" as a sign either of civil strife in heaven or of the gods' displeasure with mortals (1.3.3–14). On the further visual evidence of a man whose left hand "did flame and burn / Like twenty torches" and the lion who "glaz'd" upon him in the Capitol, along with secondhand reports of similar "prodigies" (15–32), he conflates the earlier two alternatives to the more general and ambiguous reading: these abnormal events "point upon" the present disturbed "climate" of Rome. Some critics disparage Shakespeare's hand in drawing a cynically literal Cinna in Act 1, scene 2 and then a neurotic, superstitious Cinna in the following scene, yet this split in personality seems intentional, a warning against any singular judgment on the play's characters or their world.

Cicero remains noncommittal, agreeing that the times are "strange-disposed" but suggesting that "men may construe things after their fashion, / Clean from the purpose of the things themselves" (1.3.33–36). He does not specify, though, what that true "purpose" may be. Cassius then opposes both Casca's ambiguity and Cicero's generality about the idiosyncracy of human judgment by linking the abnormalities with what Caesar has become. However, when Casca tries to pin him down (" 'Tis Caesar that you mean; is it not Cassius?"), Cassius resists a positive identification, though not convincingly, with "Let it be who it is" (1.3.57–80).

When the supernatural moves to the level of dreams, specifically Calphurnia's dream of Caesar's statue spouting blood (2.2.76–82), the problem of interpreting potential rather than present events is compounded. Calphurnia herself will offer an interpretation no less singular than Cassius's when she reads "these things [that] are beyond all use" (2.2.25) as a warning to Caesar not to venture forth on the Ides of March. In point of fact, her reading, in not identifying the portents with either the conspiracy or Caesar specifically, does not conflict with the readings already offered by Casca and Cassius. More accurate than the men in the sense that she sees the portents only as a warning of impending danger, rather than as supernatural confirmation of a political position, she is, of course, right historically, and also right in terms of what will soon happen in the play itself. Yet Caesar, already locked in as a historical character, must, no less, reject her anticipatory reading and progress to the Capitol. In an immediate sense, Calphurnia is prophetic: the bleeding statue will, within minutes, be enacted onstage as the conspirators pass their swords through Caesar's body. Moreover, Decius's reinterpretation (83–90), we all recognize, is nothing more than a stratagem. Yet in a bizarre sense he is no less right, despite his conscious intentions, since the "reviving blood" that Rome draws from Caesar anticipates not only the victory—and the peace that victory brings—of Octavius Caesar but also the more general notion of Caesarism that, whatever its liabilities, would be responsible for the rebirth of Rome from the shambles unintentionally created by the conspiracy. Decius is, in effect, blinded by the immediate and political purpose behind his alternative interpretation to Calphurnia's own.

Neither interpretation, ultimately, has any efficacy: Caesar will go to the Capitol despite Calphurnia, and it is Decius's reminder that the Senate has resolved to offer him the crown rather than any allegorical reading of the bleeding statue that prompts him to leave home. Of what use, then, are portents, dreams, and the subsequent conflict of interpretations in a play in which everything is predetermined?

ii

The Renaissance ideal holds that with our senses we take in impressions of the external world and then subject such impressions to the mind's rational faculty.[6] This presupposes, of course, that the eye, the initial contact with the external world, is sound. In point of fact, the play stresses a distinct problem with the eyes. Caesar demands, "let me see [the Soothsayer's] face" (1.2.20), but when that face materializes out of the crowd and the Soothsayer offers his prophetic "Beware the ides of March," Caesar dismisses him as a "dreamer" and the prophet fades once more into the crowd. Minutes later Cassius observes that Caesar's "eye whose bend doth awe the world / Did lose his lustre" when he suffered helplessly with a fever during a Spanish campaign (123–24). Later Caesar's confident assessment that when "the things that threaten'd" him "shall see / The face of Caesar, they are vanished" (2.2.10–12) will be reversed when the conspirators boldly face him; Plutarch tells us that it was Caesar who pulled the toga over his head to avoid the humiliating sight of his seeming friends turned enemies. Brutus is quite right when he observes that "the eye sees not itself / But by reflection, by some other things," but when Cassius offers to be his "glass" we must wonder whether Brutus can see his own eyes through Cassius's, biased as the latter is in both his conscious and unconscious hatred, and hence exclusive understanding of Caesar (1.2.52–53), 68). The act of conspiracy itself requires darkness or, at the very least, less than adequate illumination of the conspirators (2.2.277–78), yet earlier in his orchard Brutus "cannot by the progress of the stars / Give guess how near to day it is" (2.1.2–3). It is left to Brutus to voice the paradox: if conspiracy "sham'st" to be seen at night, "when evils are most free," how can it find "a cavern dark enough" during the day to "mask [its] monstrous visage" (77–81)? The solution is both simple and cynical: by day it must pretend to be its opposite, putting on an actor's face of "smiles and affability" to "hide [it] from prevention" (81–85).

Brutus, however, would idealize these same inadequate eyes, setting "honor in one eye and death i' th' other," and without hesitation would choose honor over death (1.2.86–89). He can even assure Antony that while he sees "but [the] hands" of the conspirators, the apparent confirmation of their butchery, he will in time see in "this our present act" their true "hearts," thereby acknowledging the noble motive behind the assassination (3.1.165–69). Antony appears to agree with Brutus's notion about the limitations of present vision: he was "sway'd from the point, by looking down on Caesar" (219). In the same breath, however, he ironically anticipates the ghost's appearance as he imagines what Caesar would say if his "spirit look[ed] upon us now" (195–96). Though he never adopts such a policy, he then links vision with political expediency in his cynical argument that had he "as many eyes as [Caesar] hast wounds, / Weeping as fast as they stream forth [their] blood," it would "become [him] better than to close / In terms of friendship with [Caesar's] enemies" (200–203).

Early in the play Cassius has an eyesight keen enough to recognize Cinna from afar "by his gait," while Cinna himself momentarily confuses Casca with Metellus Cimber (1.3.132), yet later the same Cassius sends Pindarus aloft to observe the progress of the battle since his own "sight was ever thick" (5.3.21). John Velz reminds us that in Plutarch it is Cassius, not his comrade, who misreads the signs of victory for defeat, and thus this change from the man earlier described by Caesar as one who "looks / Quite through the deeds of men" (1.2.202–3) to a general plagued by near-sightedness may stand as emblem of the failed or failing vision in the play.[7] The ocular instrument, the agent through which the external world is conveyed to the reason, is thus literally and figuratively defective here, and it is an exhausted and more circumspect Brutus who, near death, is relieved to know that now "night hangs upon [his] eyes" (5.5.41).

There is, significantly, a parallel problem with hearing. In a revealing departure from his source, Shakespeare has Caesar ask Antony to "come on [his] right hand, for [his left] ear is deaf" (1.2.213). This addition has been read both literally (Caesar, aspiring to godlike supremacy, is ironically afflicted with a hearing loss) and figuratively: in his arrogance Caesar only asks Antony to confirm his speculation that thin men, such as Cassius, are dangerous, and hence wants Antony to stay on his "right" or good side by playing the "yes" man.[8] We have seen, moments before, an example of Caesar's exclusive hearing when he dismisses the Soothsayer as a "dreamer." Conversely, when Cassius recognizes Casca "by his voice," he is complimented with "your ear is good". (1.3.41–42). By the end of the play hearing is as defective as sight. Titinius rhetorically addresses the dead Cassius, "Didst thou not hear shouts [of victory]?," and the response to that question is that because he failed to, Cassius "hast misconstrued every thing" (5.3.83–84). In a revealing combination of the visual and auditory, Messala observes that "piercing steel, and darts envenomed" thrust into Brutus's ears will be "as welcome . . . / As tidings of this sight" (Cassius's faulty death [5.3.74–78]). Earlier Brutus himself wishes that the ill Ligarius had a "healthful ear" to give the conspiracy (2.1.319).

Ears, even if healthy, may not function properly if the conspirators depend on others for what they themselves cannot hear or see. Again, it is Casca who interprets for Brutus and Cassius the offstage flourishes during Caesar's coronation, and yet Casca is unreliable. At the coronation he failed to understand Cicero since "he spoke Greek" (1.2.279): the pun admits the literal and the figurative. It is Caesar himself who at his death speaks what is for an English audience a foreign language: *"Et tu Brute"* (3.1.76–77).

iii

As interpreters, the characters are thus limited by what one critic has aptly termed the "failures of objectivity."[9] The reverse side of such failures is what L. C. Knights has called "the unreality of the world which they inhabit."[10] In a real sense, even if the mortal eye and ear functioned at peak efficiency, the world here is still too large for mortal comprehension.

For alongside the secular and external realm of politics exists the mystical,[11] the portents described by Casca and Calphurnia, as well as the latter's prophetic dream in Act 2, scene 2 that, in effect, takes form three scenes later. That Casca is otherwise "blunt" (1.3.295) and that Calphurnia, as she admits, is not one to stand "on ceremonies" (2.2.13) only strengthens the case for the portents' existence. Cassius may flout Casca for believing in such signs, but the stage direction for *"thunder still"* (1.3.100) undercuts his declaration of the supremacy of human will

("That part of tyranny that I do bear / I can shake off at pleasure" [99–100]), and near death he will qualify his Epicureanism and "partly credit things that do presage" (5.1.76–78). Even Caesar, the embodiment of a worldly realpolitik, "is superstitious grown of late" and, as a consequence, is now receptive to matters "of fantasy, of dreams, and ceremonies" (2.1.195–97). His first action in the play, in fact, is based on superstition as he commands Calphurnia to stand in Antony's path so that his touch may "shake off [her] sterile curse" (1.2.3–9).

This belief in the mystical, that dimension beyond the rational faculties of vision and hearing, is most often associated with women. In Casca's description of the portents it was "a hundred ghastly women" who were "transformed with their fear" (1.3.23–24). During that curious short scene (2.4) where Portia senses the imminent assassination, hearing sounds beyond the comprehension of the servant Lucius, she makes the distinction between her rational "man's mind" and her prophetic "woman's might" (8), and I would further observe that here the Soothsayer, earlier rejected by Caesar, makes his penultimate appearance. We will also recall Portia's own death in which "she fell distract, / And (her attendants absent) swallow'd fire" (4.3.155–56). If we see Portia as Brutus's other "half" (2.1.274), not only as his marriage partner but also as the imaginative side of his otherwise rational consciousness, she may be said to bequeath her powers to him through her suicide. Later Brutus will actually see Caesar's ghost, the only portent that ever materializes onstage. Similarly, in *A Midsummer Night's Dream* it was the wife, Hippolyta, who could entertain the four lovers' garbled account of the supernatural happenings in the forest, whereas the rationalist Theseus dismissed what she saw as "strange and admirable" as the mere "tricks" of "strong imagination" (5.1.1–27).

This mystical dimension coexists, I believe, with the sense of timelessness or with what J. L. Simmons calls the "eternal,"[12] that larger dimension in which the linear progress of history, the notion of an orderly sequence of causes and effects, is overwhelmed by the cyclical.[13] The play demonstrates that the rational arrangement of past, present, and future is fraudulent, for history as progress—surely the optimistic basis of Brutus's resolve to join the conspiracy—is supplanted by repetition that turns an optimistic notion of the force of human will into its pessimistic, cyclical opposite. No one fighting in the Hundred Years' War could label it as such, and in the light of subsequent history our own label "The War to End All Wars" of course seems farcical. Seeing themsevles as live men, making informed decisions in the present to alter, even to ameliorate the future, the conspirators cannot know that they are characters in a play, deterministic not only within its own confines but also as a playing out, and repetitiously so, of past and future scores.[14] He will reverse his thinking later, but early in the play Cassius unconsciously errs with his assertion of the supremacy of human will: "Men at some time are masters of their fates" (1.2.139). With the outcome of the civil war in Philippi already set by that in Pharsalia—in the former Caesar defeated Pompey; in the latter Caesar's spirit, embodied by Antony, will defeat Brutus—Brutus eloquently but no less wrongly invokes the image of history as a sea as he champions that same human will: "There is a tide in the affairs of men, / Which taken at the flood, leads on to fortune" (4.3.218–19). As audience we silently supply the necessary corrective: the same tide that also swells no less rapidly declines.

With the actual events already locked into their historical place, with the play itself known fully only by its author, Shakespeare's theater here is given, I think, to this cyclical view, epitomized in the metaphor of the tide, as corrected, and to a corresponding diminishment of men into "actors," in the more pejorative sense of that word. In the play's shortest scene (2.3) Artemidorus subordinates free will to fate with his "If thou read this, O Caesar, thou mayest live; / If not, the Fates with traitors do contrive" (15–16). This is how in this "strange-disposed time" (1.3.33) the "world . . . goes" (5.5.22). Against the monarch's "linear progress" there is what Maynard Mack has called the "cycle of kingship,"[15] and it is both ironic and appropriate that Caesar himself, however much he lacks perspective on other occasions, sees this same historic inevitability: "What can be avoided / Whose end is purpos'd by the mighty gods" (2.2.26–27), though this observation only serves as further justification for his going to the Capitol. Cassius also winds down to this position near his death, the bold proponent of man's will now seeing "the affairs of men" as resting "still uncertain" (5.1.95). In *Hamlet* the Clown's argument is that the one action man takes in which he both foresees and controls the consequences is his death, and Hamlet echoes this earlier in his advice to Ophelia that to stop a senseless existence one must forsake pregnancy either by becoming a nun or living the prostitute's non-procreative sexual life. In this light, we can look anew at Cassius's observation that every "bondsman" has at least the power to take his life (1.3.101–2), though he thinks here of suicide only as the last resort after all human policy has failed. Beyond his conscious knowledge, Cassius only seals his fate and hastens his death when he "elects" to free the state through Caesar's murder. In this sense, both Brutus's Stoicism and Cassius's Epicureanism are merely illusive paradigms, based on false premises about the significance of human thought as well as action.

The "working out" of history is here determined not by present but by past actions, and the play thus sustains the paradox that men are a factor in events but only by what happens to them rather than by what they consciously cause to happen. Cassius unwittingly suggests such repetition when he links the swimming episode, which he uses to underscore Caesar's pathetic mortality, with that moment when Aeneas bore Anchises on his back through the water (1.2.112–14). Men here seem interchangeable, playing roles that have already been fleshed out.[16] Just when he thinks the factor of Caesar or Caesarism has been eliminated, both by the actual assassination and the reasoned eloquence of his funeral oration, Brutus hears the mob cry out "let him be Caesar" and "Caesar's better parts / Shall be crown'd in Brutus" (3.2.51–52). Cassius has already found the two names interchangeable: "Brutus and Caesar": what should be in that 'Caesar'? / Why should that name be sounded more than yours?" (1.2.142–43). Moreover, it is a common observation that Brutus, in his self-inflicted and egoistic failure to see his fault in the episode involving bribes, will later resemble no one so much as the man he assassinated. Titinius's "it is but change" (5.3.51) refers immediately to the (ultimately) inaccurate assessment that Octavius has been overcome by Brutus just as Cassius has by Antony, yet this same line signals a larger motif of repetitive change, a tragic blending of roles. Late in the play Antony addresses Octaviuis as "Caesar" (5.1.24), and thus the cycle of change, though ultimately without end, is momentarily completed within the present play.

To the degree that *Julius Caesar* is a revenge play, it also partakes structurally in the cyclical nature of the genre. In Act 4, scene 3 Cassius literally enacts Caesar's theatrical gesture in offering his throat to the mob (1.2.265–66) as he presents his dagger and naked breast to Brutus to "strike as thou didst at Caesar" (100–105). At his own death he supplies the logical conclusion: life is a "compass" and "where [he] did begin [both his actual birth and his "birth" as a character in murdering Caesar], there shall [he] end" (5.3.23–25). His face "cover'd" as Caesar's was at his death, Cassius is murdered by his friend Pindarus "even with the sword that kill'd" Caesar (44–46). We will recall that Caesar himself was killed not by foreign enemies or even by those, to his conscious knowledge, of a rival domestic faction, but by his friends. Myron Taylor reminds us that "Caesar is not his own master, and neither is Cassius."[17]

Because men are not fully masters of their fate, issues of culpability are in part discounted. One acts as courageously and as self-consciously of his motives as is possible, but such courage and consciousness is at length inadequate for penetrating far into a world that is both substantial and mystical, present and also beyond present comprehension. Pindarus supplies a curious coda to this larger issue of responsibility when he exits from the stage, having assisted his friend Cassius in his suicide: he "shall run / where never Roman shall take note of him" (5.3.50). Both a coward and a wise man, Pindarus attempts to escape the play, whether it be history's or Shakespeare's.

iv

Against this cyclical inevitability, whose dominant metaphor is found in the repetition of roles and scenes, there stands the image of the playwright himself. Through language and spectacle, and in full comprehension of his subject, Shakespeare has fashioned a historical event, recreated it through the theater, to the degree that, as T. J. B. Spencer observes, twentieth-century man tends to see ancient Rome much as Shakespeare himself enacts it.[18] The playwright's view even dominates here over that of Plutarch, who lived closer to the period and served as the playwright's primary source. Nor could the admittedly greater erudition of Ben Jonson give his two Roman tragedies a comparable status.

Yet, with no less equal energy and intention, the characters, Brutus in particular, try to "fashion" (2.1.220) the present, to "play" with it for a desired end. In this sense Brutus is a failed playwright, or, as Sigurd Burckhardt argues, he, like Shakespeare, is the playwright responsible for committing an act.[19] A common complaint about Brutus's playwriting skills, however, is that he is too cold, too abstract, not sufficiently attuned to the ears and eyes of his audience.[20] He sees not so much the bodies of men but the abstraction "conspiracy" (2.1.77). Unlike his own playwright, Brutus, in fact, would divorce language from spectacle, preferring the "word" of men (2.1.125), indeed "good words" before physical action itself (5.1.29). His funeral oration is a case in point. The language is abstract, nontactile, and while there are superficial appeals to the audience for its response, Brutus's questions are actually *rhetorical* in the most limited sense of that word. He plays *to* an audience, but not in concert *with* it, and it is a telling fact that when he pauses for their "reply," the audience affirms "None, Brutus, none" (3.2.34–35). His own play, the assassination of Caesar, reverses Shakespeare's since it is based not so much on the past (Brutus has no clear present complaint about Caesar's policies) as on the future (he would murder Caesar for what he might become). Like a playwright or poet, he must also use the physical as the root for language and symbolic vision: "For Antony is but a limb of Caesar" and "O that we then could come by Caesar's spirit, / And not dismember Caesar!" (2.1.165, 169–70). Yet, in attempting to separate what cannot be separated if the theater is to work, Brutus fails to produce the very play he would fashion. Disdaining "savage spectacle" (3.1.223), he would convert the physical act of assassination, as Brents Stirling rightly observes, to a theater of "sacrificers" (2.1.166), in which, contradicting the normal balance in such rituals between the body and the service over that body, the physical source of the sacrifice would cease to be a factor.[21] Brutus's concept of both sacrifice and theater is thus limited, his play at length seen by his audience, under Antony's tutelage, as a "piteous spectacle" (3.2.198), and ultimately as only a "gallant show" (5.1.13). In point of fact, he will not "come by" ("eliminate") Caesar's spirit; nor will he avoid dismembering the body. This theatrical cleavage is the equivalent to the "gaping dualism" that G. Wilson Knight finds in Brutus as he contrasts his cold abstractions of "honor" with the physical and communal nature of "love."

In this regard Cassius is Brutus's counterpart; he would sacrifice a diminished language to spectacle. He is physical, tactile. In his opening line he asks if Brutus will "see" the "order of the course" (1.2.25) and then "observe[s]" something other than a "show of love" in Brutus's eyes (32–34). Uneasy with the symbolic, with anything other than what is here and now, and as perceived by himself, Cassius is not given to art in any exalted sense, loving neither plays nor music (1.2.203–4). Like the unplayful Tribunes in the first scene, he would "disrobe the images" (1.1.64). His language is used instead for the practical purpose of inciting others to action: "my weak words / Have struck but thus much show of fire" (1.2.176–77). Nor is he above the stratagem of having "writings" thrown in Brutus's window (1.2.316–18).[23]

Though we might want to qualify the word, Antony is a *compromise* between the extremes of Brutus and Cassius. Of "quick spirit" (1.2.29) and given to "sports" (2.1.189), with that word embracing everything from athletic contests to theatrical spectacles, he stages the offstage coronation reported by Casca, with the audience clapping and hissing the performers "as they use to do the players in the theatre" (1.2.258–61). Antony's own staged sincerity in the presence of the conspirators and his self-conscious address to Caesar's dead body ("O, pardon me" [3.1.254–75]) culminate, of course, in the funeral oration, where he combines the conceptual (the challenge to Brutus as an honorable man) and the visual. Making himself and then Caesar the object of the address, rather than attempting to justify a past event, *playing* to his audience, his speech itself is replete with highly theatrical details. When he comes down from the pulpit, lifts Caesar's mantle, and asks the mob to form a circle around the body (the otherwise formal "theater" of the oration now becoming theater-in-the-round), Antony demonstrates a sense of staging unmatched in the play. Significantly, Brutus is absent, by his own wish, during this performance. Still, even this "shrewd contriver" (2.1.158) cannot practice his theatrics so effectively as to rise above history, and at the end it will be the efficient but playless Octavius whose star is in the ascendancy.

All three "playwrights" pale, of course, beside their ultimate creator. Nor does any character have a sense of play equal to the complexities of its world. Curiously, *Julius Caesar* opens with tribunes chastising workmen for playing, for celebrating in a holiday spirit Caesar's return. The occasion for play, the feast of the Lupercal, will itself be quickly con-

verted to the arena of serious political work. Mildred Hartsock notes that
the only characters not caught up in the complexities of the world, and
hence able to see the tragic connection between man's attempt to fashion
events and history's inflexible hand, are the two poets and the
soothsayer.[24] More often, the theater is dismissed as something irrelevant to the seeming "realities" of the world: the Soothsayer is only a
"dreamer" (1.2.24), the staged coronation "mere foolery" (1.2.236), and
that imagination by which we escape the confines of the present is on a
par with a belief in "unicorns" (2.1.204). As with the trust in portents, or
the belief in a world beyond the immediate reaches of the senses, particularly the visual senses, the theater is here associated with what is
womanish and, in the almost exclusively male world of *Julius Caesar*,
unflatteringly so. Cassius dismisses those who read the portents for
supernatural commentary as being governed by their "mothers' spirits"
(1.3.83). In similar fashion Decius associates a belief in dreams with
women (2.2.99). Misinterpretation of the object of the immediate senses
is an "error soon conceiv'd, / That never com'st unto a happy birth, / But
kill'st the mother that engend'red" it (5.3.69–71).

Nevertheless, when the play metaphor surfaces most graphically, it is a
male speaker who imagines a production that will never exist, a *Julius
Caesar* having little in common with the complex play world that the
speaker himself presently inhabits. Cassius's "How many ages hence /
Shall this our lofty scene be acted over / In states unborn and accents yet
unknown" generates in turn Brutus's "How many times shall Caesar
bleed in sport, / That now on Pompey's basis lies along / No worthier than
the dust!" (3.1.111–16). Here are Romans "speaking centuries before the
Renaissance" and anticipating "a Globe audience in 1599 watching a stage
representation of their deed."[25] To be more accurate, the laudatory play
they envision never comes from Shakespeare's pen.

Only at the end of the play, near death, do these characters who
mistake themselves for flesh-and-blood people see the world of *Julius
Caesar* with any real perspective. Brutus's "I know my hour is come" ends
a speech that opens with the revelation to Volumnius that the ghost of
Caesar has twice appeared to him (5.5.20), and later when he says that his
"tongue / Hath almost ended his life's history" and that he has "but
labor'd to attain this hour" (5.5.39–42), the theatrical metaphor, so long
missing in Brutus's conscious mind, subtly reasserts itself: the actor
playing Brutus is about to end his speaking role, and he has worked for
the stage's two-hours' traffic to bring himself to this final scene. Now for
Brutus history itself becomes cyclical and cynical rather than progressive
and positive: "O Julius Caesar, thou art mighty yet! / Thy spirit walks
abroad, and turns our swords / In our own proper entrails" (5.3.94–96).
Earlier he parallels this observation with one a bit more general: "but this

same day / Must end that work the Ides of March begun" (5.1.112–13). In his own words Brutus is late developing a sense of "his life's history" (5.5.40). Just as Caesar near death was given to superstition's imaginative world—the theater in essence—both Brutus and Cassius, in now qualifying the otherwise secular, rational tenets of their Stoicism and Epicureanism, respectively, "change" their minds and "partly credit things that do presage" (5.1.77–78).

v

The ghost scene (4.3.239–308) stands as a vortex for the enlarged vision called for and yet so rarely found in the play. It is a moment when Brutus can see through, albeit briefly, to the mystical or supernatural that coexists with the natural, external world, as well as to the cyclical history encompassing his own present actions.

The scene itself does not come upon the play suddenly but rather has been anticipated, though, like Brutus in his serene moment before death, we as audience can realize this only in retrospect. Brutus himself had earlier defined the night as that time "when evils are most free" (2.1.79), as a time when he envies the peaceful sleep of his servant Lucius since he has "no figures nor no fantasies, / Which busy care draws in the brains of men" (231–32). Prophetically, he had found the sleepless period "since Cassius first did whet [him] against Caesar" or the space between "the acting of a dreadful thing / and the first motion" as being "like a phantasma or a hideous dream" (2.1.61–65).

As noted, Shakespeare couples Plutarch's spirit embodying Brutus's ill conscience with the ghost of Caesar. That ill conscience may find its origin in the Cobbler's pun on "bad soles" (1.1.13), and surfaces at length in Antony's prophetic remark at the funeral oration that "the evil that men do lives after them" (3.2.75). Several commentators have seen the ghost as Brutus's other half, as the Caesar element in himself,[26] as the embodiment of "his subjective fears and misgivings,"[27] the "proof" that Caesar and Brutus are ultimately the same being,[28] as the spirit that "Brutus cannot stop . . . because he is infused with it himself in all of its paradoxical glory."[29] Perhaps this notion of the ghost as part of Brutus, or as a manifestation of a half that has hitherto been suppressed in the play, is anticipated in Portia's description of herself as her husband's half: "am I yourself / But, as it were, in sort or limitation?" (2.1.282–83). She observes this, we will recall, after the conspirators have left, and her most pressing subject is the "sick offense within [Brutus's] mind" that keeps him from bed and restful sleep (2.1.268).

The ghost scene itself is set outside the confines of the daylight, political world, and forms part of what John Crawford has charted as the play's larger movement from the external to the internal.[30] Appropriately, Brutus observes that "the deep of night is crept upon . . . talk," and to his question "There is no more to say?" Cassius replies with a simple "No more" (226, 229). The failed playwright, as I have called him, given to language rather than spectacle, the man who attempted earlier to divorce the conceptual from the physical, is here bereft of words themselves, indeed has grown "much forgetful" (255).[31] The sure, inflexible Brutus of the Quarrel Scene is now twice given to the qualifying "I think" (274, 276). The intellectual of the conspiracy, the classic orator at the funeral, now speaks with an almost awkward simplicity: "*Bru.* Well; then I shall see thee again? / *Ghost.* Ay, at Philippi. / *Bru.* Why, I will see thee at Philippi then" (284–86).

In representing not one but two entities, the ghost itself defies normality or probability. Like Hamlet's father's ghost, both dead and living, it comes from a world not fully encompassed by orthodox notions of reality. And it must be invoked; Hamlet's "Speak, I am bound to hear" (1.5.6) is here Brutus's "Speak to me what thou art" (281).[32] Potentially a god, an angel of conscience, and a demonic spirit, the ghost demands that sense of play implicit in an enlarged vision, the ability to entertain a double, an inclusive rather than an exclusive notion of reality.[33] Nor can anyone onstage, upon waking, share Brutus's vision or, more properly, what he has both seen and heard. Like Bottom waking from his forest adventure with "when my cue comes, call me, and I will answer" (4.1.200–201), Lucius wakes with the line "the strings, my lord, are false" (291) and thus reveals that for him the time covered during the ghost's appearance does not exist, since to his own mind he has continued speaking, without interruption, from Brutus's earlier observation about slumber rewarding him with sleep as he plays the instrument (269). Nor can Brutus find anyone else to verify the appearance. As most of those who have directed the play would do, I take his questions to Lucius, Varrus, and Claudio as a tactful way of detecting whether those onstage have shared his vision, without at the same time raising suspicions that he alone has seen the ghost. After first claiming that Lucius cried in his dream, thereby making his question "Didst thou see any thing?" (297) seem reasonable, he repeats the stratagem with Varrus and Claudio. As the offstage audience, we confirm what they cannot, though Brutus, caught in the historical confines of the stage, cannot take any comfort in this "fact."

Maurice Charney's observation that throughout the play the name of Caesar becomes a kind of "talisman"[34] takes on a very special meaning in this scene that another commentator sees as bordering on "the occult," with Brutus functioning as a "tragic conjurer," working in a setting complete with bell, book, candle (and an ill-burning one at that),[35] and music.[36] Until this moment Brutus has been convinced of his own clear vision. Here his otherwise unreliable eyes help shape the "subjective apparition of Caesar himself."[37] The very play that introduces Brutus to Cassius with the subject of eyes is now flooded with reference to vision: "heavy eyes" (256), "Let me see, let me see" (273), the "weakness of mine eyes" (276), the opening questions to the ghost as Brutus struggles with the evidence of his eyes (275, 278).

By his own admission Brutus sees the ghost once more (5.5.17–18), and for us the question must be, in this play that enacts the limitations of man's vision of himself, his role in history, and of his place in a world that embraces the natural and the mystical: just how much does Brutus see? Like Othello in his final speech, does Brutus, so late in the play, achieve something approaching tragic vision? There is no sure critical consensus here. It has been argued that once Brutus's optimistic prophecy about Rome after Caesar is rejected, another "voice" in the form of Caesar's cryptic ghost must fill the void, and so here Brutus's "evil spirit" shows the prophet offering up his last sign by giving up the ghost.[38] Conversely, Brutus's subsequent behavior, unlike that of Macbeth after he has seen the ghost, is not that of a guilty man since the spirit is "another pointer to the unavoidable outcome; it signifies power rather than judgment."[39] Or the scene allows Brutus's inner self to surface briefly in a play where otherwise it is never "fully confronted or reflected upon."[40]

Though he predates him by little more than a year on the Globe stage and was, indeed, performed by the same lead actor, Brutus is surely no Hamlet. His vision of the ghost comes late rather than early, and unlike Hamlet, Brutus does not wax desperate with imagination almost from the start. If Hamlet is too circumspect, to the degree that he renders himself incapable of the decisive action distinguishing the elder Hamlet, Brutus, although an intellectual and an idealist, focuses more on the events of the world than on human motivation or questions about reality as it is intersected by the unreality of dreams and the theater. John Russell Brown speaks of the ghost as an actor's subtext—the motivation and rationale of a character existing just below the conscious, written text—which has momentarily come to the surface.[41] More often in *Julius Caesar* that subtext, as it includes the forces at once psychological, historical, mystical, and cyclical that shape human behavior, must be inferred by the audience. Brutus prefers another type of play, one where "our looks [do not] put on our purposes, / But bear it as our Roman actors do, / With untir'd spirits and formal constancy" (2.1.225–27). For him, to his conscious mind, the theater is only secular, a tool at best, only a metaphor for reality (as when we spoke during World War II of "the European Theater"), a way of picturing the abstractions of political and ethical thought and thus only their handmaiden, inauthentic in itself, let alone being a superior way of understanding reality. This concept of the theater is, I think, at once Brutus's strength and glaring limitation. His kinsmen are to be found in those public figures like Theseus and Claudius who, with varying degrees of both success and integrity, try to manage in the immediate world. Unlike Hamlet, a man given to theater, they do try to prove "most royal," having "been put on" (5.2.397–98).

Yet a serenity comes to Brutus following the ghost's appearance. We have already observed those moments near his death when he sees his life in some perspective, as a kind of theatrical "history," which, of course, is what it is. Such late-come vision is brief, to be sure, but we are no less grateful. One critic cites the paradox: "the flood [of history] cannot be gauged by the reasoning mind," and the only wisdom we can have is at the end, when the end is known.[42] Harriet Hawkins comments that here Shakespeare's audience has "the retrospective foreknowledge of a historian, a playwright, or a god," and if we misconstrue the world the fault "lies in human nature itself," when we are compelled to be actors ourselves rather than spectators.[43] No less than for us, Brutus's knowledge comes late, yet it comes nevertheless. Moments before the entrance of Antony and Octavius, Brutus can at last avert his look with impunity from the visible world, for now, and only now, obscured vision is a blessing rather than a curse: "Night hangs upon my eyes, my bones would rest, / That have but labor'd to attain this hour."

5

Macbeth:

"Mine eyes are made the fools o' th' other senses, / Or else"

M_{ACBETH}'s opening line is bounded by the first Witch's "when" and "again," implying that the past rests heavy on the play, and that it will be repeated. With the sole exception that he shows no similar repentance at death, Macbeth himself plays out a role already determined by the first Thane of Cawdor. Moreover, we confront here the mood of ambiguity that will color both the play and our response to its central characters: the battle won, the state of being fair, must coexist with the battle lost, the state of being foul. Tantalizing as the question of Macbeth's own culpability has been—are the three sisters external agents? or are they projections of Macbeth's will? or, as A. C. Bradley has it, both?[1]—the opening scene, as one critic astutely phrases it, appears to single out no one individual but rather points to a disease in the general "psyche" of Scotland itself.[2] Shakespeare's "overture" here may thus allude to conditions, both individual and social, existing before the play.[3] In a way the opening scene never dissolves, but rather "hovers" over *Macbeth*. Its infection remains general, and it is little wonder that critics and directors have had to resolve whether the disease is to be limited to the play's conscious villains, or whether Banquo, among others, is tainted by its atmosphere.[4] The past that is also present and future, the bifurcation of an otherwise single event or state, the contamination that is both singular and plural—such paradoxes spread into the waiting play, distorting and making complex even those moments when the issues of valor or ethics or human accomplishment seem most clear.

The first word of the bleeding Sergeant who reports Macbeth's victory over Macdonwald is "doubtful" (1.2.7), and if his story ends with a resolution—Macbeth's defeat of an opponent—the passage to that resolution is far from simple as he describes the antagonists clinging to each other, like drowning swimmers, or like lovers, choking "their art." Laurence Michel observes that the Sergeant's language almost gets out of hand, the fury of his rhetoric, beyond its immediate subject, suggesting that he too has been infected with the violent energy generated by Macbeth no less than Macdonwald.[5] The simple Duncan offers a simple benediction to the account—"O valiant cousin, worthy gentleman!" (24)—but his optimistic conclusion is itself overturned as the Sergeant, back on his narrative, describes the battle's irony: at the moment of Macbeth's victory, the tide turned when the Norwegians began a fresh assault, the battle just won promising to become a battle lost. The Sergeant continues to invoke the paradoxes of the opening scene: just when the sun seems to shine, promising a clear day, "shipwracking storms and direful thunders break" (25–26); the Macbeth and Banquo pronounced "valiant" and "worthy" by Duncan are now "dismay'd," like a sparrow fearing an eagle, or a "hare the lion" (33–35). And what are we to do with the "cannons overcharg'd with double cracks" (37) since the literal reading (Macbeth and Banquo, recovering their equilibrium, now redoubling their assault) admits its opposite (the cannon, overloaded, cracking and thereby blowing up its operator)?

This complexity and the ensuing confusion in what is seen and what is heard—the day both fair and foul, the cannon's retort threatening both its object and its operator, the Sergeant's ambiguous narrative—will be most fully enacted in scene 3 when the two mortal observers and auditors confront the three witches, and come away as an audience divided in its interpretation of what they themselves have just witnessed. Little wonder that, as was observed in *Julius Caesar*, the characters' problem of understanding their world becomes our own. In his study of the play's theatrical history Marvin Rosenberg uses the musical term *polyphony* to describe at once the plethora of conflicting stage interpretations extending over almost four centuries as well as the numerous possibilities that the text itself, without cease, presents actor and director.[6]

i

Duncan's curious "negative elegy" for the first Thane of Cawdor is significant in this respect: "There's no art / To find the mind's construction in the face: / He was a gentleman on whom I built / An absolute trust" (1.4.11–14). The first two lines underscore, of course, the problem of reading signs correctly, of passing without error from the face's existence to the mind's essence. However, the last two lines signal the inevitable stand against paradox, or what I would call the characters' mania for certainty, for what is clear or absolute as a defense against uncertainty. In effect, the very conditions that would delight the scholarly mind of a Hamlet, given as he is to paradox, relativity, and theatricality, terrify the "mind" of *Macbeth*, of both character and play. This stand against paradox is, curiously, almost atheatrical, unplayful,[7] as reductive and exclusive as the theater, at least on the level practiced by Shakespeare, is expansive and inclusive.

In this play that points to the actual figure of King James in attendance for a court production, it is no less true that *Macbeth* cannot be dismissed as simple propaganda, as handmaiden for a Stuart reading of history.[8] Those historical facts were not only certain but had been "properly" interpreted by none other than the King himself. Yet in the play Macbeth fights against the certainty of subsequent history, his attempt to establish a solid, Thousand-Year Reich rendered absurd by basic facts within the grasp of any theatergoer then or now: the Macbeths' childless state, the irony of Macduff's birth, the subsequent history of the realm.

Going against history, Macbeth himself most eloquently and yet perversely expresses this mania for certainty. Banquo's presence puts "rancors in the vessel of [his] peace" (3.1.66). An attempt to control fate, the double murder of Banquo and Fleance, while perfect in theory, is rendered imperfect in consequence; the desire for the finite thus receives no enactment in the play. One normally raises a question or initiates an action to resolve an uncertainty, yet as the witches well know, this desire for resolution or "security / Is mortals' chiefest enemy" (3.5.32). I take the line, purposely, from the scene that is almost surely not Shakespeare's; despite any crimes against taste that the adapter, if it was an adapter, committed in dragging Hecate into the play, I believe he managed to read this issue of certainty with clarity and conciseness.

This stand against paradox that only exposes the very thing it seeks to avoid finds its expression early in the play. Whatever complexities there are in the Sergeant's earlier narration of the battle between Macbeth and Macdonwald, the battle ends with Macbeth's fixing the enemy's "head upon our battlements" (1.2.23), the head thus "fix'd" serving as a symbol for a battle successfully resolved. The issue, however, is complicated in *Macbeth* since the second head to be fixed on a battlement, Macbeth's own "usurper's cursed head" (5.9.21), is, like the first, that of a countryman, the product of civil, not international war. The notion of Scotland's diseased psyche, suggested in the opening scene, is thus curiously linked to this mania for certainty.[9]

The Sergeant asks Duncan to "mark . . . mark" his words (1.2.28) at the very point in the narrative when the account of battle is complicated, when "discomfort swells" from apparent "comfort" (27–28). But much later in the play, when the civil poison of Macbeth has spread in a way that far surpasses whatever his former enemy attempted, that same word *mark* (with its implications of certainty, of something that can be noted and thereby recorded) is itself swept away: the reliable Rosse tells Macduff that the very same air that was once both fair and foul is now so rent with "sighs, and groans, and shrieks" that such sounds are "made" but "not mark'd." On this occasion the "mother" earth became its opposite, "our graves," and the only individuals who can now feel secure (who are "once seen to smile") are those who know "nothing" (4.3.165–170).

Certainty, security in the political sense, is located in the King, significantly called the head of state, and it is fitting that the false King, Macbeth, is denied his seat at the banquet, though his chair is set in the very center of his subjects ("Both sides are even; here I'll sit i' th' midst" [3.4.10]). Lady Macbeth begs her guests to "keep seat" (53), dismissing her husband's unaccustomed and unbecoming movements about the room as only a momentary "fit" (53–54), while Macbeth himself tries to confirm his unshared vision of the usurping King—Banquo's spirit—with the revealing lines "If I stand here, I saw him" (73). In a curious parallel to the issue of seating in the banquet scene, Duncan's first observation about Macbeth's castle is that it has "a pleasant seat" (1.6.1). The secure home, the haven from the terrors outside, has, in the Porter's judgment, turned to a hell. Richard Jaarsma observes that not only does Banquo feel this reversal ("a heavy summons lies like lead upon" him) to the degree that he cannot sleep in Macbeth's castle the night of the murder [2.1.6–9]) but he—and others—may actually be tainted as long as he remains in this perversion of a home.[10] The complex question, and one never fully resolved, of why Macduff leaves his own home may also be linked to this violation of the center of security,[11] because the "world" invoked by Macbeth, itself born of a mania for security, threatens the very foundation of the King's castle and his subject's good name.

The discussion so far, on the paradoxical opening scene and the correlative mania for certainty, sets the stage for what I would like to call the play's own negative metadramatics of language and spectacle, coupled as it is with a violation of the notion of the theater of presence. The Macbeths would, from this perspective, substitute an inner theater working against the historical world offstage and the very notion of theater itself.

ii

It is through language that the characters attempt to name and thereby "fix" a world already disordered and then assaulted further by the Macbeths. As the bleeding Sergeant approaches, Duncan first addresses him through a question to his attendants: "What bloody man is that?" Malcolm provides a more specific description: it is the Sergeant "who like a good and hardy soldier fought" against his capture. Sight precedes language here, and as the solitary figure makes his way across stage, the eyes of his audience, initially tentative ("He can report, / As seemeth by his plight"), soon focus and thus the interrogatory "man" quickly metamorphoses to "sergeant" and then to "friend." The sequence, a few seconds in length, underscores the need to locate by words whatever comes into the spectrum of the community. When Malcolm's greeting "Hail, brave friend!"[5] is used three times by the witches in the subsequent scene, his seemingly clear salutation is itself clouded. Macbeth "start[s]" and seems to "fear" the same greeting.

For that mentality outside Macbeth's own, what is seen, the "signs" (1.4.41), are to be converted to language and thereby "regist'red where every day [one may] turn / The leaf to read them" (1.3.151–52). That I borrow here Macbeth's own words, said in response to Banquo's appellative "worthy Macbeth," only makes more suspect this optimistic notion about the relation between vision and speech. From the witches' greeting on, the unilateral movement from sight to speech will no longer exist. Banquo's question "Who's there," as Macbeth approaches him and Fleance through a night when the "candles [of heaven] are all out," is met with a password whose irony is clear to us and that thereby exposes the absurdity of the very response designed to "fix" the man approaching: "A friend" (2.1.10–11). Late in the play Young Siward will demand of his fellow actor onstage, "What is thy name," and, despite Macbeth's hesitation in responding ("Thou'lt be afraid to hear it"), Siward persists, reducing the name given, "Macbeth," to "abhorred tyrant" (5.5.5–10). By this point in the play we know, of course, that Macbeth's identity is not so singular as to be confined to a name or an epithet. Siward, later to be celebrated as the flower of the reborn Scottish community, opposes his own physical force to Macbeth's grimly playful rejoinder "nor more fearful"—and, as we know, with disastrous results.

At the root of such linguistic problems is the ambiguous or insubstantial nature of the physical, or that spectacle grounding the play. Looking directly at the witches, *seeing* them, Banquo cannot be sure of just what he sees: "What are these / So wither'd and so wild in their attire, / That look not like th' inhabitants o' th' earth, / And yet are on't? Live you? or are you aught / That man may question?" (1.3.39–43). When these seemingly substantial witches "*vanish*" (SD, 1.3.78), Macbeth underscores the problem of sight and identification with "what seem'd corporal melted / As breath into the wind" (81–82). Later, for Macbeth, solid man will reappear as a ghost, in a form that only he can see and whose existence even his wife cannot comprehend.

This conversion of what is substantial, dependent on light, to the insubstantial, or the product of darkness, parallels the illusory nature of theater itself, that radical challenge to those cleaving offstage to the measurements of the real world. In *Macbeth* defective or uncertain physical sight admits the antithetical but double-edged otherworldly "sight" championed by or, alternatively, seducing Macbeth as he becomes entangled with the witches. Such double-edged sight is infectious; even Banquo wonders if the witches "may . . . not be [his] oracles as well" as Macbeth's (3.1.9–10).[12] Macbeth's own "heart / Throbs to know" more than the witches can or will show him (4.1.100).

The mortal eye is here both celebrated and overwhelmed, for only the illusory spectacle of the theater can stand as correlative for the fatal but tantalizing mind's eye, or what I have called the inner theater that the Macbeths follow and that in its negative, delusive anti-nature opposes the certainty of the God-created world and of God-ordained history. The bifocal vision of the play is literally so, showing not one but two incompatible worlds, and it is Macbeth's recognition of this double "fact" that gives the present chapter its title: "Mine eyes are made the fools o' th' other senses, / Or else" (2.1.44–45). To the ultimate detriment of Macbeth, but not *Macbeth*, the play admits both otherwise-canceling optical extremes.[13] Their vision liberated through darkness from the firmly set, daylight world, the Macbeths at the end will need the world's more mundane light: the Waiting-Gentlewoman informs the Doctor that her mistress "has light by her continually, 'tis her command" (5.1.22–23). At this moment of recognition, Macbeth depends on the image of a "brief candle" (5.5.23). The characters call for light, as Banquo does ("Give us a light there, ho!" [3.3.9]), yet within seconds after moving onstage he is murdered. Still, this loss of light or life is reversed: Fleance escapes into the darkness, accompanied by the Third Murderer's "Who did strike out the light?" (19).

These secular problems of illumination admit more metaphysical ones. After Duncan's murder, Rosse, observing that the heavens seemed "troubled with man's act," finds only opposition between man-devised time ("th' clock" that indicates the day) and the "dark night [that] strangles the travelling lamp." Nor is any answer forthcoming to his question as to the time: "Is't night's predominance, or the day's shame?" Darkness "entomb[s]" the very earth that "living light should kiss" (2.4.5–10). The unnatural acts generated by this ambivalence constitute an "amazement of [his] eyes" (19). Seeing Lady Macbeth holding her taper, the Doctor also finds his "mind . . . mated" (confused) and his sight "amaz'd" (5.1.78). Confronted with the show of kings, Macbeth commands his eyes to "start," overwhelmed as they are by the sight of eight kings whose "line stretch[es] out to th' crack of doom" (4.1.116–17).[14]

This assault on the eyes, either forced beyond their regular function or challenged by sights that can only disorient the mind, is countered by a denial or closing of the eyes. Macbeth asks the stars to "hide [their] fires," the "light" to avoid the presence of his "black and deep desires," and "the eye [to] wink at the hand." For him sight can be restored only after the fact (1.4.50–53). Similarly, Lady Macbeth would sever the connection between the instrument and its object by invoking a "thick night" to prevent the "keen knife" from seeing "the wound it makes" (1.5.50–52). This same denial of light and, thereby, moral vision, this emblem of the Macbeths' inner theater, doubles back on itself. The very eyes that Macbeth would shut will, when irritated by the "horrid deed" of the assassination, open into univeral tears ("pity") that like some second flood will drown both Macbeth and his resolution (1.7.21–25). It is Banquo's ghost, whose eyes paradoxically "glare" but without "speculation," that affronts Macbeth's sight so powerfully that he wishes the spirit could be hidden within the earth (3.4.92–95). G. R. Elliott speaks of how Macbeth's true perception, his rational faculties, are befouled by evil, yet, as we shall see, the reverse is no less true: the voyage into that evil only opens his eyes, powerfully, albeit in a grotesque and fatal manner.

iii

"See, and then speak yourselves" (2.3.73). Again, this is the ideal, the graceful transition from sight to speech, and for a time in the play the ideal holds.[21] The optimistic Duncan, responding to the Sergeant's cry "my gashes cry for help," compliments him with "So, well thy words become thee as thy wounds." The sight of his wounds (recalling Duncan's "What bloody man is that?" when the Sergeant first enters) and the nature of his narrative are then subsumed ("smack") under the word *honor* (1.2.42–44). However, Macbeth will later reverse Duncan's ideal when he denies this process of the physical leading to the linguistic with "words to the heat of deeds too cold breath gives" (2.1.61).

In point of fact, this partnership between seeing and subsequent naming comes unglued early in the play, minutes after Macbeth's first entrance in Act 1, scene 3, when, confronted with the sight of the three witches, he challenges them to "speak, if you can" (47). The command's absurdity is exposed lines later when, overwhelmed by what they predict, he brands them as "imperfect speakers" who, having told him much, now need to "tell [him] more" (1.3.65–66, 70). Whether they trap Macbeth or are projected from his own desires, with the witches the language of domestic and political discourse turns on itself, becomes punful, ambiguous, equivocal, at length theatrical, a way of naming what is not, or what has no singular, sure existence. When Banquo's ghost, unlike the witches earlier, fails to respond to Macbeth's command, "if thou canst nod, speak too" (3.4.69), or when Macbeth himself cannot speak of the apparition to anyone at the banquet except Lady Macbeth, who in turn cannot understand what he refers to as he covers the ghost's exit with "Hence, horrible shadow! / Unreal mock'ry, hence!" (3.4.105–6), he can turn only to those imperfect speakers, demanding that "more shall they speak" (133).

As Shakespeare's play abandons Holinshed, the playwright's chronicle or "speaking" of what did happen and of what was once seen by real-life observers, like that "chronicle" invoked by Malcolm who, though he did not see the execution of the first Thane of Cawdor, has "spoke / With one that saw him die" (1.4.3–40), we leave language as commerce among humans, and approach that paradoxical, suggestive, at length mysterious language of the theater itself: that speech based, ultimately, on that which is not, on illusion, a seeming world that is only a stage set to be struck by the next performance. Here is a language that responds to an illusory world, internal and thus beyond sight, a dark world related to but more immediately separate from the substantial, daylight world offstage. Lady Macbeth invokes this inner theater based on private language with her "Hie thee hither, / That I may pour my spirits in thine ear" (1.5.25–28).[17]

And yet however more expansive, symbolic, tantalizing, here is a language that, taken to an extreme, consumes itself. Coming onstage from the king's chamber, Macbeth says more than he knows when he defines what he has just seen as something "tongue nor heart / Cannot conceive nor name" (2.3.64–65). To his wife's command—though it is playacting on her part, to be sure—to "speak, speak," he accurately, albeit unintentionally or insincerely, again names this self-destroying language: "O gentle lady, / 'Tis not for you to hear what I can speak: / The repetition in a woman's ear / Would murther as it fell" (83–86). In time the trajectory of language from human to metaphysical discourses, from the word that is grounded upon the thing to the word that is "grounded" upon the stage's illusion of the thing, leads to the denial of all speech itself—to silence. Confronted with the unusual circumstances of Macduff's birth, Macbeth curses "that tongue that tells" him he cannot be killed by child of woman born. He now sees the witches' language as "palter," as language of "double sense" contradicting itself, as metaphysical "promise to our ear" that at last "break[s] to our hope" (5.8.16–22). In the world of normal discourse he now receives only "mouth-honor, breath," the source of articulate speech but nothing more (5.3.27–28). The organs and orifices of speech itself, "tongue" and "lips," become mere ingredients in the witches' cauldron (4.1.15, 29).

In time, of course, the metaphoric language of Shakespeare's positive theater as well returns to its ground in the real world. The "lie" of metaphor itself, the fraudulence involved in explaining one thing in terms of another that it is not, is justified, *excusable* only when the issue demanding metaphor is clarified, put into a picture that serves as the means for its clarification. In Murray Krieger's sense of the terms, the theater's own mirror world, self-enclosed and pleasurable, at length becomes a window back to the world offstage.[18]

If the witches embody the same principle of transformation essential to metaphor, still, in warring against the substantiality of the created world, they would overthrow metaphor itself with equivocation, whose aim, by definition, is confusion rather than clarification. The first witch, who will mislead the sailor, would transform herself not into an actual rat but a parody of one "without a tail" (1.3.9). Like humans, the witches themselves are not fully human; like men, they are not men, nor are they fully women. In effect, they embody the principle of equivocation rather than metaphor.[19] Like the theater—fictive, unreal—they are no less *unlike* the theater, a mockery of it, an instance, if you will, in which the theater, rather than turning to the world offstage, turns inward, "justifying" only itself. Blind for so long to their equivocations, eager to find an absolute in these creatures who are only superficially metaphoric, Macbeth hastens toward an inner theater that is unique, dazzling in its poetry and in its vision beyond the normal world, yet also terrifying, and at length a parody, a denial of the high public theater of Shakespeare.

iv

In this sense, the ultimate paradox in the play is Macbeth himself. Little wonder that critics, directors, and audiences are troubled by the seeming tension between the play's clear ethical basis and our fascination with the mentality of the character who gives *Macbeth* its name.[20] On one hand, the achievement of *Macbeth* is that it is not simply a chronicle, or an onstage dramatization of scenes from Scottish history, but rather the enactment of a mind that, buoyed up by the witches' prophesies, would violate the established chronology and facts of history. This is surely what separates *Macbeth* light years from, say, the *Henry VI* plays. Conversely, the theater in its spectacle and language is a presence that is, by definition, public. All that is inner must at length be revealed. There is an illustrative moment in Pirandello's *Six Characters in Search of an Author* when the family insists that a particular conversation be whispered and thereby go unheard by the audience; however absurd his character may have seemed to this point, the Director now rightly insists, much to the family's objections, that the conversation cannot go unheard. The family's demand for "realism" here must give way to the practical and, I think, philosophical principles of stage enactment. As opposed to Pirandello's frustrated Director, Shakespeare succeeds in enacting on his Globe stage Macbeth's inner world. Conversely, Macbeth's isolation in that world removes him from the same stage as perceived by the other characters, and this isolation, symbolized in the character of the childless murderer and, later, the murderer of children, is at once his ethical and theatrical crime.

In making their "faces vizards to [their] hearts, / Disguising what they are" (3.2.34–35), husband and wife thereby cancel through illusion their public self and invoke an inner self now elevated to a real self ("what they are"), or what one critic calls a region deep in their minds.[21] At the banquet Rosse speaks for an uncomprehending society with his "what sights, my lord?" (3.4.115), as does Lennox with his simple "No, my lord" and then "No indeed, my lord" when Macbeth asks if he saw the three sisters or if they passed by him (4.1.136–37).

Several critics have noted that this inner theater possesses its own language to the degree that the Waiting-Gentlewoman, who has heard Lady Macbeth talk in her sleep, cannot tell the Doctor what she has heard: "Neither to you nor any one, having no witness to confirm my speech" (5.1.17–18).[22] It also has its own visions, its "strange images of death" (1.3.97), the visual parallel to its own language or "strange screams of death" and "accents terrible" (2.3.56–57). Alex Aronson has distinguished such visions born of imaginative awareness from the ocular proof demanded by those outside its confines.[23] In asking if two men can have the same illusion, Roy Walker points to the inevitable isolation even of its two "inhabitants,"[24] for clearly the imaginative non-reality initially shared by husband and wife has at length no possibility of reaching an audience outside its idiosyncratic and initial creator, at least by the time of the banquet scene if not earlier.[25] Hence blood that is symbolic to Macbeth is only literal ("this filthy witness" [2.2.44]) to his wife, and as the husband creates a voice condemning him for violating sleep, an imaginative voice to be distinguished from the actual "God bless us" and "Amen" uttered by the sleeping grooms, she can only see him as thinking too "brain-sickly of things" (2.2.43). Macbeth equates the "deed" with himself (2.2.70), seeing himself as the product of his "strange and self-abuse" (3.4.141). Even the cries of women or the night-shriek of the owl cannot penetrate him in his isolation. Lady Macbeth asks why he "keep[s] alone," making "sorriest fancies" his only "companions" (3.2.8–9). At the banquet this mental isolation receives its most graphic enactment.[26]

v

All that has been discussed so far—the symbolic status of the opening scene, the mania for certainty, for using language as a naming device, the conflict between sight and otherworldly vision, between the Macbeths' dark inner world and the external reality inhabited by the other characters—all this is subsumed by the play's most inclusive image: the figure of Macbeth as actor pointing to the paradoxical presence of the theater itself.

At its most basic, the theater is equated here with conscious fakery for clearly political ends. Lady Macbeth's first practical advice after reuniting with her husband is a veritable catalogue of acting techniques designed to cover substance with show: "bear welcome in your eye, / Your hand, your tongue; look like th' innocent flower, / But be the serpent under't" (1.5.64–66). As the characters begin to see Macbeth's performance after Duncan's death for what it is, as their suspicions mount, the Macbeths themselves fall deeper into such performance: since Duncan's death still disturbs her husband, Lady Macbeth instructs him to "sleek o'er [his] rugged looks," and Macbeth agrees to "present [Banquo] eminence both with eye and tongue," making their own "faces vizards to [their] hearts" (3.2.27–35). Here is advice that Macbeth will be unable to follow at the banquet scene, for there his "honest" performance or emotional hysteria is itself disguised by Lady Macbeth as "a strange infirmity" or as "nothing" (3.4.85). Even as the mask is stripped from him, Macbeth, like Hitler drilling the few adolescents who constituted his "army" as the Allies stormed Berlin, instructs his servant boy to hide his real terror by "prick[ing] his face, and over-red[dening his] fear" (5.3.14). Against this increasing parody of acting, of course, the level of acting required of the play's major character remains steadfast; acting as metaphor thus pulls apart from its "reality" in the onstage performance.[27]

Macbeth's perverse acting also threatens to infect others. Malcolm's feigned profligacy is so real that, even after he admits the imposture, Macduff finds "such welcome and unwelcome things at once / 'Tis hard to reconcile" (4.3.138–39). In fact, Macduff's own concealing his true reasons for abandoning his wife and children, as well as Malcolm's pretending to be a monarch "smacking of every sin / That has a name" (4.3.59–60), may be a sign of the times in which Macbeth, like the first Thane of Cawdor, has so confused man's ability to know "what is" that others are hesitant to present their real selves.[28]

Macbeth's feigning, his play within Shakespeare's play,[29] this fraud within an imaginative creation, is at once what Clifford Leech has called the Incredible[30] and, no less, what Harold Toliver sees as an example of the limitations of willful self-creation.[31] For such feigning rests, ultimately, on air, on nothing, and this comes as no surprise in a play whose future is anticipated in its present, whose end is announced from the beginning, just as Macbeth himself only refills the mold, albeit with his own variations, of the first traitorous Thane of Cawdor. In his initial encounter with the witches he knows that in his raptness,[32] his willingness to entertain the witches' prophesy, he abandons his "single" or natural state and enters a realm where "nothing is / But what is not"

(1.3.140–42). V. Y. Kantak observes that the image of the actor sustaining him up to but only shortly after the assassination subsequently becomes his reality, giving him the false sense that what he does renders the judgment of an audience irrelevant: he is, in this sense, a good actor turned bad.[40] Macbeth is left with only the techniques of an actor, the accoutrements of theatrical costumes and props, but these only prove a "fruitless crown" and "barren scepter" (3.1.60–61). The last king with "glass in his hand" (4.1.119) holds a mirror reflecting the very audience that Macbeth would deny through a theater playing only to himself, only for its solitary actor. By that mirror's reflection the world offstage thus makes its way onstage to dissolve the baseless fabric of his idiosyncratic vision.

This "unreal" and therefore imaginative creation, which is also a "mock'ry" of responsible creation (3.4.106), receives its fullest expression, of course, in Macbeth's "to-morrow" speech (5.5.19–28). It is, surely, the darker side or the moon's other side of Shakespeare's own sentiments. As John Lawlor observes, here we see not the actor taking pleasure in his craft, or in the audience's witness of his performance, but rather the actor painfully conscious of his isolation from a hostile audience.[34] In our time it is the pathetic nightclub comedian, failing with his spectators, reduced to frenzied attempts to match their insults with insults of his own. In his self-created world of darkness,[35] Macbeth, who only manages to precipitate the very accomplishment he wished to avoid,[36] now insanely defends what G. I. Duthie has called a life meaningless to him.[37] Curiously, this nihilistic mood is Macbeth's one positive accomplishment, stripped as he will be of the position he coveted, for he dies free of illusion,[38] or in what Walter Clyde Curry calls the "doubtful calm of utter negativity."[39] Earlier the consummate "false" actor, he now abjures the role, opting for the real world, the physical as unenhanced by language: "Why should I play the Roman fool, and die / On mine own sword? While I see lives, the gashes / Do better upon them" (5.8.1–3).

His is a theater that fails at length to become a window back out to reality, to life. On its "bloody stage" (2.4.6) even cosmetics are linked with death: Lady Macbeth would use the excess blood of Duncan to "gild the faces of the groom," transforming by her fatal cosmetology the innocent into the guilty (2.2.52–54).[40] In this theater of death Macbeth, resembling Richard III in a way, must perforce be both its chief actor and its chief victim.

vi

Against Macbeth's death-bringing theater stands a theater of life that in the person of Macduff will usher in the daylight of the public world.

Terence Hawkes points out, however, that it is the ghost of Banquo who ironically, through illusions, restores reality to Macbeth's hitherto impregnable world of appearance, and, further, that Macbeth is unmanned by a real man whose birth is itself rationally improbable.[41] I think, however, the argument holding that with the emergence of Macduff the play moves from tragedy to melodrama obscures the fact that this second world was contained, implied, indeed generated by the parabolic curve of Macbeth's own antitheater.[42] Macbeth acts, as J. A. Bryant observes, as if he were the sole author of his creation; he cannot be, of course, and Shakespeare's presence as the play's immediate author reminds us of this.[43]

Still, this restoration of the daylight has its cost. If Macbeth's inner theater fails because it cannot be made public, just as Shakespeare's succeeds because his is, the surviving characters perforce reduce the tragic hero or criminal of the play we have experienced to a caricature, ethically right but theatrically inadequate. We are back once again to that comforting but also reductive mania for certainty. Hence, for them Macbeth can only be "the tyrant" (5.2.11), "the devil himself" (5.7.8), "the abhorred tyrant" (5.7.10), "the show and gaze o' th' time" (5.8.24), at best one of the world's "rarer monsters" (5.8.25).[44] "Enter Macduff with Macbeth's head"—the stage direction in the final scene presents *a* Macbeth, but not the whole being. In similar fashion the head is not the actor but only a crude simulacrum, all the while the "real" actor disrobes in the tiring house. It cannot be otherwise. The theater of presence, no matter how charmed that presence may be, is at length responsible to a real offstage presence.

Like his wife, who is, as one commentator phrases it, disdainful of the factual present for an imagined future, Macbeth denies this same theater of presence for what will be.[45] Banquo's qualified request that "if" the witches "can look into the seeds of time," they should speak to him, even though he would "neither beg nor fear" them (1.3.58–61), is not so qualified by Macbeth. If for him "to be king / Stands not within the prospect of belief" (1.3.73–74), then he will substitute an imaginative inner theater in which he can play the king. Francis Fergusson brilliantly argues that his play thereby becomes a race against reason itself.[46] Macbeth would sacrifice the sure present for an imagined future, and thus, as Emrys Jones observes, the future here becomes both a structural and a thematic device.[47] His futuristic theater, like his speculation about murdering Duncan, can only be "but fantastical" (1.3.139), and this fact is underscored by the Porter's unflattering picture of the farmer who hangs himself when his expectation of plenty fails to materialize.[48]

The present, albeit "this ignorant present" (1.5.57) to Lady Macbeth, is what we have, and if that present is to lead to a positive future we must, as in *The Comedy of Errors*, see and hear it clearly *and* in community: the thought of one spectator watching one actor is almost as eerie as that of a solitary actor serving as his own auditor and spectator. In the communal presence of his fellow characters Macbeth can find only a "present horror" (2.1.59). In Cleanth Brooks's words, their positive future *is* the child that Macbeth cannot control.[49]

While the punishments of the Macbeths are not, as we have seen, the whole play, they are nevertheless fitting once the Macbeths are forced from their inner theater.[50] If Macbeth's exhilarating voyage into his own inner darkness "hath trifled former knowings" (2.4.4), the accomplishment itself must, in time, be placed within the context of the world offstage that is at once the source of the playwright's vision and, no less, its final home. Macbeth's earlier "Mine eyes are . . . worth all the rest" (2.1.44–45) must be balanced with Macduff's final call to the audience on- and offstage to observe Macbeth painted on a pole and to see outwardly and then to hear inwardly the inscription: "Here may you see the tyrant" (5.8.26–27).

PART III

Language Private and Public

6

Richard III:

"And descant on my own deformity"

i

BOTH actors and critics admire Richard's control of language, his sense of linguistic play, and they are quick to distinguish the old-style rhetoric of his victims from his own highly individual speech.[1] Though the other characters may be flat, Richard himself is the "first example of Shakespeare's characterizing a person through language."[2] If the play still betrays its roots in the historical chronicles of the 1590s[3] and in the earlier morality plays, nevertheless it is Richard's own verbal "steel" set against the other's "soft metal,"[4] his extravagant speech that anticipates those larger experiments with language[5] which James Calderwood, among others, has charted in the tragedies and comedies of the 1590s.[6]

Indeed, Richard's linguistic achievement looms so large that he is allowed to serve as prologue to his own play. After greeting us with that opening "now," he proceeds to subvert the positive connotations of words like *summer, peace, victorious,* and *delightful* with their opposites in *winter, war, bound,* and *dreadful* —no mean achievement indeed. Curiously, however, this triumph over the normal meanings of words seems to rest on a pervasive mockery, even a negation of language. Freudian echoes notwithstanding, Richard, moments after that exquisite prologue, associates speech with what is womanish, unbecoming a man. In Leonard Dean's phrase, he pits his self-consciously theatrical pose against the "historical voice" of the play's women, his ultimately sterile "art" against procreative life as vested in the play's mothers and wives.[7] The King, for example, whose supposed obsession with the letter G drives him to imprison Richard's brother George, Duke of Clarence, is dismissed as one "rul'd by women" (1.1.62). During his verbal seduction of Lady Anne, Richard sees himself as alternately "provok'd by [Margaret's] sland'rous tongue" (1.2.97) and captivated by Anne's own mouth, which he describes in reverse fashion: "Never came poison from so sweet a place" (1.2.146).[8] It is those lips, both the orifice of words and, by the double entendre, her vagina, that makes his "proud heart [to] sue[,] and prompts [his] tongue to speak" (170).

Given his physical deformity, Richard's own conversion of the widow Anne to the wooer of her husband's murderer is surely a verbal, not a sexual triumph. Still, on Anne's exit Richard dismisses his linguistic feat with the theatrical questions "Was ever woman in this humor woo'd?", followed by "Was ever woman in this humor won?" (227–28). When divested of its association with women, language is seen here by its chief practitioner as only play, as not proper for a man, even as something childish. Queen Elizabeth describes the young Prince as "parlous" (2.4.35)—that is, verbally and intellectually precocious—but in the next scene Richard, responding to Buckingham's epithet "this little prating York," calls him "perilous" (151, 154). Language thus seems to have death at its root, and the very play whose theatrical life is initiated by Richard's own "Now" thus establishes a reverse hierarchy in which linguistically seductive women point downward to verbally precocious boys doomed to die. This same hierarchy may lend a special emphasis to Richard's question to Buckingham: "canst thou . . . / Murther thy breath in middle of a word" (3.5.1–2). Richard even forges a curious link between himself and the parlous boy when he contrasts the adult Edward, dissipating himself in a sexual liaison with Mistress Shore and other women of his kingdom, with himself, the would-be preserver of his brother inhibited by his own verbal naiveté at court: he finds himself "too childish-foolish for this world" (1.3.141).

When Richard warns the Murderers not to listen to Clarence's pleas for life, not to "mark him," since he is "well-spoken" (1.3.346–48), this association of speech with women and death comes full circle. The Murderers, appropriately, promise to "use [their] hands, and not [their] tongues" (351). We will recall Richard's earlier promise to "entertain these fair well-spoken days" by playing the "villain," since the role of "lover"—supposedly, until the following scene, at least—is denied him (1.1.28–30).

If Richard's language elevates the play in Shakespeare's early canon, it is for him only a tool with which to revise history, as when he instructs Buckingham on how to invalidate the claims of Edward's children to the throne, even at the risk of implying the adultery of his own mother (3.5.72–94). This notion of language as a tool to alter the past or manipulate the present surfaces again in Richard's conversation with the same "parlous" young Prince. The latter argues that even if written history made no mention of Caesar's being the original builder of the tower, the "truth should live from age to age," handed down orally ("retail'd") "to all posterity" (3.1.68–93). When the Prince asks Richard what the latter has mumbled in an aside to Buckingham—the aside being "So wise so young, they say do never live long"—Richard changes its first eight words to "without characters fame," coupling that altered text with the original final two words "lives long." Then, in a second aside he glosses for us just what he has done: "like the formal Vice, Iniquity" he has "moralize[d] two meanings in one word," playing on "characters" as handwriting (that is, written records) and moral qualities. The pun thereby complements the boy's observation and, beyond his present understanding, signals to Buckingham Richard's desire to murder the Prince before he reaches adulthood and has the chance to achieve a reputation. The boy's second invocation of Caesar's name provides an unintentional but deeply ironic comment on Richard's own use of language, and the play's larger devaluation of words as the basis of his characterization. Caesar's positive actions on behalf of his country (his "valor" and his "valure") were matched by his skill with the written word (the "wit" of his *Commentaries*) and thus contrast with Richard's own negative actions, especially with his own manipulation of the word.[9] The tower, symbol of Caesar's fame that survives in both written and oral history, thus confronts Richard's use of it as a place of confinement and of death.

The voice itself, the very instrument of speech, seems to be suppressed as long as Richard holds the stage. The citizens' first response to Buckingham's "God save Richard, England's royal king!" is silence; "like dumb statues, or breathing stones, / [They] Star'd each on other, and look'd deadly pale," and would respond only when, as custom dictated, they were spoken to by the Recorder, that city official charged with making such proclamations and who, on this occasion, simply repeated Buckingham's speech. Even here the verbal response was less than overwhelming: by Buckingham's count, an optimistic one we should assume, only "some ten voices cried, 'God save King Richard!'" (3.7.22–41). As Wilbur Sanders observes, these "tongueless blocks" (as Richard presently dismisses them [42]) will lie dormant until they find a spokesman in Richmond, until the play's own tongue, epitomized in that of the Duchess as "woe-wearied," "still and mute" (4.4.18), can find a voice.[10] Even at the staged coronation, whose precise text has been written by Richard or written for him through his intermediary Buckingham, these same "citizens are mum, say not a word" (3.7.3) and, when they do speak, produce only an ambiguous "Amen" (241), always said on stage without passion or conviction. The most graphic desecration of the mouth finds expression much earlier in Anne's description of her husband's "wounds / Open[ing] their congeal'd mouths and bleed[ing] afresh" (1.2.55–56). We will think here of Antony's promise to add "the voice and utterance of [his] tongue" to the wounds of Caesar "which like dumb mouths do ope their ruby lips" (3.1.260–61).

Moments before Richard enters in Act 4, scene 4 for the verbal battle with Elizabeth, the Queen raises the rhetorical question that the play itself asks in the presence of Richard's too-long verbal domination: "My words are dull, O, quicken them with thine!" Her response to her own challenge, however, is at first a negative one: she brands her words as only "windy attorneys," as "poor breathing orators" that, even if given scope, can at best accomplish nothing beyond easing "the heart." The Duchess proposes a more constructive alternative, a way beyond their present "tongue-tied" condition: together, their words joined, they will use this enlarged "breath of bitter words" to "smother / [Her] damned son" (4.4.124–35).[11]

Of more immediate importance is the fact that the Duchess's proposed speech is, like Richard's, death-bringing, and yet has nothing like his energy and fascination. Why, then, do we respond with such pleasure to this wordsmith who so devalues language?

ii

We go back to that much-admired prologue. Not until line fourteen does the audience get Richard's own psychological and physical justification for preferring "discontent" above its opposite "content," the ugliness of "Grim-visag'd War" above beauty.[12] Those justifications come late, almost as an afterthought. The humped back, of course, is not Shakespeare's invention, but this curiously reverse psychology, and indeed the entire first act ending in Clarence's death, *is*, and at best is only lightly suggested by More and Hall.[13] If Richard seems the epitome of control here, if for much of the play he seems manifestly superior to his opponents and, as Murray Krieger has argued, is thereby only prototypical of the play's fallen world,[14] he may be no less absolutely out of control here. Whether he fully comprehends the implications of his perversity, whether his simple and reductive "I am determined to prove a villain" itself covers the darker dimensions of his character, he only succeeds in invoking the normal world endorsed by any sane member of the audience. The very paradox on which he *seems* to thrive—"Now is the winter of our discontent / Made glorious summer by this son of York"— will itself defeat him, indeed *points* to his defeat. Bridget Lyons observes that the very aural and visual symbols Richard tries to appropriate to his own purposes exert a power that he cannot check once he actually becomes king.[15] A controller of language, he cannot control language. I parallel here A. P. Rossiter's observation that Shakespeare's achievement in the play is to unite the two antithetical strands of comic and moral history.[16]

Richard may push Anne, unwillingly or in collaboration with her own unspoken desires, from enemy to lover, yet he can do so only by first establishing the very world of love and sacrifice, of mutuality, that his conscious mind scorns. If he is the glamorous Machiavellian individual, the "natural" or "new" man of "thorough-going individualism" set off against a crowd of lesser lights and nobodies,[17] Richard also sacrifices himself, beyond his linguistic consciousness, for a society that he rejects because it has in turn rejected him. The very source of this individualism is, paradoxically, an accident of birth, an event over which he had no control.

Both his own creator *and* destroyer, Richard in his exquisite use of language also implies its opposite, a time before language itself, a pre-verbal world that Ruth Anderson defines as one of brutishness and fear, and Robert Ornstein as the darkness before the dawn of civilization.[18] This, I think, is the "mysterious"[19] dimension to his character. Though the world is ordered for so long by his verbal fiat, his order at length implies a parabolic curve leading to the disorder inseparable from his character, that very disorder he would invoke to supplant "this weak pipping time of peace" (1.1.24). Michael Steig cites Freud to suggest these twin and strangely compatible sides of his character: he is at once the bad father figure, taking control to such an extreme that he must be de-throned by the young hero Richmond, even as he is the symbol of a childish disorder that also must be subdued.[20] These twin poles of tyrannical order and childish disorder account in large part, I think, for our exhilarating yet frustrating inability either to accept him or to dismiss him.

Prefiguring darkness itself, he drags down inhabitants of the daylight world to "his new kingdom of ne'er-changing night" (2.2.46). His very body, otherwise the stimulus for the verbal energy he spends in reshaping the society that rejects him, is a "lump of foul deformity" (1.2.57), and the suggestion here, beyond Anne's own complex motives giving rise to the epithet, is that he represents what one critic has called "a lump of chaos thrust into the midst of the natural order."[21] Ironically, a truer portrait of the man than Clarence himself can see in the daylight, the Richard of his brother's dream pushes him into a nether world where "foul fiends . . . howled in [his] ears" with "hideous cries" (1.4.58–60).

Behind even these archetypes of the primitive or presocial stands Satan himself, and the associations of Richard with "God's enemy" (5.3.252) or the "cacodemon" (1.3.143) are not merely rhetorical.[22] In not rejecting Richard's "suit," Anne herself invokes him with "Arise, dissembler" (1.2.184). It must be observed, however, that his power is neither physical nor magical, but rather entirely verbal; here language itself is the demon/daemon. Richard ultimately is not Satan, nor is the play simply a morality play. Anne herself confuses the figurative with the literal when she cries out in Richard's presence that "mortal eyes cannot endure the devil" (1.2.45). Richard sees the issue more clearly when, acknowledging that he has "odd old ends stol'n forth of holy writ," he defines himself as one who can "seem a saint, when most [he] play[s] a devil" (1.3.336–37).

iii

Not the thing itself but a sign of the thing, language, like Richard himself, embodies the paradox of power built upon an illusion, without a physical base and yet dependent on a physical correlative in the real world. Appropriately, Richard has a peculiar hostility to the physical world or to its mother, Nature, which he finds, rather than himself, a "dissembling" creature (1.1.19). His own physical deformity may be a stimulus for his character, but ultimately it is a strangely inadequate objective correlative for what he comes to represent. When Anne falls prey to his ardor, he himself raises the comic possibility that he has "mistake[n his] person all this while," that a seeming deformity is now a symbol of beauty, of its opposite, so much so that he can now rightly "entertain a score or two of tailors / To study fashions to adorn [his] body" (1.2.252–57). If the physical, even at its most grotesque, is so changeable, insubstantial, then—handy-dandy—what is unseen, non-physical, *said* rather than seen may lay equal claim to reality, if not more. If he cannot alter what Elizabeth properly calls his "interior hate," he can change by words the "outward action," the external half that "shows itself" (1.3.65–66).

Disdaining the physical, it is little wonder that Richard is, by his own terms, a champion of shadows: at the end of Act 1, scene 2 he vows to buy a mirror so that with the aid of the "fair sun" he can observe not his body, now rendered beautiful by Anne's promise, but his "shadow" (1.2.262–63). As such, he has a special affinity with the correlatives of shadows found in dreams and sleep, and in death, sleep's own counterfeit. He says more than Anne knows, perhaps even more than he himself knows, when, parodying the romantic lover, he declares that Anne's "beauty . . . haunt[s him] in [his] sleep / To undertake the death of all the world" (1.2.122–23). Like Iago, with whom he has much in common,[23] Richard would supplant physical reality, and here a historical reality as well, with a world fabricated upon mere words. Though subsequently enacted on stage, Clarence's vision of his brother points to the imaginative, the insubstantial or dreamlike dimensions of a character who hoodwinks both his onstage opponents and, to some extent, the offstage audience as well by his seeming addiction to realpolitik, the would-be external political sphere of a Machiavelli. Stanley also "experiences" Richard in a dream through his surrogate, the boar (3.2.11). And since we know that Buckingham is feigning when he calls upon the seemingly unwilling candidate for kingship with a prayer that he be "waken[ed] to our country's good" from the "mildness of [his] sleepy thoughts" (3.7.123–24), we can reverse the linese and see in them a portrait of Richard, a creature of harsh dreams bent on translating his own chaos into the realm of daylight.

With Richard, then, we journey from civilization to a precivilized state, to the chaos linked with Satan, and at length to a realm of sleep, dreams, and death encroaching on the daylight, historical world that is the play's ostensible ground. Like Macbeth, Richard seems partly to exist in an internal, nonpublic dimension at variance with the public stage itself, with that theater of language and spectacle made manifest in time before the witness of an audience. He thereby violates in his "hidden" character the concept of theatrical presence. Conversely, like the stage itself, he champions the submission of reality to illusion. Hugh Richmond spots this "duality" when he finds Richard moving, by a "flight into subjectivity," to a private self, substituting for reality "the pure artifice of personae," indeed sustaining that artifice with "each virtuoso performance," and thereby, in a tragic parallel to his comic counterpart Falstaff, attempting "to transcend hostile circumstance and social alienation."[24] In like fashion Emrys Jones sees the play becoming an "activity [that] is all within Richard's mind.[25]

The "amorous looking glass" (1.1.15) is here a mirror reflecting not Richard in the context of society, but rather solely of himself, indeed a magical mirror that reveals not even so much his external features as his insides, or, in his own term, "my shadow" (1.2.263). This inner theater takes the form of an actual "self-cue" when, after that opening monologue, Richard addresses himself with "Dive, thoughts, down to my soul, here Clarence comes" (1.1.41)—a literal cue for the actor playing his brother, a psychological cue for the actor playing a Richard conscious of playing himself ("I am determined to prove a villain" [30]).

The irony here is that language is, by definition, a social, a public instrument, and yet the Richard that Shakespeare characterizes can be expressed only by his *abuse* of such language. Such abuse expresses itself early in his claim to "clothe" his naked villainy (1.3.335): that is, he uses speech for obfuscation rather than clarification. The task, for Richard, for the Shakespeare who writes Richard, must be at once daring and absurd: to use expressive language, the tool whose normal goal is clarity and understanding, to disguise a demonic force that, paradoxically, substitutes by words an illusory history for the true history waiting at the end of the play in the person of Richmond. In a sense Shakespeare affirms that public history by "buying" the Tudor line on Richard, taking More, Holinshed, and Hall as biblical truth, and thereby lending a credence to a Tudor dynasty greater than it deserved. Still, he elevates his theater above mere propaganda by making his perverse artist fascinating and successful, while at the same time refusing to whitewash the attendant characters. In the succinct judgment of the historian Christopher Morris, Shakespeare "shared in the assumptions of his age . . . but he transcends them also."[26]

A rival playwright to Shakespeare, a "second" to Shakespeare even as Buckingham is a second to his master,[27] Richard is, for a good time in the play, if not Shakespeare's equal, at least a fellow collaborator, for it is the dual presence of two worlds here, one deeply psychological, one historical, that distinguishes this play from the three *Henry VI*'s and that makes it the proper prelude to the second tetralogy. There the public/ private sides of man exist in the conscience-tortured Bolingbroke vowing to pay his public debt by a crusade to Jerusalem; in the contrastive public and private figures of Hotspur and Falstaff, contrasts taken to an extreme and then blended in the figure of Hal; and in Hal himself, as he both strolls among his troops, hidden in a cloak, and then leads them into battle as the ultimate in public figures.

As much as he seems in control as the demonic playwright,[28] and even as he gives his name to the play, Richard, therefore, is in no way its dominant figure. For with this private, *a*theatrical side to himself, we encounter a dimension of the character that can only be expressed in language beyond the conscious intention of its speaker, even of such a clever wordsmith as Richard. If the play is not simple, no crude melodrama or mere comic portrait of an appealing villian,[29] it is so because as audience we must work overtime, bringing this private side to the surface of Richard's deceptive public posture, even fleshing out those rare moments when he moves, fitfully, toward some deeper revelation of self. Our challenge as audience is thus identical to that of the actor who wants something more from the role than a prototype, something approaching a flesh-and-blood human in a character who, to his conscious mind, is determined to prove just the opposite.

iv

It is no surprise that, along with Richard's own dazzling theatrics, there is a pervasively negative image of the theater here inseparable from the negative attitude toward language. Again, Richard's prologue is also my point of departure.[30] If he initially associates an "effeminate" theater with his opponents who thrive in peacetime—unlike them he cannot "strut" (17) before ladies, and we will recall Macbeth's own insignificant actor who "struts and frets his hour upon the stage" (5.5.25)—he quickly turns this theatrical image upon himself, although by way of justifying his decision to play the morality Vice. He is the actor not fully made up ("unfinish'd") or costumed ("scarce half made up"), pushed too soon "into this breathing world" of the stage, and confronted with a rude audience ("dogs") who jeer at ("bark") rather than applaud him.

By the end of scene 2, of course, Richard will reassess his person, and be willing to submit himself to the stage's mirror or "glass," since it now reflects a newly discovered romantic hero. Still, the theater he champions is ultimately negative, one of "inductions dangerous" (1.1.32) and "devilish plots" (3.1.60).[31] Richard's own looking glass, of which he is so enamored, will be reversed when his mother, the Duchess, brands him as "one false glass" who has himself "crack'd in pieces" the "two mirrors" of his brothers, which now reflect in a distorted fashion only the "princely semblance" of their father (2.2.53).

This negative theater even complicates what would otherwise be fairly neutral theatrical self-references. Hastings speaks confidently about giving his "voice" for Richard, that is, for saying what Richard himself would say if he were on stage. Perhaps with a touch of rivalry for Richard's favor, Buckingham informs the Duke, seconds after his entrance, that "had [he] not come upon [his] cue . . . / William Lord Hastings [would have] pronounc'd [his] part" (3.4.19, 26–27). Within minutes, of course, Hastings will be branded as a traitor, and in a set speech, much like Clarence's and anticipating Richard's own in Act 5, will see himself as an actor, briefly onstage one moment and off the next.

What I have already called the external, political play, opposing Richard's complex, internal theater or atheater, is itself constructed on a palpably gross, old-style tragedy. Scenes 2, 3, and 4 of Act 3, for example, parallel the de casibus tragedies of The Mirror for Magistrates. In scene 2 Hastings rejects Stanley's dream of an impending fall; there intervenes the short scene 3 showing Rivers, Grey, and Vaughan being led to the Tower; scene 4 properly combines the two, picturing first a Hastings in the ascendancy and then, after an "intermission" of exits and entrances by Richard and Buckingham, in the "descendancy." This trinity itself then serves as prelude to scene 5, where Richard and Bolingbroke literally write the script and prepare the optimal staging for the coronation. This is in turn followed by the short scene 6 where the Scrivener brands the anticipated staging as a "palpable device" (11) that no audience, least of all us, is "so gross" (10) that it cannot see through. So qualified, scene 7, the coronation, can be viewed as comprehensively and, therefore, as negatively by us as it is seen in a limited and hence affirmative fashion by its chief actors. Two types of theater, old-style (scenes 2 to 4) and Richard's new style (scenes 5 and 7), seem to collide here. But, with our onstage surrogate, the Scrivener—appropriately, for this chapter on language, a man involved for "eleven hours" in writing Hastings's indictment to be "read o'er in Paul's" (3.6.1–5)—we can see the old-style theater as dramatically crude but ethically right, since it antici- pates Buckingham's and then Richard's own fall,[32] and the new-style one as theatrically sophisticated but ethically bankrupt.

That new-style theater, again, is built upon an abuse of the term for Richard and Buckingham base their anticipated success on what can only be described as a cynical attitude toward the stage. Richard parodies the tragic actor, Burbage himself, or Burbage playing Richard parodying himself: he will only "counterfeit the deep tragedian," mismatching voice and gesture ("speak and look back"), crashing about the stage in a way mocking refined stage movement ("pry on every side"), melo- dramatically adjusting his face from sudden horror ("ghastly looks") to a seeming comic joy ("enforced smiles")—and all this not for theater in any exalted sense but for theater as instrument, as "stratagems" (3.5.5–11). Buckingham and Richard even give us an immediate enactment of this crude theater when, for the Mayor's benefit, they fake concerned hosts, delighting in his presence even as they try to fend off imagined enemies threatening to charge over the drawbridge into the castle. The comedy of this theatrical turning to itself is certain, but it is a cynical comedy built on a reductive attitude toward the medium.

In Act 3, scene 7 Buckingham will play the stage manager to Richard's actor, the modest Christian king; and it is perhaps significant that Richard, who in real life has a special antipathy to women and, by extension, to what they represent symbolically in this play, agrees here to "play the maid's part" (51). There is more than just comedy in the coronation scene, however, for now, where Richard seems most to exer- cise theatrical control, the scene itself, beyond its parody, only anticipates the coronation of the play's true Christian king, Richmond.

Even Richard's new theater begins to wear down as he, increasingly caught up in the business of preserving a tottering realm, becomes more earnest, taking less joy in his own inductions, stratagems, and plots. Robert Heilman speaks of a "post-coital" lethargy in Richard's latter theatrics,[33] and in a splendid article on the play Richard Wheeler ob- serves that the Grand Mechanism of history itself proves a force more than equal to Richard's inner, self-indulgent theater, for even if Richard's earlier theatrical success is built on his perception of the wishes of others, as in his seduction of Anne, it is still only an artifice. Richard thus shows "the limits of the actor, both in controlling power and in controlling the whole person that lies behind the actor's mask."[34] In Emrys Jones's phrase, he becomes "an *umbra*—an actor-shadow from the past summoned for a time by the dramatist's theatrical magic."[35] As long as the play exists within the limits of his own dreams Richard can temporarily recreate himself, his staged self, in terms of an idiosyncratic image.[36] Still, the play must "wake" to its larger self, and, in Waldo McNeir's terms, Richard's "continuous play-acting has fragmented his personality, so dividing him that he has disintegrated into the ineffectuality of one who has lost all cohesion as an individual."[37] That earlier cohesion, I would observe, is achieved by mirrors, by tricks, by words, words, words. What attracts us to Richard is precisely its fragility: we delight in the artifice because we see it as such.

For most actors assigned the part and for most directors, Richard's "suit" for Elizabeth's daughter (4.4), a clear parallel to his wooing of Lady Anne, represents a falling-off, to the degree that in production the scene is often severely cut. Elizabeth is more Richard's match than was Anne, who herself is now able to see her earlier seduction in perspective, as a time when her "woman's heart / Grossly grew captive to his honey words" (4.1.78–79). For Richard, Elizabeth only raises a question, without giving a sure promise: "Shall I go win my daughter to thy will?" (426). Actresses generally deliver that line with a sense of cynicism rather than resignation. Richard is over-eager with his "And be a happy mother by the deed," and Elizabeth gets the last and ambiguous line: "I go. Write to me very shortly," with no hint of her capitulation (427–28). His judgment of his performance is surely overly optimistic: "Relenting fool, and shallow, changing woman!" (431) He has properly been called overconfident in the scene,[38] his tone more "neutral" in this second wooing.[39] For one critic, and for more than one director, this scene, where time stands still, seems anticlimactic, with Shakespeare having nowhere to go but to try, and unsuccessfully so, to repeat his/Richard's earlier triumph with Anne: again, the verdict is to delete the interview with Elizabeth.[40] That same verdict is based in part on the observation that after the coronation scene those two strands of comic and moral history that Rossiter had detected come undone. Surely, though, this verdict is off-target, given the catholic psychological and theatrical dimensions of the play, dimensions that are so intertwined that Richard's failure with Elizabeth is no less germane to his character than was his seemingly unqualified success with Anne.[41]

It is Margaret who had much earlier anticipated this dark side of Richard's theater and who now sounds its death knell, indeed as a sort of "dire induction," in her own words (4.4.5), to Richard's meeting with Elizabeth. Confronting Elizabeth, Margaret, in a fashion more direct than anywhere else in the play, invokes a negative theatrical self-portrait in which the play itself becomes "the flattering index of a direful pageant," "a dream," "a garish flag," "a sign," "a breath, a bubble," something serving "only to fill a scene" (85–91). She refers, of course, to what Elizabeth has now become, but in the sense that the play for so long has been Richard's creation, she also refers, I think, to the demonic play-wright who has been the shaper of Elizabeth and the other characters.

v

Yet even if we acknowledge the double-edged nature of Richard's linguistic and theatrical domination, the fact is that, despite the qualifica-tions we bring to his character, there is no force within the play capable of restraining him, let alone forcing him to share the stage of our attention. This is especially true on the level of language—in particular, the play's numerous curses that are, interestingly enough, associated with women, with that physical, procreative world for which, as I have argued, Richard has a special antipathy.[42]

Anne curses Richard's hand, heart, and blood early in Act 1, scene 2 (14–16), while he, playing on the romantic notion that she is his entire world—his night, day, life, and death—deflects her with "Curse not thyself, fair creature—thou art both" (132). Later he plays similarly with Margaret by substituting her name for his, though only to be topped by her "Thus have you breath'd your curse against yourself" (1.3.237–39). Within the context of the play these curses, concentrated in the figure of Margaret, prove correct, yet still they also stand as symbol of the con-strictive linguistic world of *Richard III*: at best they can point to a future that only redresses the past, but they cannot neutralize error, nor eradi-cate it. Buckingham observes their limited force with his "for curses never pass / The lips of those that breathe them in the air" (1:3:284–85). Leonard Dean characterizes Margaret as serving only as the ghost to Richard's own spirit.[43] An anachronism in the play, literally revived by Shakespeare from her historical time of death, she opposes Richard, standing outside the play in what Nicholas Brooke calls a "detached, Brechtian fashion."[44] Still, if she opposes Richard, she is powerless to defeat him. Nor is she able to swerve him from a fatal course of action. Albeit structurally effective, the curses are also theologically invalid, and it is Margaret who speculates, perversely, that York's curse against her family for their murder of "pretty Rutland" (1.3.177) has been answered by a cruel god in the form of the deaths of her Henry and Edward (189–92): in her own words, two adults have been sacrificed for "one peevish brat" (193). Clarence well knows that the God who will be avenged for human "misdeeds" cannot be reached by secular cries for vengeance, let alone by "prayers" from tainted souls (1.4.69–70).

Almost always associated with women, the curses are therefore sterile as a linguistic counterforce, incapable in themselves of generating an alternative speech to oppose Richard's verbal domination so long unchallenged in the "world" of the play. Richard himself understands their nature, albeit comically, when stopping short of linking himself with those who "scathe" the kingdom, he realizes in an aside that had he "curs'd now, [he] had curs'd" himself (1.3.315–18).

Margaret represents "repetition" (1.3.164), the past, a caustic but nonprocreative force. The play thus can be *delivered* from itself, from its own perverse maker, only by forces outside itself; within its own theater of presence Richard's linguistic hold is unassailable. We may choose to see this outside force either as divine or as a historical reality beyond the play.[45] Within the play's own tight confines, however, Richard is what he is, and his enemies are not liberated by their own efforts.[46] Only when he goes against the flow of "real" history is he unsuccessful.[47] In retrospect, we might see a providential design at work, with Richard as scourge and minister who is at last scourged by God's larger hand working through history. Reginald Saner suggests that coexisting with this providential scheme is a "natural human agency," a force for order and the good; but if it is vested in Richard—that is, if he undoes his worst self—he dies curiously unrepentant.[48] If that same human agency is to be identified as Richmond, it is equally clear that he is "injected" into the play, required by truth to the chronicles, and thereby serving as a sort of dramatic *deus ex machina* to deliver the play from itself. In a sense, the play's own allotted length, its two hours' traffic, is on the side of Richmond.

As a history play, *Richard III* acknowledges a past that is prerequisite to its own presence; that same history, along with the play's transitional position between the two tetralogies, anticipates a future beyond that same presence. Perhaps, then, it is the factor of time, rather than language or that spectacle which Richard would dissolve with his perverse inner theater, that must prove his undoing. Indeed, just as he perverts language and the theater, Richard would pervert the relationship among theatrical present, past, and future. He tries to arrest time, plunging the world into an eternal present on his own terms. Seeking change in Machiavellian fashion before his coronation, he is "fear-ridden" once on the throne, hostile to change, neurotically trying to preserve what history itself will take from him.[49] Several commentators have observed that Richard operates on a time schedule vastly different from that of the play,[50] and that the process of usurping or holding power supersedes either its realization or, once realized, its employment, to the degree that the political ends that Richard champions seem almost a by-product, an afterthought.[51] As one critic phrases it, Richard would "extract" from the womb of time his desires, but, once so extracted, those desires cease to interest him.[52]

When Anne argues that there is "no beast so fierce but knows some touch of pity," Richard, acknowledging that he feels no pity, "logically" concludes he is no beast, thus wiping out the past graphically represented onstage by Edward's coffin, and thereby recreating himself as the widow's "present" wooer (1.2.71–72). By those words presently escaping from the lips Richard would abolish the past by a linguistic fiat: he can, with comic and yet also serious intensity, simply "say that [he] slew them not" (89). Using nothing but words, disdaining objects, the physical, the ground of words, Richard avoids being the victim of the past, as are his opponents. Only in their dreams, that is, in a theater not of his own making, can he be forced to confront a past, *his* past. For him, however, "what I have been" always gives way to "what I am" (1.3.132), even as he "uses" his past, beginning with the accident of his birth, as justification for the role of villain he assumes in the present. If he prefers the military past to the present "piping time of peace," he will replace that present with a preferred past made present. It is ironic, therefore, that his fall in Act 5 is set within the time of All-Saints's Eve (October 31), All-Souls's Eve (November 1), and All-Souls's Day (November 2), the period of the "remembrance of the faithful dead."[53]

If Margaret through her curses is the dead past and Richard through his perverse theater a maniacal present, Richmond is the future, the "day [that] will come" (1.3.244).[54] The same ghosts who signify the past in Richard's dream on the eve of battle embody the future for Richmond. They are what Richard has avoided,[55] and, like Caesar's ghost seen by Brutus, are at once objective and subjective,[56] a reenactment of the past that he had slain in his lust for the present, as well as being the conscience that he would deny.[57]

Unlike the other characters, Richmond, the promise of the future, also brings with him at least the promise of a new language. In his hypocritical vow to Elizabeth, Richard offers "to beget / [the] issue of [her] age," to transform her tears "to orient pearl," to advance "unto the dignity and height of fortune, / The high imperial type of this earthly glory" (4.4.322–24). A manipulator of the King's English, he serves here only as the mouthpiece, unawares, for both his destroyer and the kingdom's savior. The dying "father figure," rejected, about to be sacrificed, thereby transfers his speech to the children of the play. That child reemerges in the youthful Richmond, and as his name makes its way into the play, "Richmond" itself acquires the status of a leitmotif.[58] It is appropriately through a prophecy given him by a "bard of Ireland" near the castle of Rouge-mount that Richard learns he is not to "live long after [he sees] Richmond" (4.2.95–107). The very name of Richmond distracts him from Buckingham's reminder of his promise of an earldom.

If Richmond survives, still it is no less true that Richard "begets" him as much as history itself insists on his entrance. Similarly, the linguistic dead end that Richard would impose on the play and on the present demands Richmond's entrance for our release to the second tetralogy. Richard's world is the dark depth of the ocean scattered with dead men, and yet in their skulls, mocking "the dead bones" that lay "scatt'red by," are also "reflecting gems" (1.4.26–33). The negative, dark, coexists with the positive, light. This paradox, that he himself begets the light, is the greatness of Richard's character, though it is a greatness of which he is unaware or would smother in his self-professed role of tyrant. It is his "other shape" (4.4.286). If he is the villain,[59] the successful sacrifice[60] that some commentators would see—and he is this—he also makes us thrill at his challenge, albeit unsuccessful, to that Grand Mechanism of history, that too-mechanical concept of the world in which human will, the kinetic force for good or evil, is of little account.[61] In another light, Richard is a comic Falstaff,[62] for, as with Falstaff, we delight in his company even as we realize its potential for disorder. Robert Turner observes that Richard signals both Shakespeare's need for and partial success in moving from character as illustration, or as the embodiment of a single motive, to character as affecting and being affected by history.[63]

This tension between Richard and his world, or between the two worlds that I have charted in the play, explains, I think, why his energy continues to his death: the character does not cease to develop once he becomes king, or even once he loses the kingship. Accordingly, we hear of how Richard on the battlefield "enacts more wonder than a man" (5.4.2), "seeking for Richmond in the throat of death" (5). If it became a cliché, a subject for parody even in Shakespeare's own time, his "a horse, a horse! my kingdom for a horse!" (13) is not only the actor's ultimate line, but one of the most dazzling "covering" lines for an exit in Shakespeare, and a line that makes the play's final scene seem dull in comparison.

vi

It is Richard's "What do I fear?" speech (5.3.182–206), or at least the first half of that speech, that most graphically enacts the catholic nature of his character. The speech itself is linked with the clock's most ambiguous time, "dead midnight" (180), caught between the eve and the day of battle, between All-Souls's Eve and All-Souls's Day. For a moment Richard assimilates his divided halves. His is an expression of marvelous, Faustian egoism, in which he becomes all the world, all its citizens, even his own lover ("Richard loves Richard"). In his "I am I" we hear the assertion of that will, the insistence that man and not events constitutes history, a will that, however disproved by the providential or historical design controlling the play, is because of its very impossibility, its fragility, all the more wondrous. If Richard has become preoccupied with survival in the final two acts, if the playful, engaging villain of the opening scenes has been too long absent, that character is reasserted here, as he identifies himself as his own murderer, and then rejects the possibility on the grounds that no sane man would play that role against his better self. If his murderer were present, then he would "fly" from the felon; but how can one fly from oneself? How can he revenge himself against himself, since clearly he loves himself if no one else, and is loved by no one else? Then, with a sudden insight that places the intentionally light or unintentionally profound insight of his prologue in a new context, he concludes, tentatively, that self-hatred has been his basic motive, the sole possible alternative given his incompatibility with the "good." Then his logic traps him: if he loves himself, how can he be the "fool" dispraising himself, and yet it would be no less foolish to flatter himself since flattery, once recognized, once conscious, is self-destructive.

If the play as moral or divine history is now realized, the play as comic history is no less so, here in Richard's own savage humor and in his logic where, for this abuser of words, words fall against themselves. The speech's latter half is, to a degree, anticlimactic, but only so because a word, *conscience*, which has been missing from Richard's vocabulary, now enters, thereby "adulterating" his genius. This same adulteration is compounded by the morality play scene, where he imagines himself appearing before the "bar" of God's justice, his sins serving as witnesses for the prosecution and crying "Guilty! guilty!." Then, in a striking coda, Richard justifies the absence of pity in others with the argument that he, no less, finds "no pity [in] himself." The monologue itself now sinks into a reference to the dream that moments before we have seen enacted on stage, a dream that Richard has experienced, through the actor, in a way that no audience, onstage or off, could know.

It is here Richard himself who expands as a character to embrace the counterplay, one of conscience and of historical justice, that he has so extravagantly and yet so fatally resisted, and against which he has piled a language whose energy exists as an inverse correlative to its source in civilized speech and the theater, the epitome of civilized speech. Confusing himself earlier with the entire play, in this last-minute "reprieve" he *becomes* the play, but only through a recognition, however fleeting and incomplete, that will all but destroy this fascinating creature, not entirely unlike ourselves and therefore appealing to some source deep in ourselves. No mere tyrant, he is the first "interesting tyrant"[64] on the

English stage. If the speech itself is more ritualistic than realistic,[65] it is so because Richard, by definition, has been archetypal, representative, though not in the limited, emblematic way of the characters in the *Henry VI* plays or in the historical chronicles of Shakespeare's contemporaries.

In a sense, the speech conflates Shakespeare's old style and the promise of a new one.[66] We hear now an "inner voice"[67] in which a kind of moral self-knowledge tries to break in.[68] If he dies without true recognition,[69] if Shakespeare yanks him or if Richard yanks himself back from the brink of becoming a Macbeth,[70] I think the speech and the character behind that speech are not, as one critic calls it, a dead end for the playwright.[71] Rather, by this Danteish descent into a hell of linguistic and theatrical negativity, *Richard III* ends the first tetralogy, sacrifices itself and its sense of history, so that the second tetralogy can be born. There the comic manipulator of language will be diffused in the character of Falstaff; there man, for better or worse, seems more in control of his destiny. There the abuse of language and the theater of words will be reversed in the person of Henry V, who consciously manipulates language and its theater for more public ends.

7

Henry V:
"Speak freely of our acts, or else"

I HAVE already suggested that in *Henry V* Shakespeare manipulates the theater and its language for public ends no less than Richard III would have manipulated them to sustain his own private world.[1] Indeed, when matched against the idiosyncratic speech of the history concluding the first tetralogy, the present play offers what one critic has aptly called a veritable "stylistic spectrum"[2] of public discourse. For the audience, the challenge, I think, is not to fathom the darker recesses of its central figures, as was the case in *Richard III*. Nor is the "problem" of history one of optics, as it is in *Julius Caesar*, where the onstage spectacle is beyond the individual's grasp. Rather, we confront here a play whose language is, at best, inseparable from the public nature of the theater, and at worst practical, "political," and—in the eyes of some spectators and some critics—dangerously close to propaganda.

i

It is Shakespeare's other "Richard" play, perhaps, that puts into context the nature of language in *Henry V*. For if Richard II had persisted, Shakespeare's merging of theater and history would have championed language to the level of abstraction: it is the concept of divine right, rather than physical force, that Richard would marshal against Bolingbroke. His is an error in practical policy judgment, and it is significant, I think, that the poet Yeats, who labeled Hal "remorseless and undistinguished as some natural force," took Richard as his hero for being "full of capricious fancy."[3] Richard's addition to language that is abstract, timeless, and therefore true is echoed here by the first Chorus as it laments the stage's limitations, even as it celebrates, in a revealing paradox, the efficacy of that language spoken in "this wooden O" (Chorus, 1.13): the physical deficiencies of the rounded playhouse can be overcome if the audience grants the principle of representation where, by the use of O as "ciphers," one "crooked figure may / Attest in little place a million" (15–16). The Chorus, in effect, would employ language to elevate physical "facts" to some larger and therefore more significant Platonic reality: in its view Hal is not just the single actor assigned the part, nor merely the historical figure, but rather emblematic, the "mirror of all Christian kings" (Chorus, 2.6). To the degree that Hal himself believes such abstractions, or—what is more likely—finds no shame in using them, he would appear a semi-divine figure waging a holy war that itself serves as a "beadle" enacting on earth God's "vengeance" (4.1.169– 70). Whether out of sincerity, or policy, or both, the Archbishop of Canterbury picks up this same airy notion of language as he informs the Bishop of Ely that, when Hal talks, "the air, a charter'd libertine, is still, / And the mute wonder lurketh in men's ears, / To speak his sweet and honeyed sentences." With such an ethereal concept of language, indeed of the very act of delivery, it follows that the earthly or actual ("the art and practic part of life") can only be an inferior or "mistress to this theoric" (1.1.47–52).

There is a concomitant danger in this linguistic overriding of reality. Hal would abstract his soldiers to the level of a "copy . . . to men of grosser blood" (3.1.24) and, even if we allow for the inevitable rousing of the troops before battle, his instructions seem chilling: "imitate the action of the tiger" and "disguise fair nature with hard-favor'd rage," setting "the teeth and stretch[ing] the nostril wide" (3.1.6–15). Nor does the glorious "battle rend'red you in music" (1.1.44) ever materialize. We recognize as pure hyperbole the ironic, albeit patriotic cry that the "hearts" of the English soldiers "lie pavilion'd in the fields of France" while their bodies remain "here in England" (1.2.128–29). Confronted by this evangelical concept of war fostered by the Chorus and at times by Hal himself, some of the play's most perceptive commentators conclude that *Henry V*, like war itself, brings to the surface, albeit coated with patriotism, "the animal in man," that the play shows there is "no activity so savage that men cannot reduce to sober order and to humane rules and disciplines."[4]

This tendency of the play's language toward an essentially non-dramatic, abstract level, where dramatic structure is replaced by non-dramatic tableaux,[5] is inseparable from a timelessness, also urged primarily by the Chorus, that wars against the very concept of the "theater of presence." Through language the Chorus would adjust historical time itself by "turning th' accomplishment of many years / Into an hour-glass" (Chorus, 1.30). By language's "imagin'd wing" we can displace not only the limitations of the physical but also the slow time of history itself as the "swift scene flies / In motion of no less celerity / Than that of thought" (Chorus, 3.1–3). Through such a cerebral agency the past dissolves as easily as the future, and Hal becomes not a man moving through the present but a "remembrance of those valiant deeds" that at length stand outside of time (1.2.115). The Chorus voices, in essence, our own yearning for the absolute, for a Hal who becomes the perfect allegorical abstraction, the ideal king reconstructed from the "pasts" of those other plays in the tetralogy confined to showing, on their own inadequate physical stages, those imperfect kings whose sacrifice only served to produce *Henry V*.[6] Like us, Hal would sacrifice "many of our bodies" as long as "witness live in brass of this day's works" (4.3.95–97), preferring to life itself that ultimate art which abstracts both language and time: the epitaph.

More than one commentator has suspected—even accused—Shakespeare of trying here to yoke the nondramatic epic form to the demands of the stage.[7] In observing that actual "history thus defeats those who would defy it by trying to live in a changeless present or an undiminshed youth, or in a realm of pure play,"[8] Jonas Barish cites, in effect, the problems posed by the initial Chorus. If anything, that Chorus tries to involve us as collaborators in its concept of language. We are the "gentles all" (Chorus, 1.8) who can "eche out [the] performance with [our] mind" (Chorus, 3.35) or "piece out . . . imperfections with [our] thoughts" (Chorus, 1.23), thereby surpassing the Chorus's linguistic truth with one even higher in our imaginations and, as a consequence, beyond stage representation.[9] Though the Chorus may represent only one of the play's several positions on the issue of patriotism,[10] still its call for "imaginary forces" (Chorus, 1.18) would make the audience if not the only at least the ultimate text. Not the impartial observer, we would become the godlike judge in a line of descent leading from us, the offstage audience, to this onstage audience of one, to the actors and their playwright, these "flat unraised spirits that hath dar'd / On this unworthy scaffold to bring forth / So great an object" (Chorus, 1.9–11). This same superior position is reexpressed metaphorically when the Archbishop describes the father of Edward the Black Prince as watching "on a hill" and "smiling" while he observed his son—"his lion's whelp"—who "play'd . . . a tragedy" by defeating the French" (1.2.105–9). Thus, a reality beyond history stands as the positive alternative to the "mock'ries" of stage enactment (Chorus, 4.52–53).

Eamon Grennan speaks of the Chorus as functioning like a "commissioned historiographer," shaping the physical facts for a king who in turn shapes his own image to fit a predesigned and mythical scenario.[11] Dramatic exposition in the first Chorus and first two scenes of the play would thereby become main action. That claim of the Verbal, in which we are invited to be collaborators, will have "transported" us not just to Southampton (Chorus, 2.35) but to the realms of political allegory; and more than one commentator—if I may venture to say so—has been so seduced.

ii

Though invoked in the play's opening lines, this epic "muse of fire, that would ascend / The brightest heaven of invention," cannot last. Once in the play itself, the epic hero Alexander becomes, in Fluellen's tortured King's English, Alexander the Pig (4.7.13), and if Alexander is like Hal, or Hal like him, it is as much for negative as for positive qualities. Even the most telling link between the two, the betrayal of a friend (Clytus, Falstaff), makes reference to an event outside the present play.[12] If Hal emerges from the unpromising youth of the *Henry IV* plays, then *Henry V* itself must emerge, I think, from the dramatically unpromising "youth" of Act 1. Ely's metaphor works for both parallel incidents: "the strawberry grows underneath the nettle" (1.1.60), and it is here the "faculty" of the theater itself, "its inherent power," as the Arden edition glosses the word,[13] that is initially or seemingly "unseen, yet crescive" (66). The play's fruition is posited on an initial question: what happens when an epic hero as initially depicted is subjected to the demands of reality as enacted in this medium that, like reality, rests on the productive tension between the visual and the verbal? If chauvinistic thoughts go first on imaginary linguistic wings to France, still the companion cry is "let their bodies follow" (1.2.130): Hal's verbal court of Act 1 must inevitably give way in Act 2 to the shipyards of Southhampton.

Words cannot be all. The same Fluellen who deflates Alexander as an epic, nondramatic hero observes that in the camp of Pompey the Great words must share the stage with action, and, in fact, on the night before battle, when talking may give away a position, "there is no tiddle taddle nor pibble babble" permitted (4.1.70–71). The movement to France is metadramatically a freeing up of the stillborn epic posed by the Chorus. It will be Harry, not the idealized Christian King, "like himself," as enacted onstage by Burbage, who will "assume," but *only* assume, the bearing of Mars (1.5–6). The world of abstract "givens"—"miracles" in Ely's words—"[is] ceas'd" and "therefore we [those onstage, as well as the audience ratifying the play offstage] must needs admit the means / How things are perfected" (1.1.67–69). A man of the theater, Shakespeare, as eager as his Chorus seems reluctant, must "force a play" (Chorus, 2.32), bringing the "theoric" to what Nym—one careful, perhaps too careful, with his words—sees as the necessary "conclusions" (2.1.24). If the fields of France seem initially too "vasty" (Chorus, 1.12), at issue now is not the literal recreation of Agincourt but a theatrical compromise where we at once see Agincourt, though admittedly on a more limited scale, and—

much more significantly—*experience* what one commentator properly
calls history "recreated, evoked, preserved."[14]

What *Henry V* cannot be, or cannot be exclusively, points to the new,
fuller theater to be presented here. The play's own initial "anti-theater"
is not so much dissolved as it is transferred to the French, who are
nothing if not verbal, and self-indulgently so. Even Hal fears that the
"air of French / Hath blown [the] vice" of empty rhetoric into him
(3.6.151–52). Nor will *Henry V* be a "green" or pastoral comedy; once
committed to the French campaign, Hal will find no forest of Arden.
Bringing the biases of the pastoral to the play, one scholar finds it—
understandably—an anti-war drama where the French campaign is a
"violation of natural law revealed in a landscape that forfeits both beauty
and utility"[15] I think Joanne Altieri provides a more circumspect account
of the pastoral when, wrestling with the genre of the play, she finds its
pastoral patterns, while upholding an idealized notion of kingship, coexisting with a realistic appraisal both of the actual soldier king and of the
exclusive claims of such pastoral romance.[16]

In the context of the *Henry IV* plays, we miss, of course, the Falstaffian
element, those tavern scenes celebrating play, both verbal and theatrical,
at the expense of the demands of a public role, but surely Hal's education
as a private being is now complete. William Babula suggests that Hal
moves here from a man evading responsibility in the opening act, to one
struggling to unite words and action, to the competent king, able to
compromise, one who through his experience in France is "created
verbally as the hero."[17] Though an essential element in Hal's early
education, playing is now merely frivolous, and it is the reported death
of Falstaff that frees the present play from the public/private axis of its
predecessors. That scene is, without doubt, touching, and one observer
speculates that Shakespeare himself identifies with the dying man;[18]
another, that Falstaff's death echoes in parody that of Socrates.[19] For
present purposes, however, the Falstaff who exists through the Hostess's
untrustworthy description expires verbally. The captivating garrulous
seducer of *Henry IV* is here an invalid who can only babble, and if that
babbling is about the appropriate topic of one's salvation ("green fields"
[2.3.17]), the hostess has advised Falstaff that there is "no need to trouble
himself with any such thoughts yet" (21–22). Nor can we take seriously
the attempted, albeit understandable whitewashing of his character. He
cried out, predictably, for sack, but the Hostess's insistence that he did
not also cry out for women is undercut by the Boy, who also proves
himself on other occasions a good observer. To use Bardolph's words,
Falstaff's own "fuel is gone" (2.3.43).

However, his spirit in limitation may be here. We have already observed that parallel between Alexander and Hal as betrayers of their

friends. Joseph Porter makes an intriguing link between Falstaff and the Boy, suggesting that the Boy's knowledge of Falstaff, and his cynicism about language as contrasted with Hal's own positive attitude, allow him to stand in for that youthful Hal linked earlier to Falstaff. Still, if Falstaff dies, the Boy must, also. We will recall Hal's anger here when the French kill the boys in the English camps; Porter argues that the present Boy is one of those youthful victims.[20] The critical consensus, however, would have Hal representing the Protestant ethic that is required by the present play, and Falstaff opposing that ethic, albeit granting its heavy price.[21] Robert Kelly even suggests a parallel between the death of Scroop and that of Falstaff in their successive scenes (2.2. and 2.3): both represent those spirits of discord, public and private, that Hal must challenge.[22] Even a defender of Falstaff like A. C. Bradley saw the rejection of the comic knight as revealing at once the pleasant and unpleasant side of Hal's character: Bradley found Shakespeare overshooting the mark in Falstaff's character and undershooting it in Hal.[23]

If Hal does try a disguise, reminiscent of the stratagem so effective in exposing Falstaff in the Gads Hill robbery, the result is more dubious.[24] When the king is "unmasked," the common soldier Williams proves, at the very least, his intellectual match. The entire episode has what John Wilders calls a "morally disturbing context."[25] Hal "wins" on the twin issues of separating the private sins of his soldiers from the King's personal responsibility and the right of the soldier-king to claim an allegiance absolving him of guilt for the deaths in battle. However, he cannot answer, or he evades answering, Williams's question as to the justness of the war itself. Perhaps still smarting under his "bitter terms" (4.8.42), Hal demands that he keep his promise to strike the man wearing the matching glove, yet Williams scores again and, in doing so, shows at once why Falstaff must be rejected and why the character of Hal in the present play demands its own special context: the king "came not like himself . . . but . . . as a common man," and therefore what Hal "suffer'd under that shape" was his own "fault" (50–54). In short, Hal has here only a public personality. It is unfair, I think, to suggest that he can function any longer as a private person, especially on the eve of an international battle.[26]

This is why we see so little of the "interior" Hal in the present play, and this fact rivals Falstaff's absence, from the perspective of some commentators, as being the play's chief defect. The Hal as described by Bates and Williams—full of ordinary fears, like other men—cannot really exist in *Henry V*.[27] He can "play" at being like them, yet no longer with the intensity, or even with the sincerity such playing had in Falstaff's tavern. Tracing the disguised-king motif in Elizabethan drama, Anne Barton concludes that Hal ultimately has no private dimensions: he is now the royal "we." In France he consciously plays the role of fellow soldier, but only as a stratagem. Thus, his is the "dilemma of the man placed at a disadvantage in the sphere of personal relations by the fact of a corporate self."[28] It is not so much the case, I think, of Hal's consciousness being "restricted,"[29] or his being less interesting than Richard II, an intensely private person to be sure.[30] And Hal is no Hamlet,[31] nor is he meant to be. If he hurts inwardly from the "fault / [His] father made in compassing the crown" (4.1.293–94), that fault will not be, like Hamlet's, an irritant infecting and, in the same process, enlarging the consciousness until its bearer adopts a nihilistic attitude toward the public world of the court. Rather, Hal will absolve himself of the past by building "two chauntries, where the sad and solemn priests still sing for Richard's soul" (301–2). He himself will not be among the mourners.[32] And if his one soliloquy, following on the heels of the complex conversation in disguise with Bates and Williams, shows a man petulantly complaining about his position, even condescendingly wishing to be the "wretched slave; / Who with a body fill'd and vacant mind / Gets him to rest" (268–70), it is simply a fact that he does not, like Lear, give up such "ceremony." It is his "brother Gloucester's voice" (307) that pulls him out of the reverie on Richard II, and Hal soon destroys even this fleeting glimpse into his conscience with the authoritative "I know thy errand, I will go with thee."

Robert Egan observes that the soliloquy at once reviews and, no less, concludes Hal's *psychomachia*.[33] He may indeed be shaken by the camp debate,[34] or may be becoming the "controlled" like his father,[35] thereby demonstrating that the man of forceful political action is at length humanly inadequate.[36] Indeed, we may think of these negative dimensions of Hal as a temporary subtext functioning in its way just as powerfully as the text itself. In this sense, the soliloquy voices our own concerns about what Hal is becoming in the present play, given the claims made on him by the public world. Moreover, his public self is no more real than the private self at length submerged here: Hal himself sees the king, defined by ceremony, as only a "proud dream" (4.1.257).

iii

Though it must be confined within the parameters of this study, I would now define the play's purpose as that of enacting on the public stage man as a public being, acting in the *polis*, where language is at once both a determinant of reality (if not *the* determinant) and the source of a relativity that in turn makes reality itself an exercise in individual will.[37] *Henry V* is thereby an extension of the concerns in *Richard II* and the two *Henry IV* plays, and yet, metadramatically, in everything from its attitude toward stage language to characterization to its relation both to the audience and to the historical/present reality encompassing the stage, the play is new,[38] unrelated to its predecessors.

Far from outdistancing spectacle or even serving as a metaphysical extension of physical reality, dramatic speech here must form a partnership with the visual. This same partnership forced by the play's public concern allows, in retrospect, for a more neutral assessment of the Chorus's appeal to the audience's imagination: "Think, when we talk of horses, that you see them / Printing their proud hoofs i' th' receiving earth" (Chorus, 1.26–27). Bernard Beckerman has argued that increasingly in his career Shakespeare calls for the audience's visual collaboration, as he himself becomes more certain of the strength of his own dramatic language; the present play duplicates this pattern, releasing us from the dominant but static verbal bias of the first scenes.[39] As audience, therefore, we are no longer a verbal collaborator with a Chorus longing for epic significance but rather a disengaged spectator functioning with heightened aural *and* ocular powers. The earlier "claim of the verbal" is met with a no-less-insistent "claim of the physical." Like the Boy, who has "observ'd" the three comic holdovers from Falstaff's world and finds in them no relation between word and actuality (3.2.28), we must "sit" in the playhouse (Chorus, 2.36) as observers, and if as collaborators, then as collaborators of the playwright working with a dramatic form striving to be as inclusive as the larger reality that is its subject. Like Macmorris as advised by Fluellen, we must be sage interpreters and not "take the matter otherwise than is meant" (3.2.125–26). One scholar observes that, accordingly, the patriotic Chorus becomes more and more dubious and shallow.[40]

The play is thus an exercise in forging a *public* language. Dismissed as linguistically and culturally "barbarous" by the stylistically pure French (3.5.4), it is the English, these "bastard Normans" (3.5.10) who, in spite of their verbal plurality, will succeed. Indeed, if there is a fault, it rests on the side of the linguistic conservative, for the play, like the theater itself, is a public medium, subject to a variety of tongues. When Nell, that murderess of even minimal King's English, bids her husband a French "adieu," we know that the French cannot help but lose (2.3.64).

The play, in fact, represents a conflation of competing tongues: there are scenes in English; scenes involving the various dialects of the British empire in English and ranging from courtly high to comic low; scenes in French (or at least Shakespeare's French); scenes involving translation from one language to another; and—as in the movie without subtitles— scenes involving Frenchmen speaking English. In some very perceptive comments on the play's language, Joseph Porter observes that, even while recognizing the plurality of dialects, the playwright's purpose seems to be that of finding the common language that men actually use and can use.[41] Given its purer, more formal speech, French is "a less perfect medium for the king's word than the English society as an organic whole." Hal epitomizes his nation's "illocutionary force," and his speech-acts (speech that implies and then leads to action) parallel the function of the theater itself in combining dialogue and action. With its plurality of tongues, the play recreates a sort of modern-day Babel—I use Porter's term here—even as it seeks a coherence out of the potential chaos of language.

To forge this common tongue the play first attempts to mirror the multifaceted nature of public reality itself, a reality to be distinguished from our own idiosyncratic interior world, and one admitting plural interpretations because that exterior world can be nothing less, no less inclusive. Hence the play can be viewed positively as manifesting the epic spirit, even as it offers an uncritical glorification of its epic hero.[42] That second, seemingly negative judgment admits a bias for the more complex, introspective central character that another commentator finds lacking here, precisely because the play at once deletes the comedy of its predecessors in the tetralogy even as it avoids the questioning of public order that characterizes the tragedies.[43] From one perspective Hal is praised as being the handbook-perfect officer, and that definition admits that the morality of war is not the same as that of peace.[44] Yet, adjusting the focus, he becomes a real person in a play that straddles the line, offering neither "panegyric [nor] satire."[45] Is *Henry V* many things because it is not unified?[46] Does the subplot deflate Hal's character,[47] or, conversely, does the subplot added to the main plot allow for a fuller response to his French campaign?[48] On the one hand, Shakespeare, it is argued, here attempts something not fully belonging to the theater;[49] on the other hand, the complex response we have to Agincourt anticipates the dichotomous theater of Brecht.[50] The playwright takes the form of tragical history to the extreme here and then exhausts it,[51] or the play is so wide-ranging that it eschews singular judgment, whether of its central character or its genre.[52] If we could only unveil the form (or even forms) of this generic puzzle[53] we could find Shakespeare's position; conversely, discussions of genre are irrelevant.[54] One critic brands the play as exclusive, limiting;[55] another sees in it a wide-ranging analysis of the political mind, at once realistic and cynical, and therefore truthful.[56] Revising an earlier estimate of the play, Norman Rabkin finds *Henry V* going in two opposite directions, like a Gestaltist's drawing, and, in so doing, daring us to decide.[57]

In suggesting now that none of these views is wrong, I am not arguing for formlessness in the play, or for a conscious exercise in paradox on Shakespeare's part. Rather, after the initial enticement by the Chorus to read the history as epic, the play shows epic for what it really is. If Shakespeare, if Hal, has only his language, as that language defines and, in turn, shapes the physical world, we also, the audience responding with ears and eyes, have nothing but that language, that same double-edged inheritance. In revisiting the past as recorded by Holinshed and Hall, *Henry V* discloses, in its theater of presence, a public figure no less complex than those figures of the tragedies, but one faced primarily with the external world rather than the world of self.

This plurality is expressed most prominently in the Archbishop's analogy of a kingdom with a beehive, from which he makes the inference: "That many things, having full reference / To one content, may work contrariously / As many arrows loosed several ways / Come to one mark; as many ways meet in one town" (1.2.205–8). The play itself moves structurally from England to France to England, but it is an England linguistically changed to which characters and audience so return. This same inclusiveness itself allows for yet goes beyond parody, as when Hal's "Once more unto the breach" (3.1.1) is followed in the next scene, again at the first line, by Pistol's "On, on, on, on, on! To the breach, to the breach." The Chorus's admittedly narrow focus itself becomes part of the pluralistic vision of Hal.

Rejecting at once the courtly, nonactualized language of the French and the self-indulgently playful language of the Falstaffian low-life characters, the play seeks a language that can shape, that can give coherence and permanence to this public reality.[58] As the Archbishop well knows, the bill endowing the Church with power can in turn be invalidated by a second bill that would "strip" from the same Church "the better half of [its] possessions" (1.1.7–11). Henry understands the potentially disastrous consequence of a textual misunderstanding as he cautions the Archbishop in reading the Salique law not to "fashion, wrest, or bow [his] reading, / Or nicely charge [his] understanding soul / With opening titles miscreate" (1.2.14–16). Carol Sickerman traces Hal's own recognition of language's power, from his playful tavern speech to the formal verse of the opening scenes, to a "personal legality of language" where, strengthened by the Saint Crispin speech, he learns of the link between words and deeds, and how each validates the other.[59]

This recognition of language's power accounts, I think, for the emphasis in the play on both names and oaths: names as they locate a person's stature in the political world, and oaths as an expression of the contractual bonds of citizens in the *polis*. It is in God's name that Hal vows vengeance on the French (1.2.290), and, in his judgment, the name that becomes him best is "soldier" (3.3.5–6). He in turn confers names, naming the battle for the "feast of Crispian" and then invoking that battle, once named, five times (43, 46, 48, 57, 67). Conversely, Scroop loses his Christian name, and Hal speculates that his seducer's only "instance" for tempting him was "to dub [him] with the name of traitor" (2.2.120). Even when Hal drops his name in disguise, he still manages to assume a name with a double meaning: "Harry le Roy" (4.1.49).

This naming permeates even to the comic characters. That remnant from Falstaff's days is spoken of as "Doll Tearsheet she by name" (2.1.77). When Fluellen, representing the more responsible comic characters who replace Pistol, Bardolph, and Nym,[60] makes his link between Alexander and Harry as soldiers betraying friends, he recalls Hal's "fat knight" but confesses that he has "forgot his name" (4.7.50–52). The "three sworn brothers" from Falstaff's day (2.1.12) come to ruin: Bardolph is executed for stealing the "pax"; Pistol disgraces his office with bribes; Nym retreats into silence. Violating their military oaths, losing either their figurative names, their reputations, or, in Falstaff's case, a literal name, they fall from Hal, whose assumed name, Harry le Roy, becomes actual when in Act 5 he is named "*Henri, Roi d'Angleterre, Heritier de France*," and then renamed in Latin "*Rex Angliae, et Heres Franciae*" (339–42).

Joseph Lenz speaks of the relation between oath-taking and honor as the "socioreligious myth" of the play.[61] I would observe that it is through this linguistic "naming" as expressed in the oath-grounded or contractual relations between persons that the play establishes its own secular mythology, its public metaphysics. Abjuring the interior dimensions of the tragedies or the implied ritualism of the comedies, *Henry V* still seeks a larger significance in the *facts* of public life, in seeing "this history" (Chorus, 1.32) as more than a collection of details.

Devouring time, the force that the Epilogue underscores in noting that Hal's actual reign was tragically brief, is the historical factor with which men and playwrights must contend. Against this force Shakespeare sets the art of public language. Weighing "time / Even to the utmost grain" (2.4.137–38), Hal knows full well that if he fails his punishment will be a verbal one: his bones will then be "tombless, with no remembrance over them" (1.2.229). The alternatives are to be spoken of "freely" by the "full mouth" of "history," or, like a "Turkish mute," to be consumed by the "tongueless mouth" of the grave, and not "worshipp'd with a waxen epitaph" (230–33). This experiment in language for a stage mirroring our own public world thus confronts what Fluellen identifies as the "mutability" of Fortune (3.6.30–38). If Fortune is more properly Providence, then, like his King pictured here, Shakespeare effects—depending on one's point of view—a "happy compromise"[62] or an "uncomfortably precarious balance"[63] between the facts of existence and the human will that battles those facts, both politically and dramatically, with language. A necessity for political stability in the real world, this political language is, I think, the goal, the "necessity" of *Henry V*."[64]

iv

Act 5, the "conclusions" of this experience, has five distinct movements: the Chorus, the first scene, the initial meeting of the French and English in the second scene, Hal's wooing of the Princess Katherine, and the return of the French and English courts coupled with the Epilogue.

I have observed above that the language achieved here, as it seeks its counterpart in the real world, at the very least blurs any clear distinction between theatrical and political speech. Act 5 links the completion of the play with the actual treaty-signing that ends the conflict between the French and English. We are, in effect, "dissolving"—to use the movie term—into reality, both that predating the play, as detailed in the chronicles, and the actual event, the treaty marking the end of Hal's final public education that has been the subject of *Henry V*. Significantly, the Chorus informs us that Hal now forbids any theatrical presentation of his accomplishments: "Where that his lords desire him to have borne / His bruised helmet and his bended sword / Before him through the city. He forbids it" (17–19). Earlier antithetical, the visual ("behold") and verbal ("thought") are now coming to rest, even as the play returns to its thematic and actual origins: "Now in London place him" (22–23, 35). Appropriately, the Chorus, who had earlier tried to confer epic significance on the bare boards of the Globe, now metadramatically uncovers itself by announcing that it has but "play'd / The interim, by remembering you 'tis past" (42–43). Announcing the role dispels the fiction, by definition, even as "'Tis past" signals the fictive nature of a present enactment itself based on facts that are now only historical.

Pistol's appearance in Act 5, scene 1 spells the final dissolution of *Henry IV* and of his own counterlanguage,[65] as he loses to Fluellen, the play's new breed of responsible, low-life, dialect characters whose regional peculiarities are themselves sacrificed to that national language now achieved in peace. Compelled to eat the leek, Pistol, in essence, is forced gastronomically, *fundamentally*, to swallow the physical symbol of oath-taking, and hence, of united purpose. The "counterfeit" (5.1.69) standing against the marriage of visual and verbal symbolized by that leek, his crime is itself linguistic: Pistol erred, according to Gower, in assuming that since Fluellen could "not speak English in the native garb," his verbal difficulty was a sign of physical difficulty ("You thought . . . he could not therefore handle an English cudgel" [75–77]). His own epiloguelike farewell, delivered alone onstage and thus stressing his isolation from the unified assemblages of the next scene, recalls the crimes and the puns of Falstaff's world (he will "steal" to England to "steal") and parodies, though without effect, the play's concern for a meaningful interaction between the visual and the verbal: he will put "patches" on his "cudgell'd scars" and then "swear" he got them in the "Gallia wars" (88–89). If, like his former master Falstaff, he represents the life force,[66] it is only life at the low level of a bawd.

With Pistol's unsavory exit, the twin courts take the stage in Act 5, scene 2, and the stress is clearly on the visual and physical. Burgundy describes the monarchs as having "congreeted" with "face to face, and royal eye to eye" (30–31). Peace, the "dear nurse of arts," is mother to the "joyful births," the restoration of life now possible in "this best garden of the world / Our fertile France" (35–37). We now enter the male, chauvinistic world of realpolitik, where language as persuasion turns to force: Hal's right to dictate terms, to speak unilaterally.[67] Language in its less practical or more imaginative dimension is now housed with the feminine. Queen Isabella suggests: "Happily a woman's voice may do some good / When articles too nicely urg'd be stood on" (93–94). The wooing of Hal and Katherine will now take the stage and, given the accord of the participants on their return, we may assume that her more subtle tongue has prevailed.

That wooing scene has provoked a variety of responses. Its forced marriage is said to blacken the name of romance; Hal's amatory conquest here is merely an instance of domination. The would-be union is a shallow one since Hal and Katherine cannot speak the same language, either linguistically or conceptually.[68] Despite his verbal sophistication elsewhere or the Archbishop's praise of his scholarly English, Hal's pose as a plain-speaking soldier represents a lapse on Shakespeare's part, a cheap attempt for an effect, a capitulation to the convention of the blunt militarist. More positively, the wooing is said show Shakespeare valuing action over characterization, perhaps even restoring the now worldly wise King to the more carefree, engaging stance of his youth.[69] Or it stands emblematically for the merging of the political and social spheres.[70] In the context of the present comments about the play's dissolution of its own imaginary or theatrical language, I would observe that both Hal and Katherine give the illusion of denying the transcendent language we otherwise associate with Shakespeare, thereby parodying the very hand that creates them. Hal is now modeled after a man of the world and no longer imitates the poetic sun or the Son of God from the days of his reformation. The seeming dispraise of playwrights or poets is thus dictated by the demands of this unique play in the canon, and we might therefore take as both proper and ironic the notion that the "tongues of men [playwrights?] are full of deceit" (117–18), the disdain for "verses" (132), for those fellows (surely like Shakespeare himself) of "infinite tongue" (56). As *Henry V*, by its author's design, veers back to reality, our perspective on the function of dramatic speech must be adjusted, and whatever the immediate political/sensual designs of his spokesman here, Shakespeare himself can momentarily brand an eloquent poet, such as Richard II, "but a prater," and the soaring verse of *Henry IV* "but a ballad" (158–59). We also recognize that Katherine's inability to "speak [Hal's] English" (102–3) and Hal's bad French serve as the best possible correlatives for the speech that the play itself has championed: artlessness becomes an art in a public world working against the introspective nature of conceptual language.

The demands on the actor are the same as when that actor plays that fellow of infinite speech, Hamlet himself: Hal's thematic sense of timing remains inviolate.[71] Nothing is ever absolutely "plain" or actual on the stage (124), and there is still "music" in this "English broken" (243–44), though it is the music of the same public speech Hal himself defines in his speech lesson to Katherine (220–46): "take me by the hand, and say, 'Harry of England, I am thine' " (236–37). The reward for such speech is a kingdom, if not the romantic love we expect—even demand—in the comedies.[72] Just before the reentrance of the once-rival courts, Hal makes a telling marriage between the physical/visual and the conceptual/verbal, as well as a distinction between the static French language depicted earlier in the play and the English that evolves under his tutelage: "You have witchcraft in your lips, Kate; there is more eloquence in a sugar touch of them than in the tongues of the French council" (275–77). If this is not fully romantic, it is as romantic as public personages are permitted.

With the return of the united courts the practical language of the wooing scene takes a "holiday," as Hal himself, encouraged by Burgundy's playful remarks about Cupid, gives way to a courtly speech more at home, say, in *Love's Labor's Lost*. Then, just as suddenly as it has appeared, such talk is swept away by the "terms of reason" (329–30) of the international contract.[73] The conferring of French and Latin titles on Henry is itself lifted almost verbatim from Holinshed (330–42); the language now is legal, contractual, anticipatory. If in the wooing scene the dialogue had approached at least a semblance of the private sphere, such domesticity is itself now a metaphor for the public ending: the union of Hal and Katherine is likened to the newly formed marriage between France and England; the joining of bodies in marital consummation stands for a public harmony in which "English may as French, French Englishmen, / Receive each other!" (367–68).

Like Puck's or Prospero's epilogues, the Chorus's final appearance is more than merely a dramatic convention. We are perhaps suspicious of the now repetitious disclaimer of a theater whose author has "pursu'd the story" with only a "rough and all-unable pen," unless, of course, Shakespeare comically casts himself in the role of a nondramatic chronicler. If Hal's special virtue has been to read the times and, in turn, to alter them through that reading, then Shakespeare has done no less in reading Hal, from a trinity of texts extending from the "real" past to the chronicles to the first three plays of the second tetralogy. Thus the phrase *mangling by starts* (that, is, botching up Hal's life by the play-wright's arbitrary selection or omission) actually serves to define Shakespeare's technique rather than to condemn his work.

Even this inverse definition of art is itself swept away by the Chorus's sudden acknowledgment of the brevity of Hal's reign, as the author's productive "mangling" is metamorphosed to the poor "managing" of the realm under Hal's son, Henry VI. History works prospectively, with the troubled, divided realm of Hal's father leading to Hal's reign ("Small time; but in that small most greatly liv'd"), that in turn was dissipated under the next monarchy with the loss of France and "bleed[ing]" of England. But art works retrospectively. Shakespeare's stage "hath shown" earlier the realm of Henry VI: the time covered by the second tetralogy follows in the canon the later historical period covered by the first. The special paradox of the history play, a genre to which Shakespeare would not return until the end of his career, and then probably only in part, rests in the fact that it is at once subject to and yet free from time. Its mirror image is, by definition, inferior to the reality so reflected, yet that reality, for those who live in it as well as participants and the spectators in the theater of its enactment, is itself a construct of language. The issue then becomes: what language is most compatible with the inherent meaning of an event, a meaning at once relative to the perceiver, no less than the playwright, and subject itself to the "acceptance" and hence ratification of the "fair minds" in the audience.

Shakespeare here has his vision of the public world, and if that vision is itself encased in a dramatic illusion, still, against the brevity of Hal's accomplishment in real life stands the finality of his linguistic achievement in "this" present play. Perhaps this distinction between art and life accounts for what the poet Charles Williams calls the "legerity" of spirit in *Henry V*, the last expression of this spirit before the tragedies.[74] Not uncritical of Hal's success, Robert Ornstein observes that Shakespeare's art here lasts longer than Hal's empire,[75] and of course art is long, life short. I would prefer to qualify the statement by thinking that Shakespeare reads, realistically, the meaning of his King's life, a life rendered significant because of Hal's own collision course with his destiny as forged equally by language and by time. *Henry V*, a public play on the public stage, enacts in its language and spectacle an existence that is ultimately to be found outside the theater and yet one that, by definition, must be the theater's preeminent concern.

PART IV

Presence and Resolution: Onstage and Off

8

The Merchant of Venice:
"The virtue of the ring"

SOMETHING is wrong poetically in Antonio's opening lines, in his twofold complaint that he is sad and, what is more, troubled ("It wearies me") because he cannot account for the source of his sadness. For the audience, the lines may sound curiously imprecise, almost a denial of what exposition is supposed to mean. In the larger play, almost until the final moments of *The Merchant of Venice*, that alliance between language and spectacle, essential to the theater's ability to mirror the verbal and visual dimensions of life outside its stage, is more accurately a misalliance. It is Portia, the character most given to play, who here restores that lost unity, and hence comedy, to a divided world.

i

Perhaps Antonio's lines reflect his fear that Bassanio will desert him for Portia.[1] Or he may, if one chooses to act him in this fashion, be suppressing a homosexual desire for his friend, though Solanio's "Why then you are in love" (46) is abruptly dismissed, perhaps—to stretch the point—because it refers only to heterosexual love. Since his "ventures are not in one bottom trusted" (42), we may assume that Antonio's worry is not fiscal. Still, Antonio's "malaise,"[2] whatever its source, is expressed in a kind of "groundless poetry" suggesting perhaps that he speaks for an entire society of an infection, born of their self-satisfaction and physical comfort, that "wearies" his countrymen no less than it "wearies" him (1.1.2). Like a ship becalmed, he and his fellows seem inert, static, in a phrase, without meaning, without purpose.[3] Until they learn of Shylock's "merry sport" (1.3.145), whose object is a pound of flesh, this well-off mercantile society, epitomized in Antonio, has surfeited, paradoxically, to the extent that since the physical world has ceased to be a problem, their language is itself no longer clearly grounded in the physical, but is now at best abstract, at worst lacking that collaboration

155

between idea and object which we associate with Shakespeare's dramatic poetry. Without this collaboration, here denied by the gap between Antonio's physical weariness (the disease he "caught" or "came by" [3]) and its source, the explanation for his sadness, or his malaise, can only be expressed negatively: he is "sad / Because [he is] not merry" (47–48).

Nothing "holds" in this world. Salerio's misdiagnosis of Antonio's condition proves accurate as a description of the state's general malaise: the "mind" of Venice is at present merely "tossing on the ocean" (8). Without a real ground, the Venetians' metaphors lead nowhere, or point in a negative direction: hourglasses are "shallows and . . . flats"; the church's own "holy edifice of stone" is "dangerous rocks"; the breath "cooling . . . broth" is a wind fanning a storm at sea (22–31).[4] Incapable of silence, Antonio's friends struggle to find words to "explain" his sadness that has wearied them also. Disdaining that "sort of men" who would "a willful stillness entertain" (88–90), Gratiano speaks even if to no purpose so as to prevent the unwanted alternative of saying something after a practiced silence and thereby "damn[ing] those ears / Which hearing them would call their brothers fools" (98–99). Yet Gratiano belittles his own speech by calling it an "exhortation" (104), and on his departure Antonio confirms the fact: his friend speaks an "infinite deal of nothing" (114).

Nor are the linguistic difficulties confined to the Venetian males. The suitors who fail with Portia are likewise abusers of language: the Neapolitan prince who talks only of his horse, the County Palentine frowning but saying nothing, the French lord who starts capering "if a throstle sing" but says little himself of substance, and the English Falconbridge dismissed by Portia as "a dumb show" (1.2.39–73). To use Lorenzo's words when he chastises the verbally indulgent servant Launcelot, we are in the presence of men whose surface accomplishment in being able to phrase "a tricky word" is at the expense of "defy[ing] the matter" (3.5.69–70).

These men who deal in the transport of commodities thus ironically speak a language that, as yet, finds no referent in the physical world about them. When they do use their profession as the ground or objective correlative for an idea, the image thus created reveals the end-product of their malaise that awaits them once Shylock takes the stage two scenes later. In Salerio's shipwreck image the rocks merely grazing the "gentle" vessel's side would "scatter all her spices on the stream, / Enrobe the roaring waters with [her] silks" (1.1.31–34). There is a tension in his picture between the "conspicuous consumption" of the image, as he adorns the ocean with such finery as spices and silk, and the gentle ("gentile"?, to invoke a recurrent pun in the play) ship of state ruined by only a slight contact ("touching but") with its stony adversary.[5]

Bassanio takes to the extreme this cleavage between the physical and verbal characterizing the mercantile society. By his own admission, he has "disabled [his] estate" (1.1.123), and indeed, as he later admits to Portia, he is without property or goods (3.2.259). Though his suit to Portia is based on a hierarchy of motives, his initial purpose is to regain that lost estate.[6] Bassanio also seems infected with the Venetians' linguistic illness: Antonio finds that his friend's longish metaphor about recovering a lost arrow with a second arrow merely "wind[s] about [his] love with circumstance" (1.1.153–55). "More matter with less art," as Gertrude would say.

In this light, Shylock appears a less troubled, surely a more literal and single-minded practitioner of their profession, and he is rooted in the physical in a way that they are not.[7] A physicalist, as the trial demonstrates, Shylock is, correspondingly, as conservative and efficient with language as the Venetians are prodigal. His speech, as Sigurd Burckhardt argues in his pioneering article on the play, is for use,[8] and located in the world of commerce and action, the one world open to this foreigner in a Christian society. His first lines, like Antonio's in scene 1, characterize him immediately. In place of the latter's abstract "in sooth" (or truth), Shylock opens with the recitation of the sum, the "three thousand ducats," that Bassanio has just requested. Careful with language, he is also able to manipulate it. His "well" conveys satisfaction at Bassanio's specificity even as it anticipates, perhaps beyond Shylock's present consciousness, the sum's serving as prelude to that larger, but no less specific debt wherein money gives way to flesh. He also adds his own darker meaning to Bassanio's more neutral "bound." For Shylock, language is not an abstraction but something to be employed, a commodity, like food. Following his discussion of Antonio with Bassanio, it is revealing that he greets the former with: "Your worship was the last man in our mouths" (1.3.6).

Against the Venetians' airy dialogue, his always points below the surface so that even a cliché like "Fast bind, fast find" (2.5.54) can reveal a minority view rebelling against both the prodigality and affability of the Venetians, as well as a maniacal desire to ensnare Antonio, the surety for Bassanio's loan. Our ethical judgment for or, more likely, against Shylock is less an issue here, I think, than the fact that in him that rudderless, becalmed ship of Venice meets one of those "petty traffickers" whom Salerio has dismissed, fierce because he has been excluded, and calculating. From their perspective his cry "My daughter! O my ducats! O my daughter" (2.8.15) only confirms the judgment that Shylock's values, fiscal and filial, are misplaced. We might also take the same lines, their Marlovian source notwithstanding, as more symbolic than ethical: two valuable commodities have been stolen.[9] Likewise, his line "no tears but a' my shedding" (3.1.96) depicts at once his isolation and, in a more complex sense, the self-sufficiency (we recall that Shylock himself judges men according to whether or not they are "sufficient" [1.3.17, 26]) that is both his strength and his undoing.

If language and spectacle are, by definition, prerequisite, coequal values in the theater, then Shylock, this "new man"[10] advocating self-reliance wherein each man should get "as much as he deserves" (2.9.36), subordinates the verbal to the physical. His speech, albeit concrete, even skillful, is ultimately reductive. Nor can it serve as the expansive counterpart to stage spectacle. If Shylock's larger poetry exists, if there is a play that, seen from his perspective, would, like Iago's, prove superior to that in which the Ventians flourish, such poetry never makes it to the surface. Shylock would "stop [his] house's ears," and yet, taking "house" as the head, we in the audience cannot do so, cannot so close down language, if we wish the stage enactment to be more than "spectacle" in the most pejorative sense of that word. Even that mildly metaphoric "house" is reduced by Shylock to "casements" (2.5.34).

If there are faults on both sides,[11] Shylock's is one of deficiency. The linguistically excessive and hence prodigal Venetians, through Portia's tutelage at the trial and, in Bassanio's case, through her father's trial, can learn to recognize the claim of the physical—the Claim of the Real, as Shaw would have it. But with his reductive language Shylock requires new growth rather than pruning. Only on the surface can the famous "hath not a Jew hands" speech (3.1.59–73) be a plea for humanity.[12] Ultimately, it projects man in Shylock's own image; we are nothing but a mass of hands, organs, dimensions (that is, bodily proportions), senses, affections, passions—animals whose day is occupied with hunting and being hunted, feeding and sleeping.[13] Whatever the instigation for that speech, be it the persecution that Shylock has experienced or has invited at the hands of the Venetians, it does not end as it begins: the movement is downward from recoiling at an insult, to appealing for the common, but physical basis of Christian and Jew, to a fallacious justification of revenge: "The villainy you teach me, I will execute." Responsible to himself, in direct contrast to the Venetians, who presently flounder collectively in a shallow society, this self-reliant man ends by disclaiming responsibility: he is *their* creature. Within two scenes Shylock will change their curse into a fact: "Thou call'dst me a dog, before thou hadst a cause [a debatable point at best], / But since I am a dog, beware my fangs" (3.3.6–7).

ii

Linking the apparently separate worlds of the play—Christian and Jew, insider and outsider, the prodigal and the miser, Antonio and

Shylock—is money, here both a measure of individual effort and a bond for society, valuable at once in itself (or in the credit that stands behind it—the Fort Knox principle) and in terms of the valuation placed on it. Money is thus at once literal and symbolic,[14] and this duality is at one with the interdependence of language and spectacle in the theater.[15] Money is the play's reality, and this Shylock's presence underscores; but money is also a means to admit values beyond itself, beyond the economic as narrowly conceived. As Bassanio rejects the gold and silver caskets, he does not reject the value of the metals in themselves; rather, he speculates on them, and hence *with* them, to win Portia, whose value is even higher. Money is not the end—even Shylock affirms this when he chooses Antonio's death over repayment of the loan—but a means whose destination will be positive or negative as we construct it. "Thus ornament is but the guiled shore / To a most dangerous sea"; but on that shore, as Bassanio knows, can be either death or "an Indian Beauty" (3.2.97–99).

Too careful or too careless with money, with the play's own physical base, Shylock and the Venetians thus have complementary qualities; incomplete men when separated from each other—and perhaps this is the cause of Antonio's malaise until Bassanio introduces him to Shylock—they *belong* to each other.[16] In Shylock's words, "Well then, it now appears you need my help" (1.3.114).[17] It is significant that, whatever his deeper motives and whether or not he is conscious of them, Shylock meets the Christians here on the level of friendship since, in lending the ducats without interest, he treats them as his own religion instructs him to loan money to friends.[18] Indeed, when Antonio charges him to lend the ducats as he would to an enemy, Shylock takes the hint and acknowledges the "rightness" of Antonio's injunction against "breeding" barren metal.

In the Laban story Shylock's "skillful shepherd" becomes for Antonio an instrument "sway'd" by the hand of heaven (1.3.71–95). However, the latter's challenge to his opponent's example of Jacob's ingenuity can be right only if one accepts the premise of an all-powerful providence and then supports that premise by the principle that "growing" money through interest represents blasphemous creation.[19] For Shylock, Antonio's rebuttal is beside the point, and the negative answer implied in Antonio's rhetorical question, "Or is your gold and silver ewes and rams?", is answered positively, or rather metaphorically, by his adversary: "I make it breed as fast" (95–96). Antonio, in effect, brings external arguments to an example that for Shylock is self-contained, internal; a social world here collides with one purely individualistic. Moreover, Antonio's deduction from the argument, that the "devil can cite Scripture for his purpose" (98), is never answered by Shylock, who immediately returns to the issue of the three thousand ducats. And when

Antonio, perhaps saying the line sarcastically or condescendingly, abandons theological logic and enters the world of Shylock—"Well, Shylock, shall we be beholding to you?" (105)—he only sets up Shylock for a diatribe against the Christians' lack of charity, even as he fans his opponent's anger by promising to continue such treatment. In this way Antonio calls Shylock into being, even though his intentions of countering what he takes as a scriptural misreading may be well-intended. A disagreement over what Shylock takes as an ancestral example of thrift thereby becomes the means of bringing these incomplete men into conflict.[20] Antonio is theological, metaphorical, symbolic; Shylock, secular, literal, and symbolic only to the extent that he finds in the Laban story an exemplum of commendable thrift. As Antonio offers his flesh as surety for a friend's romantic quest, his ideal in which the concept of friendship outweighs his own physical safety is here, as we have seen, the stimulus for Shylock's own violation of his normal business practice, where his addiction to the physical takes precedence over any religious and social convictions. A pound of flesh now assumes, for both, a metaphoric value.

iii

That Portia's first scene separates Act 1, scene 1 and Act 1, scene 3 assures us that the Venetian/Shylock dialectic is not beyond resolution, and it is the movement toward Portia made by both Shylock and Antonio though Bassanio that rescues the play from groundless language or unredeemed spectacle.[21] This movement is, in a sense, existentially binding: to rescue his fallen estate, Bassanio needs capital from Antonio, who in turn needs an outlet for the expression of his friendship, be it challenged or not by Portia's presence; that outlet in turn "creates" the need for Shylock; that need then allows Shylock, though perhaps unconsciously at first, to revenge what is initially a general hatred and then, with Jessica's elopement, a specific cause of grievance against the Christians; Bassanio's freeing of Portia from her father's will also brings Portia into collision with Shylock; and that collision in its turn allows Portia through her sacrifice of money and sexual identity to confirm her love for Bassanio. Moreover, this same existential venture is also the playwright's, since the play, beginning with a misalliance between language and spectacle, also begs its own resolution.

Despite his verbalism, Bassanio's earlier metaphor of the arrows further suggests that the recouping of the past[22]—a lost arrow is found by shooting a present arrow to "recreate" that past—is at one with the play's, and the playwright's, own recouping of a past. That *past* embraces not only the earlier misalliance of the verbal and the visual, but the play's prehistory, implied in the opening scenes and breaking through, as we have seen, in the text and subtext: one of a drifting, purposeless, smug Venetian majority, and its scapegoat, Shylock, festering from what he perceives as former injustices.

Shylock's phrase "merry sport" thus plays between past and present, and between the radically different mentalities spanning those two designations of time. The past, both of the characters and the play, must be dealt with, even as Portia is bound by the living will of a dead father. It is the shallow Gratiano who suggests a cynical alternative to this concern with restoration or resolution with his appropriately nautical example: the "scarfed bark" sets out gaily from her native bay but returns with "over-weather'd ribs and ragged sails" (2.6.9–19). The play itself, however, will work in the opposite direction as the term *theater of presence* here both acknowledges the past and anticipates a future in which the necessary "half" that Shylock represents will be dealt with, even as it is refined and accommodated.

If the play has perhaps been subjected to some overly fine religious allegorizations, still there is a sense of movement here, I believe, from the Old to the New Testament, and I would observe that without the Old Testament the Bible is incomplete for Christian no less than for Jew.[23] If Shylock is in part an object of anti-Semitic satire—and there is commentary enough that this now seems an irreducible possibility—the Old Testament, the "Bible" of Judaism, itself is revered. It is fitting that Shylock's own invocations of the past are either shallow or self-serving. The "guess of [his] memory" (1.3.54) serves only as a ruse to convince Bassanio that the moneylender will have to borrow the sum from Tubal, and when he cites the historic persecution of his race it is in response to his daughter's absconding with two thousand ducats (3.1.85–86).

This movement, in which the old is accommodated in the new, or in the presence of the theater, is manifest in the characters' relation to the play's various fathers or father-figures.[24] Portia's father had "good inspirations" at his death (1.2.28), leaving her both a will setting forth the conditions of the lottery and the caskets themselves.[25] Jessica is also bound to her father but, as she argues, by blood and not by manners. The contrast, then, is between the verbal will of Portia's father, restrictive on the surface but ultimately liberating, and the physical will of Shylock, expressed most graphically in his attempts to shut Jessica within doors.

The Launcelot Gobbo scene (2.2) further enacts in comic fashion this infusion of the past into the present. Significantly, it follows upon Launcelot's break with Shylock, as he abandons a fiscal father only to encounter his natural one. Old Gobbo seeks his son, but initially through Shylock, and when the directions given by Launcelot "in disguise" prove too complex, the father asks directly for the son's residence. Announcing his own death, the son is metamorphosed from the Launcelot "that was" to the "son that is" and then, once father and son are reconciled, is reborn as the "child that shall be" (85–86). Past thus comes into present, and the present, as enriched by the past, leads in Launcelot's example to a more promising future. Some commentators have even suggested that Antonio is the father figure, the patron, that Bassanio himself must leave as he moves, like *Lear*'s Cordelia, from a "filial" to a marital union.[26] Thus, with the sexes reversed, Bassanio's liberation forms a parallel to Jessica's leaving Shylock for Lorenzo.[27]

iv

Shylock *uses* and Portia *is* gold, and *The Merchant of Venice* accommodates the former even as it moves toward the latter. This movement requires, therefore, a sense of "play"—transference, metamorphosis, conversion—with the physical, but not its denial.[28] While we may choose to view Jessica's throwing down moneybags to the courtiers as an unfilial theft,[29] it also represents play, as well as being the prelude to the masque or play, a transference from a home where money's value is only literal— where gold is gold is gold—to a new home in Belmont where gold can be a gift of love or friendship.

Thus there is usury—here defined as a multiplication of the literal or physical—and there is a venture to be equated with play or the theater generally, the investing of one's self through one's physical capital for a profit that is mutual rather than individual, inclusive rather than exclusive.[30] Bassanio "hazards" (1.1.151) himself no less than Antonio's wealth—we will recall the stiff penalties awaiting those suitors who fail— yet his goal is marriage, and one not simply for money, however much money may initially have been a factor. As a result, Bassanio himself is converted, *transformed*, in the venture. Neither Morocco nor Aragon is able to "hazard all he hath" (2.7.17); like Shylock, they expect a guaranteed return on the expenditure. Shylock's own seemingly interest-free loan to Antonio at once parodies this notion of venturing and, ironically because of his unaccustomed offer of friendship, violates the practice of usury itself.

Physical security, such as Shylock regressively craves, and the potentially disastrous mercantile and linguistic venturing that initially characterizes the Venetians coalesce into the image of the bond or contract, an agreement in which two parties are bound to each other for their individual and mutual profit. One gives and takes. One plays and is played with. In terms of time, a contract is a past agreement, qualified by present behavior, anticipating a future good.[31] The very language of the contract enhances the physical, fiscal transaction involved: as each party lives up to the terms of tendering and repayment, he justifies the literal or philosophic notion of contract and, by extension, the principle of society itself. The stage, in small, and the world, in large, equally represent such a transaction, a contractual trade-off between what is and how we value it.

The skill required for managing in these contractual worlds of the theater and society is, of course, linguistic, the ability to read with equity a text, both literal and figurative.[32] In the words of the legal scholars, one first needs to be able to grasp the "original intention" of the contractors: Nerissa reminds Portia that the suitor "who chooses [her father's] meaning chooses you" (1.2.30–31). Language is here an instrument to extract or excavate essence, but not its equivalent: the word is not the thing. Gratiano, predictably, is dismissed as "too wild, too rude, and bold of voice" (2.2.181); his presence, if unqualified or unmoderated, would cause the suitor Bassanio to "be misconst'red" and thereby to lose his hopes (2.2.187–88). Words become a way of playing to free up essence; language is ongoing, not static. Hence, as we have seen, Morocco and, to a lesser degree, Aragon fail precisely because they work from fixed positions—as Shylock will do later—however clear their logic. Portia's reference to her own "living will," or desires, being controlled by a dead father also admits with the word *living* that the will itself, like the notion of contract advanced earlier, is ongoing, subject to the combined "readings" of father, daughter, and suitor. Jessica, in contrast, can only use *will* in its restrictive patriarchal sense when referring to her father (2.5.10).

Language and a contract constructed of language are by definition social acts, a mutual recognition between speaker and listener, actor and audience. As Launcelot Gobbo and his father move from a fictive separation by a falsely reported death to a union, Bassanio conflates their separate attempts to enter his service with the command that "one speak for both" (2.2.141). At his moment of choosing the correct casket, Bassanio defines his emotional pleasure as a "confusion" or union such as occurs when, after "some oration fairly spoke / By a beloved prince," the audience, brought together by his words, abandons its sense of being individual members and is "blent together," their separate speeches or responses losing their autonomy ("every something") and being converted to "a wild nothing, save of joy," a moment when all possible contingencies are included, "express'd and not express'd" (3.2.175–83).

Portia best understands the elevating power of this contractual—or social or, for present purposes, theatrical—language when she speaks of the suitors' "hazard[ing] for [her] worthless self" (2.9.18). In herself she, like the money of the play, is nothing, inert; it is Bassanio's interaction with her that confers worth. Her own expression for such interaction is appropriately based on a visual metaphor: his eyes have "o'erlook'd" and "divided" her (3.2.14–15), and by this curious human "mathematics" have multiplied her worthlessness. In what is at once a parallel and a contrast to the settlement or contract *forced* on Shylock at the trial, Portia freely gives "one half" of herself to Bassanio and then offers the "other half" (16), and if she refers immediately to her lover in the phrase "owners and their rights" (19), the same phrase is self-reflexive: Portia's right is to be "owned" by Bassanio since such mutual possession alone produces value. The object, Portia or the lead casket, has value precisely because it has lost the appearance of value through transference to its interior; it is therefore the casket's "paleness" that "moves [Bassanio] more than eloquence" (106). We sacrifice all to win all: here is venture capital in the extreme. Rejecting the principle of chance, merit, or social parity advanced by the two unsuccessful suitors, Portia announces her life-conferring position: "I stand for sacrifice" (57).

We have only the ongoing social or mutual process of valuation, not value absolute; the way in which each suitor reads the text outside the three caskets "determines" the content: there are, in a trinitarian sense, three caskets parading as one. Of inherent worth, her essence contained within the casket of her own body, Portia demands a language of proper choosing and hence proper linguistic valorization.[33] Not denied, the physical is thus enhanced, and the lead casket announces a death of the physical as understood reductively or idiosyncratically by Shylock, or his surrogates,[34] as well as its potential reevaluation or rebirth through language.[35] In that rebirth spectacle meets language on an equal footing.[36] As Bassanio moves toward his choice, he is at once linked with the past as a bankrupt turned fortune-hunter and elevated beyond it. He thereby encounters Portia "with no less presence [that is, nobility of physical appearance], but with much more love" than Hercules, whose motive in saving Hesione was fiscal, not romantic (3.2.54–57). To win Portia one must sacrifice oneself: suitors who lose must abjure their flesh through celibacy, while Bassanio's loss would involve the sacrifice of Antonio's flesh as well. But Portia is also the flesh-and-blood woman of his desires.

Once he chooses rightly, Bassanio finds that words themselves are sacrificed: when he most has need to speak he is "bereft" of words (3.2.175). However skillful she will prove with language, Portia for the time sees herself as a "maiden [who] hath no tongue but thought" (3.2.8). To read Portia's text rightly one travels beyond words to that moment when essence assumes form. The couple now epitomizing Love generates its (or their) mirror image in Gratiano and Nerissa; the latter's "fortune" was dependent upon that of Portia and Bassanio (3.2.196–208).[37]

v

Portia thus requires a sense of play, with both language and spectacle, in which process takes precedence over conclusion, fluidity over consistency, hazard over fixity. Indeed, she not only requires play but represents its essence, and is, equally, both an artist, or player, and the subject of the artist.[38]

Her portrait within the lead casket, like the statue of Hermione in *The Winter's Tale*, represents an art playing so seriously and convincingly with life that it at once aggravates and resolves the Renaissance debate between Art and Nature (3.2.115–48). As Bassanio observes, the artist is like *The Winter's Tale*'s Julio Romano, a "demigod" who in the excellence of his "counterfeit" rivals natural creation itself. His drawing at once prefigures nature and points to the essence behind the physical likeness: counterfeit eyes that, observed by the viewer's own eyes, seem to move when their image is reflected on the retina ("riding on the balls of mine"); lips parted with a sweet breath that reminds Bassanio of partings between friends; and hairs that spiderlike would entrap a man's heart. Even Bassanio's eloquent praise of the artist falls short of this creation or "shadow," and, in parallel fashion, the portrait itself, like his praise, falls short of Portia herself, the "substance." Visual art overwhelms words, and is itself overwhelmed by Portia; and once Bassanio adds the portrait's text to his own response, these combined texts lead, indeed encourage him to kiss the real Portia.[39]

Appropriately, as he embraces Portia, Bassanio imagines himself as an actor, hearing applause, assuming it is for him, though not fully certain of the fact. An actor fairly convinced he has performed well, he still needs the ratification of an audience: "As doubtful whether what I see be true, / Until confirm'd, sign'd, ratified by you" (147–48). The verbs here are at once legal, economic, and theatrical. Gratiano and Nerissa, who "have stood by and seen" (187), fill out this audience. The movement from Shylock's unenhanced physical world, to an art balancing the visual and the verbal, to its product in the union of the play's romantic couple then comes full circle, and theatrically so: for Gratiano at once asserts the physical in its most literal sense, signals the theater's own self-reflexive dimension and parodies Shylock's nonmerry "merry sport" as he promises to "play with them, the first boy for a thousand ducats" (214).

Once chosen, once liberated from her father's will, and, in a larger sense, now surrounded by a play world in which the visual and verbal, actual and symbolic, exist in a productive relationship, now Portia is herself free to play.[40] The boy actor, so far playing a woman, will now play a woman playing a male. The men of the play, whose weariness and prodigality had set the tone and who find in Shylock both an extension of their own mercantile selves and an opponent whose literalism threatens to prove fatal, will now be subjected to Portia's play and, equally so, will be impersonated, *played with*, by her. Her disguise and that of Nerissa will, like the art of the portrait painter, prove such an effective imitation that "they shall think we are accomplished / With what we lack" (3.4.61–62). The reference is at once sexual and theatrical; the illusion of masculinity at once parodies the males' sexuality, celebrates the art of illusion, and confirms the literal basis of play: in playing a boy, the actor playing Portia, as well as that actor playing Nerissa, only confirms his offstage reality. Portia even offers a director's advice to herself: to impersonate a man one must carry a dagger "with the braver grace," modulate the voice between that of a boy and a man, change "two mincing steps / Into a manly stride," and, in general, imitate "these bragging Jacks" (65–78). If the "device" (81) represents a theater so self-reflexive that it follows a parabolic curse to the literal fact behind the production (a boy does play Portia; Portia is in reality a male actor), it also puts in perspective the status of men in the play, ranging from Antonio or Bassanio through Gratiano and Salerio-Solanio to Shylock. Without Portia, theirs is ultimately a world of conflict ("frays") inhabited by creatures given to "puny lies." Not the full truth, to be sure, but an assessment of a human condition that, without Portia's infusion of play into the dialectical mercantile world of Venice, has something of the truth about it.

vi

The play's two "trials" are both the sequential "products" of this movement or realliance I have been charting, as well as its enactment.[41] Having served its purpose, Shylock's physicality, formerly a counterbalance to the Venetian's prodigal language, is now blatant and unrelieved. If he was at worst an incomplete man before, now he is "an inhuman wretch" (4.1.4), bordering on the bestial, a "currish spirit" that in some former life was "govern'd by a wolf" (133–34). Shylock's rigidity now caves in on itself for in pressing for his "right" to Antonio's flesh he absurdly outweighs a counteroffer of 36,000 ducats (85–87).[42] In a grim parody of the notion of inherent worth, that symbolic valuing of what is initially only literal, Shylock has elevated what he calls his just "penalty" (322) to a mythic status. Opposing the notion of play or relativity, he is now the symbol of rigidity as he "stand[s]" (103) for judgment, even threatening to convert those who "stand within" his "danger" (180) into his own image. The character is literally going out of the play and is also figuratively out of play. His exit may remind us of Goneril or even Iago, characters whose acknowledged potency is at length dissolved by that renaissance, however qualified, of the very people whom they have victimized. He is suddenly "not well" (396), and his last request is both literal and theatrical: "give me leave to go from hence" (395).

If his language has earlier been reductive, it now moves against itself and toward silence. No word can "rail the seal from off [his] bond" (139), nor can he be altered by any "power in the tongue of man" (241–42). Like Iago, whose last words are the petulant "what you know, you know: / From this time forth I never will speak word" (5.2.303–4), Shylock, whose physical universe has already been defeated, now threatens speech itself: his "I'll not answer that" (42) assaults the very principle of stage dialogue, let alone human discourse. His subtextual psychology and motivation now curiously surface, though in so cryptic a form that the words themselves, while welcomed, seem beyond reasonable explication: we learn only that his hate is "lodg'd" (60)[43] and that he justifies the claim to the pound of flesh by the single word *mine* (100).[44] If for the audience this increasingly nonverbal man is compelling, even appealing, his attraction, I think, is created in part by the absurd power of a self-consumed and self-consuming character; there is a sort of amoral brilliance expanded in his energy.[45] Nor will the more understandable but incomplete earlier character fade from our memories.

Clearly, Portia is the ultimate actor and hence provides a commentary on what Shylock "represents" here, for to defeat him, even to transform him, she must "play" him, *be* him.[46] As she takes his literal language to its logical, absurd extreme, even as she herself represents a contrastive mercy or equity, in playing Shylock she recognizes the literal, the physical, the nonsymbolic, what Shylock himself calls sufficiency or judgment, not as an antithesis to mercy or equity but as a complement, part of a larger response prerequisite to navigating successfully in the world. She is both the Old and New Testament, the means between Shylock and Antonio: Bellario in his letter observes that "Balthazar" is "old" in head and "young" in body (163–64). By this playing, through which an outsider assumes the role of another outsider, she thus can "mitigate" (203) this play of contraries and "deliver" it from its earlier misalliance. Since no "power in Venice / Can alter a decree established" (218–19), her power is, if not divine, at least theatrical, a power not fully bound by reality as narrowly understood.

As a conscious player, she can read Shylock's seemingly legal/literal text in a way that he cannot, not only in extrapolating on its apparent clarity (the specific pound of flesh) but in adding to it by invoking the law punishing a foreigner for conspiring against the life of a Venetian, and thereby showing that death would be the contract's logical conclusion.[47] Her performance, besides, is generative: one member of the onstage audience, Antonio, brings a sense of charity and equity[48] in viewing Shylock's situation that we have not before observed in him.

Nor do her theatrics stop with Shylock as, still in disguise, she continues to play both the lawyer to whom Bassanio proffers his ring (or *her* ring, rather) and a stand-in for herself when she ironically justifies a wife's claim to that same ring: Bassanio's wife, she speculates, surely knows "how well I [that is, the real Portia from our perspective, and from Bassanio's if he were more sentient] have deserv'd this ring" (446).[49] The short scene (4.2) concluding the act demonstrates that the ring, a literal and figurative bond, like Shylock's own earlier merry sport, has not yet been fully realized, not fully enacted as a symbol of the larger human contract advocated by the play. Metadramatically, it is the bond between the present trial and its mellowed sequel in the final act.[50]

vii

Many commentators have suggested that the society depicted in the final act is not a perfect one, that it is fragile.[51] Thus Lorenzo's proof of music's power over beasts—"If they but hear perchance a trumpet sound, / Or any air of music touch their ears, / You shall perceive them make a mutual stand, / Their savage eyes turn'd to a modest gaze" (5.1.75)—may comment on Belmont no less than Venice: man is eternally capable of savagery no less than of responding to the divine. And if the phrase *mutual stand* is an equivalent of the social contract, it also implies its opposite: Shylock's asocial, potentially destructive isolation that is also a constant in human affairs.[52] The lovers enumerated in Lorenzo's list, as many have observed, bring tragic stories with them, of betrayal and death, at the very least of having to choose between conflicting priorities. As the final scene begins, the business of the rings is left to be resolved, even as Shylock rankles in our memories.[53]

However, as mistress of Belmont, Portia calls not for escapism, nor for an unqualified ideal to overshadow what Shylock represents, but rather for a sense of proportion, of the interdependence of all things, a balance between individual accomplishment and that larger accomplishment possible only in society. In the 1960s this stance would perhaps have been labeled "situational ethics." Portia's "crow" and "lark" (102)—whatever our estimate of their respective worths—are both constituent parts of society: Shylock must be a factor in our human equation no less than the preferred Bassanio (102–10). Night and day, darkness and light, even tragedy and comedy, if you will, are, when separated, unrealistic extremes: "This night methinks is but the daylight sick, / It looks a little paler, 'Tis a day, / Such as the day is when the sun is hid" (124–26).[54] The labor of mastering Shylock coexists with the happy accident by which Antonio's ships, presumed sunk, are restored.[55] In terms of the theater, reality and illusion are themselves absorbed into a larger context, just as the theater itself is "real" in its spectacle but complements that physical basis by its illusory language.[56] In a parallel equation, the pleasant theatrics of the scene are for the onstage characters also pleasant realities. The adulteries that shock the newlywed husbands turn out to be fictions, while the threats to sleep with the lawyer and his clerk are realized, to the satisfaction of all onstage. The sense of play earlier, that serious tool with which Shylock has been handled, invokes here its opposite: pleasant play, both verbal and physical. The otherwise serious Bassanio, who had missed the masque, now joins this playing with theatrics and flexible language when he promises to make the "sweet doctor" his "bedfellow," even as he agrees that the doctor can lie with his wife during his absences (284–85). If Antonio seems a marginal character here, he can also now escape his weariness, perhaps even his fascination with the death wish, and rejoin the world of "life and living" (286).

The silence promised by Shylock in the earlier trial is counterbalanced by music, so often in Shakespeare the cosmic extension of speech (83).[57] The lover Lorenzo, in charge of Portia's estate, is also the one responsible for bringing the musicians onstage (53), and it is Jessica, the main escapee from Shylock's world, who takes their music so seriously ("I am never merry when I hear sweet music" [69]) that even those commentators who accuse her of filial ingratitude or, at the least, of shallowness or materialism (in daring to buy a monkey with the money from the sale of her mother's ring) must either admit a deeper dimension to her (perhaps fostered by her introduction to Portia) or claim that Shakespeare has altered her character in this final scene.

Still, despite such restorative music, the scene is realistic, not pastoral. If the act is pervaded by an increased music, both instrumental, social, and linguistic, Lorenzo reminds Jessica that our brief glimpse of the heavens, or of the divine in man, is more often blocked by our own bestial nature, by our flesh, "this muddy vesture of decay / [That] Doth close it in [so that] we cannot hear [or see] it" (64–65).[58]

The women here—Portia, Nerissa, and, under Portia's influence, Jessica—hold the upper hand, not only in the playful illusion they cast over the men but also in their affinity with enhanced speech and vision. Mercantile masters give way to the domestic "mistress of the house" (38), the prodigal or, alternatively, reductive language of the men to music and to Portia's nonverbal, yet gracious hosting that, as she modestly admits, "must appear in other ways than words" (140). The competitive masculine language earlier in the play is dissolved in Lorenzo's description of this second night "when the sweet wind did gently kiss the trees, /

And they did make no noise" (2–3). Antonio, whose petulant, groundless poetry opens the play, admits in the presence of his good fortune, as miraculously announced by Portia, that he is now "dumb" (279).[59]

Equally so, the physical is now redeemed. Antonio offers his body a second time (249–53), yet now as surety that his friend Bassanio has not broken his marriage vows, or, rather, "will never more break faith advisedly" (251–53). His offer here is as realistic as it was unrealistic earlier: he only promises that if Bassanio commits an error, it will be a sin of omission rather than of commission. Such realism also admits its playful alternative, as Antonio, parodying his earlier self, is in turn parodied by Nerissa: Portia promises not to deny her body to the lawyer (227–28), while Nerissa offers Gratiano her body "without a fee" (290).

This comic play, bringing into a meaningful relation the play's previously unbalanced physical and verbal dimensions, admits a sense of balance, and of mutuality. The romantic poetry, for example, is met by the earthiness of the final lines, as sexual union becomes the final topic: will there be time for love with dawn about to break? The issue of bond or contract, earlier a tragic issue, is now expressed by a metaphor built on ocular interdependence: Bassanio swears his fidelity and good intentions by Portia's "fair eyes, / Wherein [he] sees [himself]" (242–43).

The ring itself is emblematic of the new visual and verbal geography of the play.[60] It binds the past to that present as informed by Shakespeare's theater of presence. Still under the illusion that Balthazar was a male, Bassanio charts its literal history, or rather the history of its loss as he interprets it: "If you did know to whom I gave the ring, / If you did know for whom I gave the ring, / And would conceive for what I gave the ring, / And how unwillingly I left the ring" (193–96). His flawed history, fortunately, is countered by Portia's sense of the ring's true historical significance, as the bond between a husband and wife who, by her own decision, were to remain separate until Shylock and what he represents were put into perspective: "If you had known the virtue of the ring, / Or half her worthiness that gave the ring, / Or your own honor to contain the ring" (199–210). A physical object, the ring literally surrounds the flesh, encircles it, adorns it, even as it bears symbolic meaning, its essence embodied in the language of the marriage vow and, as Portia pointedly reminds Bassanio, in the actual dialogue with which she bestowed the ring. Like the theater itself, like Shakespeare's own "little O" or Globe stage, it is a visual object valorized by language, a contract between bestower and wearer, like that contract that exists between actor and audience. In being an object whose meaning is assured by a dual or mutual investment, it is like the legal contract whose potency is dependent on the good will and respective behavior of the parties involved. Thus the ring, like a contract, like the theater, is a way of providing order, roles, and therefore meaning in a world whose components can all too easily be misaligned. Language and spectacle, offstage and on, are here the coequal partners of existence, onstage and off.

If the play ends with Gratiano's bawdy promise to keep "safe Nerissa's ring," that anticipated physical consummation will occur within the context of marriage, and is thereby granted a meaning through language and its extension in the imagination. Marital union is now at one with the theater's own union of language and spectacle. In turn, these thematic and theatrical resolutions only mirror how members of the audience, in both their private and public lives, must navigate between the necessary, inevitable physical world and a meaningful existence that is created and defined by language. Portia seeks what we ourselves seek, and though her resolution occurs within the confines of the stage, it is an equivalent, nevertheless, for what we desire. In *King Lear*, I believe, what occurs onstage is even less confined, even as the tragedy's paradoxically open-ended resolution suggests at once the limitations and the achievement of Shakespeare's theater.

9

King Lear:
"I would not take this from report; it is"

MAYNARD Mack implies the metaphor of the play's being an individual when he speaks of *King Lear* as "inexhaustibly patient of the images of ourselves we thrust upon it."[1] If we take the history of its commentary as, no less, a personified being, that "patience" has been rewarded, for the same catholicity, the sense of its inclusiveness that led Dr. Johnson and Charles Lamb to find *Lear* unsuitable for the limited stage, and that earlier led Nahum Tate to redo the play so that it would be actable, has now found its match in a plurality of critical responses. Those responses, especially in more recent times, suggest that we too, though in our own way, find *Lear* both challenging and challenged by life itself.

Even as they superseded the eighteenth-century argument that *Lear* was too great, the suffering of its central figure too painful for the theater, the antithetical positions of A. C. Bradley and, in our day, Jan Kott have themselves been superseded.[2] Though we sometimes forget his own reservations about pronouncing Lear's death an ecstasy of joy, Bradley's "optimistic" reading has been absorbed, indeed taken to less qualified readings by Christian and, more generally, mystical readings. Cordelia's presence is said to be "visionary," a sign of there being "something more" to her character than is "explained by the explicit contents of the play."[3] Her silence reveals a divine origin,[4] and though Cordelia is explicitly a pagan, through her Lear, and perhaps the audience, can penetrate mysteries without revelation.[5] If she is initially a secular being, she grows through her trial into the embodiment of "mysteries,"[6] and Lear, in his purgatorial growth toward her, is at length rendered as unfit for the secular world as he is fit for the sacred.[7] No less, Jan Kott's absurdist view, where *Lear* becomes a "gigantic pantomime" in the tradition of Beckett's *Endgame*, the "pessimistic" counterpart, in effect, to Bradley, has itself been expanded. In Lear's failure during the closing moments, his inability to comprehend both the facts of Cordelia's death and a vision that would ratify such facts,[8] the audience, identifying with the father, also experiences what it is like to be nothing,[9] to inhabit a world reduced to zero.[10] The play catapults us at once toward the "nothing whence we spring and the infinity in which we are swallowed up."[11] *Lear*'s greatness lies precisely in its negation,[12] its annihilation of what Shaw would call that Vital Lie by which our existence is otherwise made bearable. Kott's view is itself part of a tradition: years ago Levin Schücking found that play working out the process of dissolution to the last stage.[13]

These very extremes have in turn been united. Lear must descend "into the original chaos of Nature out of which the order of justice in society, as well as the order of the human mind itself, must be formed and reformed."[14] In his *Tragic Meanings in Shakespeare,* Thomas McFarland finds the play embodying both "Reduction" and "Renewal": once the play has acknowledged the absurdity of the whole realm of human values, the basis is laid for a return of love and human concern.[15] Such inclusive readings, accommodating both Bradley and Kott, lead inevitably to a position holding that the play's "insistent inclusiveness"[16] resists the type of criticism that works with other plays, including Shakespeare's own tragedies.[17] Our attempts to "anatomize" it can only fragment a catholic work;[18] and the failure of our critical tools has itself been anticipated by Shakespeare who, within the play, mocks any similar attempt to order its universe.[19] Only by resisting our own mania for order can we respond to this work presenting "a set of perceptions of demarcated aspects of existential complexity."[20]

Growing, as it does in my reconstruction of the play's critical history, from the extremes to which the optimistic and pessimistic readings have been taken, this thematic catholicity finds a parallel in arguments for *Lear*'s theatrical inclusiveness. In a well-received article, Katherine Stockholder examines the play's "Multiple Genres,"[21] and suggests that such multiplicity establishes a pattern that, in the words of another critic equally concerned with the work's theatrical inclusiveness, overturns "all conventions, justice, expectations and hopes" we bring to it. This vertigo produced by its plurality of forms, or by the play's resistance to a single form that would order its world, only takes "us down and down and down."[22] Wylie Sypher can thus ask, "how much background noise can a work of art tolerate or accommodate?"[23] For Eliseo Vivas the answer is affirmative: *Lear* represents "unmitigated tragedy."[24] Or, as John Danby has argued, tragedy, as practiced in *Lear*, is always whole, always inclusive, rather than being merely "a view of life."[25]

This thematic and theatrical breadth is no longer seen as the inevitable product of Shakespeare's rustic genius or—to put it negatively—his inability to rein in his vision. Rather, in overturning every expectation we bring to the play,[26] in offering us this uneasy coexistence of the comic and the tragic,[27] Shakespeare consciously and magnificently offers a play "stretched to the limits of tonal capacity,"[28] or one pushed beyond its own identity.[29] Such arguments, curiously, take a parabolic curve and return to the earlier strictures against the play's fitness for the stage. The inadequate stage itself stands as symbol for the limitations of man and his reason. Our uncertainty about Lear's status at the end—is he a visionary or only deluded?—stems from the fact that "in a flash of intuition" beyond theatrical representation Lear may, or may not, "pierce with a mystic certainty the limits of life's stage to find a cruel or gentle author" who might make sense of a world that our limited vision only obscures, or that we see darkly through the theater's own magic.[30] The "pictorial simplifications" of the subplot establish it as a conventional theater pointing by its exclusiveness to the unconventional theater of the main plot.[31] It is that main plot, as Margaret Webster explains, that is unstageable, at least in part.[32]

This concern with the play's inclusiveness and the corresponding arguments about the limitations of its artifice lead inevitably to speculations that the play struggles to make its way out of the theater and into the real life, to the reality offstage. D. G. James anticipates this possibility in *The Dream of Learning* when he conjectures that if *Lear* is a great play, perhaps the greatest of plays, then it must be because "Shakespeare . . . show[s] things more as they really are than all other modern writers."[33] Can a play, can *Lear*, be closer to the nature it mirrors than that art which is its genus? The possibility that *Lear* breaks the confines of the stage and rejoins the life offstage has been expressed in a variety of ways. Paul Alpers, for example, cautions against seeing its references to eyes, sight, and blinding as metaphors for insight. Rather, when its onstage characters see or fail to see each other we have an equivalent to that same social contact in real life initiated by the eyes. For Alpers, the play presents "experience" itself that is "ordinary, physical, down to earth," and there is, correspondingly, nothing "cosmic," let alone symbolic about its direct action.[34] This reaction to mystical and nihilistic readings expresses itself in arguments that the play is neutral, "untheatrical," and therefore concerned with humanity itself in all its sublime and terrible dimensions.[35] Actuality is "as incredible as anything the theater presents," and *Lear* is "the ultimate embodiment of incredibility, and therefore the most exacting image of life itself."[36] Lawrence Raab finds the play treating "life for life's sake," even while recognizing that such a concern must be filtered through the artifice of the theater.[37] Even a metadramatic critic like Robert Egan holds that it is to life itself, offstage, that the play's artifice is sacrificed, found inferior: "art can in no way alter the primal conditions of existence" and this is the play's final position.[38] In his *An*

Essay on "King Lear" S. L. Goldberg claims that amidst the limitations of the otherwise closed world of the theater "life keeps breaking in": the "reality we experience remains, as it must, open."[39]

Though she has comparatively few lines in the play, and is absent (or, alternatively, represented by the Fool) from the vast middle section of the play, Cordelia is often identified as this life force, as the earth mother,[40] at once threatened by Lear's theater of rhetoric in the opening scene even as she exists beyond the artifice of the play itself. Joyce Carol Oates sees Cordelia as Nature itself which, "given the freedom to act spontaneously," would upset the play's own "ritual" as she rises "in rebellion against masculine authority." Beyond the confines of artifice, indeed opposed to that artifice embodied in the male characters, Cordelia, by definition, must be murdered in *and* by the play.[41] Lear himself has been linked with this life force, bearing the "gift . . . of the colossal power of life itself." It is to this energy that Edgar (or Albany) pays tribute in the closing lines: "we that are young / Shall never see so much, nor live so long" (5.3.326–27).[42]

Other commentators take one step farther this notion that the play struggles to embody a life or nature incompatible with the limitations of the stage. At its end, the play "renounces its own meditations of morality and madness alike" and points to—though it can only point to—a "reality that exists prior to and remains unavailable to both."[43] Here "the ostensible inadequacy of art makes us feel even more directly the unspeakable experience before us."[44] John Reibetanz, examining the play within the context of the theatrical conventions of Shakespeare's day, finds that "*King Lear* directs us to a realm of meaning that exists outside" the tragedy.[45]

Such commentary, pointing to an extradramatic origin or destination, founded on what John Lawlor would call "the pathos" or inadequacy of illusion,[46] has itself taken that parabolic curve: if the play struggles but fails to embody reality—as perforce it must—then we are forced to return to *Lear* itself, to experience "what happens" within the play, without overt attempts to find symbols or establish significances. It is argued that at issue, indeed the only issue, is what I have called "presence." What happens is what counts;[47] the "dramatic experience" itself supersedes the play's own "aphoristic formulations" that serve only to "support" that experience.[48] Even the metadramatic critics, often condemned for too much emphasis on the workings of Shakespeare's art, speak of nature or life as here being superior to art. Life itself, as embodied in the play, "frustrates the instinctive desire for order in experience."[49] Shakespeare's method here of straining the art of poetic drama, of demonstrating the limitations of his medium, is thus the "key" to the play's power.[50]

When we take this commentary, now almost three centuries old, as a personified "text" that with time has at last duplicated the dazzling, perhaps even humbling or terrifying breadth of the play, and then juxtapose it with the trinity of concerns in the present study—language, spectacle, and theatrical presence—a number of questions emerge, especially in light of my own critical method, which stresses the reciprocity between the onstage illusions and that offstage audience both present for Shakespeare's theater of presence and matching the play's verbal and visual dimensions with its own ears and eyes. Given the direction of its critical history, and defining that history as a reconstruction of the play once its stage life is over, how inclusive can *Lear* be and still remain art? Can Aristotle's fear and pity operate if a work proclaims its own inadequacy in the face of life? Clearly, *Lear* finds no kin in the tightly constructed classical French comedy, nor in that narrowly fatalistic world of Senecan tragedy. But to what degree is it exclusive? Or, to rephrase the question, to what degree *must* it be exclusive? The inevitable gap between the audience's actual ears and eyes and the verbal and visual metaphors within the play's world depends on some degree of exclusivity in the drama. Nor, when we speak of a theater of presence, do we mean that Lear or Cordelia is actually present. At its root, that presence is linked with time only: the actor conveying Lear's struggle toward Cordelia, albeit a fiction, occupies the same time-frame that it takes the audience to view the onstage action. The theater's own self-commentary serves to "disillusion" us from any leap of faith in its actuality.[51] In the eight plays so far considered the language and spectacle of the stage are only analogous to real-life language and spectacle. That analogy or metaphor is the very strength of a play, aided as it is in being performed by live actors before a live audience. Through the metaphor of vision and speech we can be at once engaged and disengaged with the dramatic enactment. However, if the play struggles to approach experience itself, then distinctions between experience proper and the metaphoric phrase *dramatic experience* are collapsed. We choose, I would assume, life over art, but without art that life remains unexamined because unperceived.

With such questions, I propose now to examine the status of language, spectacle, and, by extension, the theater in *Lear*. Upon that examination, I want to consider the play's "fictive" life, or life force, in terms of that presence or real life which, as Hamlet tells us, the theater is designed to mirror—but, as his own metaphor implies, cannot duplicate.

ii

If Lear *is* the history of its critical reception in a way that surpasses any other of Shakespeare's plays, it is no less true that, like *Julius Caesar*, it is pervaded by efforts among the characters themselves to interpret its world.[52] The play opens on this very note. Kent submits for Gloucester's assessment an opinion that Lear has preferred Albany to Cornwall; Gloucester, who earlier would have agreed with Kent, now finds Lear more impartial. Indeed, it is presently uncertain whether Lear, as understood by Kent as well as Gloucester, has changed his position, or whether it is the inherent and equal worth of the two subjects that has forced the change. In the complex, interpretive language of the play, the only thing certain is that now "curiosity in neither can make choice of either's moi'ty" (1.1.1–7).

Visual interpretations follow on the heels of this exchange as Edmund, though not yet so identified for us, completes the trinity of onstage characters. To the clear-sighted Kent's question, "Is this your son, my lord?", Gloucester responds with what is more like interpretation than fact: Edmund is indeed his son, but not his son in the legal sense. Gloucester's embarrassed, convoluted language—"His breeding, sir, hath been at my charge" (8–9)—is beyond Kent, who now cannot "conceive" him. Then follows Gloucester's wretched, cruel (if Edmund hears the entire conversation) pun on *conceive*. That pun, of course, clarifies everything for Kent, and yet Gloucester's flippant explanation of Edmund's status as his "son" will itself be reinterpreted tragically when, near the end of the play, Edgar, whom Gloucester himself has "misinterpreted" for Edmund, pronounces the judgment: "The dark and vicious place where thee he got / Cost him his eyes" (5.3.173–74).

This shifting visual and verbal base, by definition making interpretation difficult, expands to the entire first scene in the form of Lear's own eagerness to impose his own "play" of interpretation upon the daughters: he believes they love him, is ready to reward such love with the division of his kingdom, but first wants data, verbal professions of love, to assure him that he acts rightly.[53] He is, as we know, at once deceived and self-deceived by their language or, in Cordelia's case, by her paucity of language. As we ourselves try to interpret his actions, Lear's phrase "our darker purpose" (36) can only explode with meanings. His "trial" of the daughters may, below the surface, be a self-trial, perhaps unconsciously so. Denying the pathological need for affection that he may only semi-consciously sense, he sets himself up here for failure, already "knowing," though not to his rational mind, that only the daughter he loves best will speak truthfully, even though her present response appears curt and unloving.[54] If we take "Lear" as the play itself, then this darker purpose thus anticipates the chaos that waits beyond the opening scene, where Lear's demand for verbal assurance of his daughters' affection is quite normal, and Goneril's and Regan's responses disclose, at most, daughters of materialistic, but not yet demonic mentalities.

Single interpretations, however, are soon gone with the wind in this play. One moment Cordelia is Lear's "joy," the next a pariah, and France must wonder how Lear can so suddenly and, to his mind, irrationally "dismantle" (1.1.217) what has clearly been a long-standing "view" of Cordelia. Conversely, Lear's perverse interpretation of Cordelia's "nothing" and the subsequent loss of her dowry only serve to allow the suitor to interpret her paradoxically, yet rightly: she is "most rich being poor" (250). He thus comes to a conclusion about her present state quite opposed to that of the now-unwilling suitor Burgundy.

The second scene, involving Gloucester and Edmund, grounds this theme of interpretation in a more emphatic manner. No less obsessed with the desire to resolve ambiguities (he "would unstate [himself] to be in a due resolution" as to Edgar's alleged villainy [1.2.99–100]), Gloucester, like his progenitor Lear, misreads the "nothing" (1.2.31) of Edmund's feigned letter as something. Edmund is curiously, though maliciously truthful when he replies to Gloucester's demand for both verbal and visual evidence of Edgar's villainy ("Found you no displeasure in him by word nor countenance?") with "None at all" (1.2.156–58). The absurdity of seeking the truth through such superficial verbal and visual data comes home late in the play when a blind Gloucester will confess, in response to Lear's order that he "mark" or see the "penning" of his challenge, that "were all thy letters suns, [he] could not see" (4.6.138–40).

The fact is that in this play all constructions of reality are relative and, further, can be overturned by conflicting, more powerful constructions. Goneril's and Regan's reading of their father, though not without some truth, at least early in the play, will prevail over Lear's reading of himself precisely because he has relinquished power to them. Hence Goneril "stages" her own play counter to Lear's when she instructs Oswald and his "fellows" to put on a "weary negligence" when he arrives (1.3.12–13).

Even as the field of critical interpretation has broadened in our time so that we now see Lear and his play as a lifelike morass of competing scenarios rather than as a simplistic fairy tale or a basic lesson in conduct for fathers and children,[55] so Lear later in the play will move toward a more open-ended, neutral, less prescriptive questioning of his world. The rhetorical questions of the first scene with their preselected answers ("Which of you shall we say doth love us most" [1.1.51]) will be refined to less prescriptive and, correspondingly, more profound questions, whose object is not the questioner himself but mankind generally: "what art thou?" (1.4.9); "Dost thou know me, fellow?" (926); the even more catholic "Is man no more than this?" (3.4.102–3); and the most basic of all questions that we all ask when confronted with the inexplicable tragedy of death, "Why should a dog, a horse, a rat, have life, / And thou no breath at all?" (5.3.307–8).

iii

Words, both as spoken and as received, will not hold place here.[56] The problem, of course, is sounded early with Cordelia's "nothing." In a way, she obstructs Shakespeare's or, more properly, Lear's verbal and visual theater. Taken to an extreme, her problem with speaking—how can she express a love "more ponderous than [her] tongue" (1.1.77–88) and, if she could speak, what would be the fate of such words in the linguistically corrupt air of her sisters?—would convert the play into a speechless mime. In the insincerity of their expressive rhetoric, but one whose logical fallacy they still manage to override, even Goneril and Regan echo this problem. Goneril loves her father "more than words can wield the matter" (55), and when she manages to surmount an apparent verbal impasse, her sister Regan, perhaps coyly, perhaps insincerely, perhaps both, finds that even those words come "too short" of the truth (72).

Superficially, the fault lies with court speech, bound as it is to ritual and decorum, artificial as it must be, in a certain sense men speaking such public language cannot be real "men o' their words" (4.6.104). Yet the play's own "darker purpose," as I have played on "Lear" as both central character and play,[57] is closer to that of tragic linguistic manipulation than insincerity. Lear—again, both as character and, by extension, as play—tries to impose an exclusive and therefore fraudulent "reality" over life, even the life of the opening scene existing as it does beyond the conscious intentions or comprehension of all the characters. Literally, no character ever "knows" himself or herself in the theater, nor do we, as audience, know them fully until the final line is spoken. Regan's judgment that Lear has "but slenderly known himself" (1.1.293–94) thus may not stop with her father. Like Bottom's wanting to speak all the parts in *Pyramus and Thisby* to the degree that he would usurp the lines and even the voice of the actor playing Thisby, Lear is a tyrant with his own idiosyncratic langauge. Cordelia is instructed to "mend [her] speech" when her qualitative "nothing" opposes her father's demand for more than what he takes to be a quantitative "nothing" (1.1.86–94). She is to "speak" and then to "speak again," but Lear, buoyed up by the compliance of her sisters, can allow no deviation from a prearranged "script." In a revealing pun, he similarly finds that Kent, in opposing him, has come "betwixt our sentence and our power" (1.1.170). It is as if he would collapse the productive tension between language and spectacle, the central issue in this book, to a state where words themselves become physical entities. Lear would thus replace regal power with a verbal equivalent.

If Othello needs "ocular proof" (3.3.360) from Iago, Gloucester, like Lear, needs "auricular assurance" (1.2.92) from Edmund, this play's Iago, whom Gloucester misreads as grievously as Othello does his lieutenant. Edmund, in turn, gives Gloucester the words, the assurance, he demands, offering to this man, who would unstate himself to be resolved, both written (the letter) and aural proof. Like Iago's arranging things so that Othello can overhear a conversation between Cassio and himself that supposedly concerns Desdemona (4.1), Edmund's promise is to "place" his father where he can overhear a conversation between the brothers (1.2.90–93).

It is also curious that the play makes no distinction between good and bad characters in their use of a deceptive language. Kent, besides changing his name to Caius, will "other accents borrow, / That can [his] speech defuse" (1.4.1–2), and it has been quite rightly observed that he becomes infatuated with an assumed role to the degree that he leaves the play not as his real self, a courtier, but as Lear's servant: "My master calls me, I must not say no" (5.3.323).[58] Edgar himself assumes a role, and in the course of the play is a veritable storehouse of accents and dialects. By definition an act in verbal deception, since characters are not speaking spontaneously (nor, as Hamlet admits to Claudius, are "these words" their own [3.2.96–97]), the theater here, with both good and bad characters, only doubles the linguistic deception.

There is a corresponding dismantling of both the organ of speech and of words themselves. Kent would confine the serviceable Oswald "in Lipsbury pinfold" (2.2.9), that is, caging him in a mouth or getting him between his teeth. And among the injuries inflicted by Edgar's foul fiend Flibbertigibbet is the "hare-lip" (3.4.118). In his opening soliloquy Edmund challenges the efficacy of words themselves, questioning the ground for "base," "baseness," and "bastardy." For him, the distinction between "legitimate" and "illegitimate" that so preoccupies Gloucester and Kent in the opening scene is itself swept away. *Legitimate* is nothing more than a "fine word," and Edmund's own fraudulent play, his "invention" (20), will reverse its meaning ("top th' legitimate" [21]) once he himself changes the status of both Edgar and, as a consequence, himself.

Even this verbal dismantling is not all. Three hundred and fifty years after *Lear*, Samuel Beckett would elevate silence to the level of a presence in his plays, the abyss that we avoid only by naming it, the inner world or what Beckett calls the "dark zone" in all of us that remains incommunicable, that with its unheard, counterlanguage threatens the shallow discourse of the public world. *Lear* moves in this same direction, away from its own language. To "love" Lear, Cordelia must also "be silent" (1.1.62), and at the end he can love her fully only as death silences him as a speaking character.[59] Kent, who equates wisdom with silence or near silence (1.4.15–16), rightly identifies Cordelia as one whose "low sounds / Reverb no hollowness" (1.1.153–54). Conversely, the court is an arena of "machinations, hollowness, treachery and all ruinous disorders" that follow man "disquietly" (1.2.112–14). Cordelia strikes, then, a counter-movement away from speech, and it is significant that the "all-licens'd" Fool (1.4.201), who like Yorick is granted a freedom of speech that Lear would deny to anyone else, pines away in her absence (1.4.74) until he is finally silenced by his unconventional exit halfway through the play. Once Lear himself moves from the tyranny of language, he can proffer money to Gloucester with which he is to "seal th' accuser's lips" (4.6.170).

In various ways, then, the play seems to erase language.[60] The verbally adroit Oswald, who in his role as messenger denies, by definition, his own particular speech, is dismissed by Kent as an "unnecessary letter" (2.2.64). As Kent enters in his disguise as Caius, itself a denial of his earlier self as defined by his speech, Lear exclaims, "I will be the pattern of all patience, I will say nothing" (3.2.37). Bessy, in the Fool's doggerel, is a woman who "must not speak" (3.6.27). This very motif of avoiding speech, seeking silence, and canceling language culminates in Lear's strategy "to shoe / A troop of horse with felt" (4.6.184–85), and at length in the silent Cordelia brought back onstage by her father.

Yet the play cannot be a mime. No less, its larger sense of theatrical presence opposes the verbally shallow, melodramatic plays of power politics and adultery foisted on us by Goneril, Regan, and Edmund. Such "inner plays" are increasingly at variance with *Lear*'s own "darker purpose," the absence or white space as expressed in these motifs of verbal negation and speechlessness. Melodrama and mysteries beyond stage enactment are thus both sacrificed to this presence.[61] Accordingly, out of such silences and negation there emerges a new language, one generated by the larger play itself in much the same way that the conflict between actors and characters in Pirandello's *Six Characters in Search of an Author* "produces" Madame Pace, a character made necessary by the aborted story that the characters and the actors struggle to enact and yet who, properly, does not exist in the *dramatis personae* fronting the play itself. The Knight's sense of duty, he informs us, "cannot be silent" (1.4.65). Nor can Kent's, even though his opposition to Lear's own verbal tyranny is futile until Lear himself is able to "hear" Kent. Such hearing, significantly, occurs offstage and is reported to us by Edgar, Kent's copartner in the positive use of linguistic manipulation and disguise. For an enlightened Gloucester, the hairs on his chin, on that beard so violently plucked by Regan, "will quicken and accuse" her (3.7.38–39). And it is no small irony that it is Goneril, an agent from what I have called that melodramatic plot at variance with the real center of the play, who will serve as Regan's executioner. If Cordelia earlier cannot heave her heart into her mouth (1.1.91–92), we hear—again from a messenger's report—that she was later able to do just this: "she heav'd the name of 'father' / Pantingly forth, as if it press'd her heart" (4.3.25–26).

This new language, emerging from the play's verbal erasures and addiction to silence, finds its origin in nature, in the court's antithesis. Lear's new voice is like that of "the vex'd sea, singing aloud," and, appropriately, we hear that his royal crown has been replaced by one composed of femiter, furrowweed, and various other "idle weeds" (4.4.1–6). The shallow Edgar in purging himself by impersonating a natural, Poor Tom, locked out from the castle and wandering the heath, must literally assume the accents of men of far lower stations before he can regain his normal speech. When Gloucester detects that Edgar's "voice is alter'd," that he speaks "in better phrase and matter" than he once did (4.6.7–8), we simultaneously encounter a slippage from his role-playing (which Edgar quickly denies, except for a change of garments, so that he can sustain the illusion) and a figurative sign that the character forced into the role of feigned villain by the play's actual villain has now, in this same slippage, regained, through the silencing of his real, albeit shallow self, his own verbal heritage and particularity. It is the same Edgar who will command an altered, now affirmative Gloucester in a way that rebalances Lear's own command in the opening scene to "speak" (4.6.64).

The dispossessed characters—Cordelia, Kent, Edgar, Lear, and Gloucester, in that order—can now return once the verbal erasures and silences have discredited court speech, carrying with them a new, almost childlike, reformed langauge. Lear's pathetic, perhaps even misdirected wish, "O, you are men of stones: / Had I your tongue and eyes, I'd use them so / That heaven's vault should crack" (5.3.258–60), both discredits the play's old speech, now seen as absurdly challenging providence, even as it signifies this linguistic transference. That old speech is now silenced like stones and yet will, in Lear's closing lines, be replaced by a new speech, so allusive, so imaginative, so open-ended, that the audience, both onstage and offstage, will have trouble hearing it, just as Lear experienced self-inflicted trouble "hearing" Cordelia, Kent, and France in the opening scene. Lear's closing compliment to Cordelia is that her "voice was ever soft, / Gentle, and low" (273–74). Paradoxically, if the play must work itself away from court speech and, no less, the silence and erasures of a counterreaction, and then return to a language of presence, that return itself only generates a new speech that at once "works" in the reordered world of the last act and yet, in its indeterminacy that pushes against the auditory confines of the stage, threatens this very enactment of presence.

iv

There is a corresponding problem and also a reformation in the play's visual dimension.[62] If Lear is eager for verbal declarations of love, Gloucester is no less eager for visual affirmation when he demands of Edmund, "Let's see, let's see" (1.2.43). Edmund will, of course, offer him ocular proof of Edgar's treachery (the feigned wounds on his arm). Such visual deception is at one with the larger problem of vision in the play. The undowered Cordelia "deceives" Lear since he assumes, as does Burgundy, that outward poverty reveals inner poverty. Again, it is France who penetrates the deception through paradox: she is more rich, being poor. Visual deception is a norm here, affecting good and bad characters alike. Kent is forced to "raze" his "likeness" (1.4.4), as is Edgar, and when Edgar challenges Edmund, the master of visual deception, he himself must appear razed, masked, and, significantly, nameless.

As with the organ of speech, the instrument of the eye is sullied here. Cordelia condemns both the "tongue" of her sisters and their "still-soliciting eye" (1.1.231–32). A repeated image of human vanity is that of one who is "glass-gazing" (2.2.18), one who has "made mouths in a glass" (3.2.36). Yet even the innocent Cordelia is forced into the Fool's image of that fair but vain woman when Lear presses a glass to her mouth to detect signs of life. As the play moves toward silence, toward mime, it also attacks the theater's own spectacle, its visual dimension. We will, of course, think most immediately here of the blinding of Gloucester. Gloucester, without sight, is solicitous of Lear's. his justification for coming to the king's aid is that he "would not see [the] cruel nails [of Goneril and Regan] / Pluck out his poor old eyes" (3.7.57–58). Even at the end of the play, Lear, despite his insistence that the other characters "see"—"Look there, look there!" (5.3.312)—confesses to having faulty vision: his eyes "are not o' th' best" and his sight is correspondingly "dull" (5.3.280, 283).

The Fool's description of Lear is prophetic: he is "an O without a figure" (1.4.192). An equivalent to the silencing of speech, we have here a denial of physical form itself, literally a zero without another digit in front of it, figuratively a denial of physical presence. Since by his own decision he can no longer appear as king and yet has no alternate form, Lear becomes in a sense psychologically invisible. As the negative challenge to vision, to the play's own physical presence (itself part of that trinity composed of verbal and temporal presence, as I have defined it), he assumes the new role of a revenger who would attack vision, specifically the eyes: hence his calling upon the lightning to "dart" its "blinding flames / Into [Goneril's] scornful eyes" (2.4.165–66).

In the play's challenge to sight as something "deficient" (4.6.23), to the eyes as capable of being deceived and therefore unable to see "what is," we confront the paradoxical vision itself, the spectacle informing the larger play. "Vision" is here both literal (or physical) and, if you will, metaphysical. The extremes of this paradox are embodied, I think, in Goneril's otherwise insincere phrase "dearer than eyesight' (1.1.56) and Lear's petulant threat to "resume the shape" that his daughters think he has "cast off for ever" (1.4.309–10). Of course, in reality Goneril has no such transcendental love for Lear—she is willing to play his game, offering rhetorical exaggerations for a third of the kingdom—and Lear promises the impossible since he can never regain a role he has contractually divided between Goneril and Regan. But in this curious, parabolic play, out of the negative comes the positive. For present purposes, the two passages, despite the conscious intentions of the speakers, serve to define the gamut of what vision—or eyes, eyesight, seeing—means in *Lear*.

On the one hand, the play implies an existence beyond the physical, and therefore beyond the reach of the mortal eye. Once the seemingly substantial court world, the realm of Goneril, Regan, and Edmund, is dismissed as a "trifle" (5.3.296), this other dimension, captured in Gloucester's own ironic phrase "the quality of nothing" (1.2.33), rises in its absence. We cannot see this existence; we can only "feel" it, as Gloucester recognizes when he is able, after his own visual purgation, to "see it feelingly" (4.6.149). Here is indeed a metaphysical world, a dimension of that larger world only a part of which is visually enacted onstage and for which one does not need "spectacles" (1.2.35). It is akin, again, to Cordelia's qualitative "nothing." Paul Jorgensen observes the paradox of that word for the Renaissance: *nothing* embraces zero, idleness, futility, but also the imagination (as the poet creates *ex nihilo*) and solace (to see this world as nothing, as vanity, represents the first step toward serenity).[63] Holding Cordelia's letter before him, Kent pronounces that "nothing almost sees miracles / But misery," (2.2.165–66). A possible reading here is that only those who are miserable, deprived of comforts, shut out from the court, reduced to the nonstatus of the unaccommodated man, can in the absence of the things of the world have visions. In effect, by denying them the basics of a minimum physical existence, the persecutors unintentionally expose the persecuted to an alternative world of miracles, of mysteries beyond our normal comprehension.[64]

The latter part of the play is flooded with references to this world beyond stage enactment, beyond the eyes of both onstage characters and the audience. Gloucester acknowledges that he has had a vision of Edgar, this in the presence of a disguised Edgar and the mysterious "Old Man" who has led him to his son. I say "mysterious" with an eye—is the pun excusable?—toward the Old Man who cautions Faustus moments before his damnation to seek Christ's grace. In the morality plays, of course, that same Old Man is often an earthly surrogate for God. Though we are right in branding Edgar's restoration of Gloucester at Dover Cliffs as a "pious fraud,"[65] it is no less true that his salvation depends on a loss of sight, as well as Edgar's success in driving Gloucester to imagine an otherworldly dimension inhabited both by a "fiend" or devil whom Gloucester has escaped and the "clearest gods," who have intervened to perform a miracle (4.6.72–74). This visionary world, of course, can only be suggested. When it is "present," as in Edgar's words just quoted, it makes its way into the *Lear* world only through a trick, through theatricalization. Or, as in the Gentlemen's description of Cordelia, shaking "the holy water from her heavenly eyes" with tears that are "as pearls from diamonds dropp'd" (4.3.22–30), we hear about it by messenger, but do not actually witness the scene. Shelley's skylark, whose presence is confirmed by the ear but not the eye, is here Edgar's "shrill-gorg'd lark" that is "so far" distant that it "cannot be seen or heard" (4.6.58–59). As Murray Krieger would argue in *Theory of Criticism*, though, Edgar's lark is still part of "The Presence of the Poem."[66] Saying the word, employing a metaphor, confers an existence, however insubstantial. In this sense we might see an irony in Lear's otherwise cynical advice that, like the "scurvy politician" or trickster, Gloucester should acquire "glass eyes" so that he can see the things that are not really there ("To see the things thou dost not" [4.6.170–72]).

However, such metaphysical vision is counterbalanced, perhaps even outweighed by the play's more literal, physical, worldly spectacle. Here, what is, *is*; like Desdemona, Cordelia never changes: she is always the faithful daughter, always exactly what she seems to be. At fault is the vision of others, whether it be a husband such as Othello or a father such as Lear. For all its tantalizing metaphysics, the play seems no less earthbound, as "presence" itself takes on a more literal, antimystical meaning. Lear, ironically and tragically, would remove this very presence in his command that first Cordelia and then Kent "avoid" his "sight" (1.1.124, 157), and it is Kent who cautions Lear to "see better" (158). Paul Alpers may be citing only a half truth, but in the play's critical history, which otherwise stresses insight, it is an often-neglected truth: the play is, metaphysics notwithstanding, about literal vision, our need to look at, to confront each other, to see the other as he or she really is, rather than as constructed in our own idiosyncratic scenarios.[67] Kent, particularly, as the earthbound counterpart to the saintly Cordelia, asserts this immediate, physical presence and present. When he asks the Gentleman to "show" Cordelia a ring if he "shall see" her, he means and we take the command literally (3.1.46–47). If it is a moot point whether Lear has a transcendent vision in the closing moments, it *is* a fact that, once abandoning his own perversely imaginative construction of the opening scene, he exposes himself, both his eyes and his body, to this same physical presence, to the heath's "naked wretches" (3.4.28). Granting that ethics and imagination are only assumed entities existing tenuously and existentially in the mind, the one unassailable fact is that man's existence is entirely physical: deprived of his metaphysics, he is "no more than this," "the thing itself" (3.4.102–3, 106).

Increasingly, the play emphasizes Gloucester's "feeling" in the more literal sense of "touching." By stage practice, Lear puts his arm around the Fool and instructs him to "go first" into the hovel (3.4.26). Gloucester yearns to "touch" Edgar, anticipating that such physical contact would make him "say [he] had eyes again" (4.1.23–24). He further defines the "superfluous and lust-dieted man" as one who does "not see / Because he does not feel" the "ordinance" of heaven; but such an insensitive man will "feel [heaven's] power quickly" (4.1.67–59).

If the play, then, suggests a visionary presence, it also emphasizes, increasingly, restored physical sight. Cordelia commands her officer to "search every acre in the high-grown field, / And bring [Lear] to [her] eye" (4.4.8). The reward she promises the officer is "all [her] outward worth" (10); her inward worth, we might suppose, is reserved as a gift for her father. Like Gloucester, who yearns to see Edgar, she wants "soon" to "hear and see" Lear (29). Physical vision even becomes overwhelming. To Edgar the sight of Lear is "side-piercing" (4.6.85), and Lear's first sight of Cordelia after the opening scene is so traumatic that for a moment he hallucinates: he is in some sort of hell, "bound / Upon a wheel of fire," while she, "a soul in bliss," must have strayed from her proper realm (4.7.45–47). And we will recall that Lear ends his life demanding that the onstage characters "look on" Cordelia, seconds after Albany has cried to them to "see, see" the tableau of father and daughter (5.3.305–12).

Its mundane function challenged by a visionary presence, even as it is manipulated positively and negatively by characters given to optical distortion, the eye itself is at once condemned as a "vild jelly" (3.7.82) and yet, once "wash'd" (1.1.268) or "wipe[d]" clean (5.3.23), its "anguish" removed (4.4.15, 4.6.6), it is celebrated or "bless[ed]" as "sweet" (4.1.54), as "precious stones" (5.3.191).

v

Lear offers, then, a divided response toward language and spectacle, and this same response is inseparable from the fact that as audience we are presented with literal details, both verbal and visual, conveyed through a medium that is only an assumed reality, an imitation of a world outside its confines. This paradoxical sense of presence, I believe, is inseparable from an equally divided attitude toward stage enactment itself.

Predictably, the bad characters at once define and employ a limited, destructive, negative "theater."[68] Edmund cynically links Edgar's timely entrance with that of "the catastrophe of the old comedy," seeing it as his own "cue" for "villainous melancholy," after which we hear and see, in a sort of perverse metadramatics, an actor impersonating Edmund parodying Gloucester: "O, these eclipses do portend these divisions!" (1.2.134–37). His lover, Goneril, similarly dismisses Albany's demand that she petition him if she wishes to marry Edmund as "an enterlude" (5.3.89). If such negative theater is technically appealing at first, as Edmund "fashion[s]" (1.2.184) material, both as manipulated by him or as it "weaves" itself to his purpose (2.1.15), it later becomes appalling. No stranger to such manipulative theatrics, Goneril admits that if she loses Edmund to Regan "all the building in [her] fancy" thus lost would make her life "hateful" (4.2.85–86). Kent spots the limitations, the crime of such self-serving theater: Goneril—and by extension the two members of the adulterous triangle—is little more than an allegorized "Vanity," the "puppet's part" in a morality play, while he, the king's ambassador, plays the role of "royalty" (2.2.36–37).

Even the good characters, in adopting this same theater of deception, find it limiting, and potentially corruptive. Confronted by his blind father, and yet obliged to continue his disguise as Poor Tom, Edgar confesses in an aside that his "tears" at the sight threaten to "mar his counterfeiting" (3.6.60–61). He struggles to stay in character, being unable "to daub it further" (4.1.52) in the presence of what, for the onstage character, is actual suffering.

In a way, we might take Lear's angry response to the Fool, "nothing can be made out of nothing" (1.4.133), as a restatement of the Puritans' objection to the theater: in constructing a seeming world out of feigned language and vision, the playwright blasphemes God, the ultimate playwright who alone could create a cosmos from nothing.[69] I also think here of the critics like Richard Fly, cited in the opening section of this chapter, who discuss those moments when the theater, the very concept of play, seems inadequate, limited, an imperfect medium for the play's more catholic (one might add lifelike) vision.[70] There is a strangely self-reflexive, second meaning to Lear's otherwise emotional "This is not Lear" (1.4.226) or the Fool's description of himself as "Lear's shadow" (1.4.231). Regan brands Lear's sarcastic impersonation of the suppliant father ("on my knees I beg / That you'll vouchsafe me raiment, bed, and food") as "unsightly tricks" (2.4.155–57), and at that point in the play her judgment has some basis. Yet later, Edgar, the play's multitalented actor, turns the accusation against himself: "Bad is the trade that must play fool to sorrow" (4.1.38). In addition, more than one commentator has been uneasy about Lear's own plan to be one of God's spies, an audience securely observing the ups and downs of persons in the mundane world.[71] It is surely a cruel fact that soon he will stagger back on stage, announcing that his daughter is dead, and that he, rather than some intervening benovelent god, has killed the slave who hanged Cordelia. This impatience with the theater, the sense that it cannot tell or enact all, may even explain why the Fool's reference to Merlin (3.2.95–96)—that is, a character who lived after the time period covered by the play—seems to break the confines of *Lear* itself.[72] His violation of chronology, in effect, serves to disillusion our engagement in the present play.

Yet as Dean Frye observes, some artifice is necessary, whether it be the particular construction by which each of us orders the world, or that structure, however minimal, which distinguishes the play from reality.[73] Characters like Edgar and Kent use artifice, the theater, for positive ends. Nor does the double-edged sword of theatrics[74] inhibit Edmund until, exposed in his fraudulent role, he pants for life and tries to undo the pernicious artifice he has woven (5.3.244–48).

Still, the fragility of artifice, of assuming a role that ultimately cannot ward off reality, is a pervasive motif in the play. In the role of Poor Tom, Edgar finds that he is "worse than e'er [he] was" as a real man (4.1.25–26). Lear's own inner play, the trial he stages in Act 3, scene 5, is aborted by Lear himself when he denounces any attempt at such judgment with "None does offend, none, I say none" (4.6.168).[75] And though he says "In nothing am I chang'd / But in my garments" (4.6.9–10) in order to allay Gloucester's suspicion that the man with him of the edge of Dover Cliffs is not the same peasant who led him there, Edgar's "defense" itself asserts the primacy of reality over theatrical illusion. From our vantage point as an audience with eyes intact, we would also admit, however, that Edgar, Poor Tom, and the peasant are all illusory.

Thus, the theater, like its constituents language, vision, and presence, is neither affirmed nor denied, but rather qualified, with each weight added to the scale's positive side balanced by an equal weight on the negative side. If it condemns the sign, Lear's own famous line, "this great stage of fools" (4.6.183), condemns the signifier as well. If we were in the impoverished theater of Beckett, where the theatrically reflexive metaphors are delivered directly to the audience, as when Estragon looks over the edge of the stage and labels us a "bog,"[76] we would be even more secure in seeing a theatrical irony in such lines as Lear's "What place this is" (4.7.65) or Kent's gloomy question, "Is this the promis'd end?" (5.3.264).

vi

It is the presence of life, of nature, to which this self-sacrificing theater points, that same life suggested by those critics whom I surveyed in the opening section of this chapter, suggested by the very breadth of the play and by its own rigorous examination of the theater's prerequisite language, spectacle, and presence. It is this *life*, however elusive the term, that paradoxically inhibits and yet is celebrated by the play. We recognize, to be sure, that what distinguishes Shakespeare from all other playwrights is the scope of his canvas, the inclusive nature of his theatrical "worlds." Accordingly, his plays are "lifelike."[77] But then, the theater *is* a live medium, in a way that other "theaters"—the cinema especially (which presents a checkered history of attempts to adapt Shakespeare's plays[78]), radio, and television—cannot be. The term *theater* itself extends beyond the stage. Our existential dilemma is precisely the conflict between our actions and our consciousness of those actions that converts them into roles, ourselves into actors, the real world into a stage. Role-playing as a metaphor thus becomes actual once it leaves the stage.

The motif of life is sounded early in the play. Admidst the stultifying, masculine atmosphere of the court, where the status of one's own child depends on a father's interpretation, we hear of Gloucester's wife conceiving and growing "round-womb'd" (1.1.13–14). Lear himself would balance "nature" and "merit" in the division of his kingdom, though of his three daughters one is branded "unnatural" by his divine fiat (53). Even if Lear's darker purpose may extend beyond his consciousness, clearly part of that same purpose—though we learn of it only after the fact—was to "set [his] rest / On [Cordelia's] kind nursery" (123–24). In this light, that touchstone phrase *nothing will come of nothing* itself points to Lear's initial denial of life and, both literally and figuratively, his choice of death. Yet there is a paradox here. Despite Regan's judgment that "Nature" or life in her father "stands on the very verge / Of his confine" (2.4.147–48), Lear, as several commentators have observed,[79] is suffused with energy, misdirected to be sure, impulsive, but clearly so much in contrast to the affected, conservative postures of Goneril and Regan that there is a certain rightness in their seeing him as senile, childlike, as violating the "normal" demeanor of old age.

If the heath is taken as the original chaos from which more sophisticated life emerges, as a wellspring of powers beyond human construction, inimical to the tawdry life of the court, then there is also a certain rightness in Lear's expulsion. As for Kent, the heath is the "new" country in which one can "[re]shape his old course" (1.1.187). When he swears "by the pow'r that made me" (1.1.207), Lear thereby invokes his origins, bringing upon himself the life that is his source. His invocations to nature, to life, *especially* when they are negative or self-serving—"Crack nature's moulds, all germains spill at once" (3.2.8)—only call attention to this force at the root of his character, a force he opposes and yet with which he feels a kinship when, bereft of political power, he summons this force, albeit absurdly, to his defense. Early in the play he sadly acknowledges that his (to him) just interpretation of Cordelia's "small fault" has "wrench'd [his] frame of nature / From the fix'd place" (1.4.268–69), and I would suggest that this fixed place is embodied in the heath. The court, appropriately, shuts out nature, literally so when Cornwall advises that the doors be shut to keep out the very storm into which Lear has charged. I note that in Kozintsev's film version this same closing of the door, keenly dividing the court from the heath outside, marks the half-point in that movie.[80] As long as he retains even a particle of his court "mentality," Lear assumes that nature is his servant, an alternative force at his command, and yet his first line after Edgar's "O thou side-piercing sight!" is "Nature's above art in that respect" (4.6.85–86).

It has often been observed that the play, and especially its central character, seems overwhelmed with a loathing of sexuality; taken to an extreme, the argument goes that Lear tries to suppress in himself such desires, even for Cordelia. From the perspective of this section, however, this emphasis on the physical establishes a countermovement not only to the growing perversion of love at court but to the artifice of the play itself. The guarantee of life, of existence itself, sexuality is inseparable from the play's focus on the body, not only when wracked with pain (and thus a testament to human cruelty) but also as a more neutral entity, a ground that persists despite the artifice of construction, be it that of characters, the playwright, or the audience. Earlier the Fool compares Lear with an eggshell, with its contents, literally its life, in the possession of Goneril and Regan. At Dover, Edgar first describes his father's body in falling off the cliffs as an egg shivering in the air. Then he quickly notes that Gloucester is substantial, "hast heavy substance," is whole, "bleed'st not," and "breathe[s]" (4.6.51–52). On this body, alive, whole, he makes, even in the presence of an artifice witnessed by us, his affirmative argument for life, for continuance. Gloucester is asked to acknowledge this same body; if he cannot see, he can still "feel" his legs (65). To Lear, Gloucester will announce optimistically that if physical sight is denied him, he can still "see now this world goes" "feelingly" (148–49). In Cordelia's presence, Lear can also "feel this pin prick" and can see his hands—and on this basis asks for more confirmation that he is alive in the present world: "Would I were assur'd / Of my condition" (4.7.54–56). Earlier, he had invoked "necessity's sharp pinch" once he determined not to return to Regan (2.4.211). This stress on the physical, on life, may even allow an altered reading of Lear's seemingly mystical reference to "the mystery of *things*" (5.3.16; my italics).

What I have called the melodramatic, conventional, inner play of Goneril, Regan, and Oswald conspires against this life. The (to our knowledge) childless Goneril would "breed from hence occasions" (1.3.24), and when she condemns the "milky gentleness" (1.4.341) of Albany, we will remember Lady Macbeth's similar adulteration of a mother's milk. Goneril brands Albany a second time as a "milk-liver'd man" (4.2.50), yet it is Albany who will grow in the play from a compliant husband to his wife's adversary.[81] If it is asserted by indirection, as in these instances, this life often forces its presence upon the characters. Attempting at the eleventh hour to reverse his command for Cordelia's execution, Edmund "pant[s] for life" (5.3.244). Even Lear, in announcing that he will "die bravely," invokes the Renaissance pun on die with a simile based on procreation: "like a smug bridegroom" (4.6.198).

Presence itself, a body whole and breathing, standing, seen by other bodies, is the unassailable fact celebrated by the play. Cordelia stands as a (mostly) silent commentary on her sisters in the opening scene, and yet Lear, who denounces her "little seeming substance," still acknowledges her physical presence for Burgundy with "there she stands" (1.1.197–98). Edgar's line, "I would not take this from report; it is" (4.6.141), elevates Gloucester's physical presence over everything he has heard, over language itself, and it is this presence, beyond the artifice of language and its messengers, that "breaks" his heart (142).[82] It is this same presence that Lear searches for with the feather applied to Cordelia's lips, and his last line, "Look there, look there!", even as it invokes conflicting interpretations from audiences off- and onstage, also celebrates what is here, *actual.*

This physical presence is inseparable from what several critics have called the play's "survival ethic," the assertion that life is good, a certainty, the one sure thing in a world otherwise floundering in complexities, interpretive and existential. This presence is our "human situation," the object of our efforts, of our energies,[83] and we must be patient of this life, taking existence on its own terms.[84] This, the richest of Shakespeare's plays, the most complex, is also the most basic. We are to learn to avoid, even to destroy all that threatens life, whether it be the "fiend" or "vermin" (2.4.159)—or thus Poor Tom defines the twin poles of our metaphysical and physical enemy. We avoid suicide, and cling to life itself, no matter how minimal. In Albany's words, anyone falling short of this ethic, anyone who would "sliver and disbranch / From her material sap, perforce must wither, / And come to deadly use" (4.2.34–36). His observation once made, Goneril, using a revealing term for critics, dismisses it with "No more, the text is foolish" (37). In the midst of "this tough world" (5.3.315), "ripeness is all," a ripeness, like Hamlet's "readiness" (5.2.222), whose aim is "to endure" (5.2.9–11).

If this motif of life, or presence, survival, preservation, breaks the confines of the play's own limited artifice, it is, paradoxically, inseparable from the fact that art itself, whatever the gloomy, absurdist, or even nihilistic presuppositions of its makers, is affirmative to the degree that such physical and psychological desecration as we observe in *Lear* is not infinite, unchecked, but instead confined within the form of the play. The play is a step away from disorder, from destruction and confusion; poets, as Yeats well knew, are always gay, even though the tragic curtain falls on the stages of their Hamlets and Lears. In avoiding death, we acknowledge "our lives' sweetness" (5.3.185). Peter Brook's production of the play, even as it underscores the savagery that a half-century of romantic interpretations would have concealed, perhaps erred in deleting the slave who, present at Gloucester's blinding, "thrill'd with remorse, / Oppos'd against the act" (4.2.73), though at the price of his own life.

The heart, more than the eyes and ears, bears the symbolism of the play's celebration of life. Lear early acknowledges its primacy when he describes Kent's words as invading "the region of [his] heart" (1.1.144–45), and Edmund, ironically and deceptively, hopes that his brother's "heart is not in the contents" of the feigned letter (1.2.67–68). We *are* our heart, and when our heart is injured we lose ourselves; part of the Fool's corrective, comic surgery is to "outjest / [Lear's] heart-strook injuries" (3.1.16–17). When Lear is most not himself, he misinterprets Kent's request that he enter the hovel with "wilt break my heart?" (3.4.4). Kent's own "Break, heart, I prithee break" (5.3.313) refers to the death he seeks now that Lear is dead, even as it acknowledges that with Lear's condition now beyond repair, that heart, at first so proud, then later so forgiving, may now properly break. Life is located literally and figuratively in the heart. We learn in Edgar's report that his father's heart "burst smilingly" (5.3.200), and Lear's modest request, "Pray you undo this button" (310), may indicate that since his heart is about to break, to ease the pain of death he needs more breathing room under his doublet.[85]

vii

The present chapter had as its "processional" the play's critics, an articulate "audience" extending over three centuries and the audience to which my own "performance" is directed, all those who have struggled with a play that from Dr. Johnson to the present seems to burst the confines of its theater. The present "recessional" also involves that audience as it considers *Lear*'s own ending. In the simplest sense, how are we to read the "sacred pieta"[86] of the closing moments, the tableau of dead daughter held by a dying father, calling us to "look" at the stage with eye and ear?

Both those extremes to which that earlier Bradley/Kott dichotomy have been subjected offer closures, though of radically different natures. Some hold that, his terrestrial journey complete, Lear will now be joined by Kent on a new one to a transcendent realm, the character having literally absolved himself of the cruel, secular world of the play.[87] With father and daughter reconciled, that secular world is, in effect, "shut out."[88] If Bradley was hesitant about the ending, others have been less so: Lear, we are told, dies in ecstasy, believing Cordelia is alive.[89] Conversely, it has been argued that here we see the End of the World, the first step in a "progressive transformation into chaos."[90] At the end Lear's material view fails him just as his moral vision had failed him earlier,[91] and as audience we must avoid being led by him into that same folly.[92]

Other commentators find the ending beyond explication. In Cordelia's death is reflected the inexplicability of the world as viewed through mortal eyes.[93] In point of fact, the comments of those onstage provide little guidance for any interpretation, either negative or positive.[94] We have no evidence other than Lear's own word.[95] Rather, the ending is open, "divergent,"[96] and the last scene is unbearable not because it denies but rather because it give us the complex, relative justice that we want, even beyond our conscious wishes.[97] Our frustration in not having closure, or a single, albeit complex tool for determining if this or that reading is more or less correct, leave us with a response that is "painful and profoundly depressing."[98] Michael Goldman speaks of our exhaustion in these closing moments.[99]

This relative response to more optimistic or pessimistic views has led, in turn, to speculation that Shakespeare's own art form is superseded here; we experience "a conclusion that in its painfulness is almost beyond the experience of tragedy itself."[100] Berel Long argues that what would be a "normal space of inference" in other works, our distance from the tragic hero, is here "a line of identity," and, therefore, just as Lear's focus has changed from himself to Cordelia, we too experience "a consciousness coming alive": as the central character becomes an audience like us, we enlarge our own perspective and look beyond the play to that life waiting outside the theater.[101] Even H. A. Mason, who is critical of Shakespeare's artistry in *Lear* and identifies the Gloucester plot as "the real thing" of the play, concludes that in this "significantly blank" ending, where Shakespeare finally is able to manage his portrait of Lear, Lear "thus dies in the real."[102] One critic rephrases the conclusion more graphically: despite what we may think, "what Lear sees at the end is life."[103] The play seems to shake off its own form, its own artifice; in its closing moments *Lear* does not "yield a new style" but rather proclaims "the absence of styles."[104] In the words of a fine metadramatic critic, the father is now without a role, and as he and the play are absorbed by the life waiting just outside the theater's exit doors, both onstage and off, Lear is "unable to articulate a fully elaborated self-conception with its own appropriate language, its own recognizable voice."[105] The play at length shakes off the rituals of drama itself.[106]

And yet we still want to interpret the ending. C. F. Tucker Brooke suggests, for example, that only by imagining the spiritual salvation of Lear and Cordelia can the spectator see beyond the play's own unacceptable victory of physical evil.[107] If Lear's seeing Cordelia alive represents "subjective mythologizing," that unwarranted vision can nevertheless be universalized by our own leap of faith.[108] But Madeline Doran cautions us against accepting Albany's "simple" allegorization of the events.[109] Could the play's final statement be as unassuming as: death stops pain?[110]

The text *is* there. Or, with an eye to the current controversy, we have a choice of texts. Though it is now fashionable—and I use this word in an entirely neutral sense—to deconstruct that text, its matter, I would argue, cannot be destroyed entirely, especially the text of a play that in its catholicity, in its exhilarating yet potentially stern challenge to the playwright's own artifice, celebrates at once the gamut of life and the physical basis on which the idiosyncracies of metaphysics so depend. Life may be so, but art is not random or infinite, at least that art bounded by the presence, language, and spectacle of the stage. In Murray Krieger's terms, the text *is there* and so is our actual experience of it, even as that text points outside itself to that world for which it serves as a window.[111]

Some years ago I proposed in an article, "*The Tempest* and Shakespeare's Last Plays: The Aesthetic Dimensions," that if in Prospero's abandonment of his art and magic island and in his subsequent return to Milan we see *The Tempest* as celebrating real life at the expense of the play's illusory world, or Milan itself as representing reality (or, if one is so inclined, Stratford), then we must also acknowledge it is no less Shakespeare's highly conscious artistry that allows for such a conclusion.[112] Simply, when art most seems to celebrate life, it celebrates itself and thus justifies the presence of artifice. Surely, the ultimate, the only *real* language and vision of the play are those of its audience, and the final *presence* is that real-life time in which we witness the performance. But these same verbal, visual, and temporal dimensions of our existence are activated and, what is more, enhanced by the artifice of the stage. All of the plays considered here, all theater rightly understood, opens back out onto life. As a precious undergraduate student of mine says, "It's good to go to the theater, but it is also good to leave." If *Lear*'s final goal is life itself, then the play celebrates, even as it sacrifices its own form for, that larger reality. We see in Lear and his daughters our own father, our own children; our fellow mortals, onstage and offstage, assist us in the experience, sharing it with us. My own graduate teacher and spiritual father has told me no less: "This larger meaning gives our tears the dignity of an act of ratification and gratitude: to these still figures we have pitied we owe the gift of feeling pity."[113]

Conclusions
A Coda on *A Midsummer Night's Dream* and *Othello*:
"If this be not a dream I see and hear"

I HAVE so far avoided talking about the nine Shakespearean plays discussed in my *When the Theater Turns to Itself,* but in this final chapter I revisit two of those plays, *A Midsummer Night's Dream* and *Othello.* For me they can no longer be the "same" plays since, as I mentioned in the preface, the more theoretical metadramatic approach of that earlier book has been mated here with a more practical performance criticism. I employ the metaphor *coda* in this chapter's title since, like a musical composition, my remarks here both repeat and then offer variations on the issues of language, spectacle, presence, and the role of the audience that have informed the preceding nine chapters. And why these two plays? In *When the Theater Turns to Itself* I used them as a contrasting pair, arguing that *A Midsummer Night's Dream* celebrated the artist's uncovering a larger reality than could be grasped by reason, or by the mentality of a Theseus. *Othello,* conversely, offers in Iago a negative portrait of the artist, for, however appealing, even exhilarating his sordid antiplay of adultery might appear, Iago himself parodies, in a sinister fashion, the Renaissance ideal of the playwright as one who, as William Webbe once described him, "could bring men together, create good fellowship."[1] However, these same two plays, when seen from the perspective of the present book, are much more alike since my four issues here imply a continuum, a ground of elements prerequisite to theatrical enactment and one that is thereby unaffected by the glaring thematic differences between the two plays. Discussing *A Midsummer Night's Dream* and *Othello* thus allows me to readjust an earlier critical approach even as it offers a chance to summarize and then push a little farther those conclusions reached in a discussion that has made its way from *The Comedy of Errors* to *King Lear.*

i

When Bottom wakes from his adventures with Titania in the forest, he is only dimly aware of what has happened, sure only of one fact or, more properly, one nonfact: an instant before, the members of his company were with him in rehearsal, and now they have vanished, "stol'n hence" (4.1.204). We have been a conscious audience to Bottom's forest adventures, as well as those of the four Athenians, who spend even less time than Bottom trying to recreate the mysterious something that has happened to them, an experience that has, in point of fact, radically changed their lives. They went into the forest mismatched, with two men pursuing one woman and the second woman abandoned; they exit neatly arranged in marital pairs. Now, as Bottom tries to recount his dream, his senses become hopelessly confused: "The eye of man hath not heard, the ear of man hath not seen" (211–12). This reversal of the eyes and ears echoes the passage in 1 Corinthians 2:9, and, in more general terms, the notion—the very dilemma of Tiresias in Eliot's *The Waste Land*—that when in the presence of the supernatural, at the very moment when we should be most articulate, we experience either dumbness, like Eliot's character, or sensory confusion like Shakespeare's. We know what Bottom does not know: that during this midsummer's night his eyes have been enchanted and his human ears displaced by those of an ass.

There is a moment in *Othello* that offers a tragic counterpart to Bottom's waking. In Act 4, scene 1 Iago arranges things so that Othello can overhear a conversation between Cassio and himself. It is a stage recreation of our own experience in the theater: Othello is told where to sit, or rather where to "encave" himself so that he can "mark the fleers, the gibes, and notable scores / That dwell in every region of [Cassio's] face" (81–83). This is a bit of audience preconditioning for the "tale" that is about to be told "anew" on the makeshift stage (84). Othello, though, is too far upstage to hear the start of that conversation: he sees only the animated, suggestive movements of the speakers. In effect, he witnesses a dumb show rather than a full-blown play with dialogue. Iago's role is that of a presenter, Othello's untrustworthy guide to the action. When Othello moves close enough so that he can use his ears as well as his eyes, he can only take Cassio's insulting remarks as slurs against the wrong woman, since Bianca's name has long since dropped from the conversation.

Bottom's confusion of eyes and ears is, paradoxically, a fitting symbol for his mystical experience, a *clarifying confusion,* to invoke an oxymoron in a play pervaded by oxymorons. As the play moves back to Athens, back to Theseus's domain of the rational or the unimaginative, however, such confusion evaporates. When the oxymoron does reemerge in the parodic *Pyramus and Thisby*, it seems only a dim, sanitized echo of the real thing: as Pyramus, Bottom himself speaks of seeing Thisby's "voice" and of hearing her "face" (5.1.192–93). Moments before Puck has transformed Bottom into an ass, Quince, concerned that Bottom has made an unplanned exit during rehearsal, comforts Flute with "he goes but to see a noise that he heard" (3.1.91). Nervous in the presence of Theseus and his court, the rustic actors thus participate, unknowingly, in reducing a mystic confusion to the comic. Near the end of the production, when Thisby reverses her lines so that the "tongue" is instructed to "lose [its] light" and the "moon" to "take [its] flight" (5.1.304–5), the actor playing Moonshine leaves one line too late. Seconds later Bottom, no longer in character, asks if Theseus would like to "see the epilogue, or to hear a Bergomask dance" (353–54). The epilogue that Theseus refuses may have been the very "ballet" titled "Bottom's Dream" that Bottom promises, on waking, to get Quince to write, an account—assuming that Quince would be more articulate than the inarticulate Bottom—of a supernatural evening that, in Bottom's scheme, would have been sung at Thisby's death "to make it the more gracious" (4.1.215–19).

Othello's own confusion symbolizes that obscenely imaginative world, the tale of adultery with which Iago supplants the wholesome reality of the marriage of black and white, old and young, pagan and Christian. Thus what is positive and illusory in the comedy becomes no less negative and illusory in the tragedy. If Othello's ears are activated too late in the conversation between Iago and Cassio, they have already been distorted by Iago, whose own scheme is "to abuse Othello's ear" (1.3.395) or to "pour this pestilence into his ear" (2.3.356). If in *A Midsummer Night's Dream* it is the eyes of the characters that are assaulted, in *Othello* it is the ears, and if language creates reality, rather than vice versa, then Iago very clearly embodies the position of modern linguistics. Brabantio, who misreads the nature of his daughter's marriage, also misreads the potency of words when, rejecting the Duke's attempt to comfort him, he sarcastically exclaims, "But words are words; I never yet did hear / That the bruis'd heart was pierced through the ear" (1.3.218–19). Othello, whose ear has clearly been abused by Iago, speaks ironically about the "ear-piercing fife" (3.3.352), whose music he will no longer hear now that Desdemona's alleged infidelity has rendered him impotent as a soldier, robbing him of his "occupation" (357). The visual distortions induced by the love potion in the comedy lead to the verbally inarticulate Athenians and Bottom once they are expelled from the forest. Iago's verbal distortions in turn distort what Othello "sees," despite his demand for "ocular proof" (3.3.360) before he doubts Desdemona. Othello fears earlier that blind Cupid will "seel with wanton dullness / [His] speculative . . . instruments" (1.3.268–70), and in a sense he is right: he loves Desdemona "too well" (5.2.344) to consider rationally Iago's trumped-up charge of adultery. Yet the opposite is also true: it is not love but an absence of love, not Desdemona but Iago who, through language, ruins Othello's vision so that the honest wife becomes dishonest and the dishonest lieutenant "honest Iago."

Theseus disclaims, albeit unawares, against the very theater that gives him his life when he pictures "the poet's eye, in a fine frenzy rolling, / [Glancing] from heaven to earth, from earth to heaven" (5.1.12–13), for this is precisely what Shakespeare does, offering us a universe extending from the rustics to royalty to the supernatural, from the mundane to the cosmic. Thus the vision and the speech championed by Theseus, which he clamps on the play by refusing to grant any credence to the lovers' stories, is as bound to earth as is his own precious "cool reason" (5.1.6). Only in the inner play that Theseus suffers through can "sweet eyes" and "lily lips" be cherished by an imaginative Thisby. In Theseus's unconscious outer play the instrument of vision is literally reduced by Bottom when he advises the actors to eat no onions the day of the performance. Hippolyta alone can sympathize with the lovers' stories, seeing their fantastic but identical experiences as growing to "something of great constancy" (5.1.26). Still, even her account of that "one mutual cry" (4.1.117) produced by dogs and echo in conjunction when she hunted the bear with Cadmus and Hercules is itself supplanted by Theseus's more prosaic "music of [his] hounds" (106), and is parodied in turn by the dialogue of the self-conscious actors whose "speech [is] like a tangled chain; nothing impair'd, but all disorder'd" (5.1.125–26). The comedy ends with Puck's call for silence, for sleep, as a way of escaping the "serpent's tongue" (Epilogue, 433).

If the return to an Athens dominated by Theseus represents a reduction in the nature of vision, the final scene of *Othello*, conversely, allows for a liberation from Iago's perverse linguistic control. By his own confession, Othello is "rude" (1.3.81) in speech and hence hardly a match for a wordsmith like Iago. Cassio says more than he knows with his "O God, that men should put an enemy in their mouths" (2.3.289–90). Iago's corruption of Othello's speech, displacing the eloquent speech that, in spite of Othello's disclaimers, initially won the heart of Desdemona, is manifest in Othello's epilepsy as he "foams at the mouth" (4.1.54). But if Iago's inner play is perverse directly in proportion to its being an illusion, an instance where the demonic artist literally makes a seeming something out of nothing, his creation is also fragile. Othello enters the bedchamber in that final scene acting in Iago's stead, convinced of the justness of his "cause" (5.2.1), thus becoming Iago's man just as Roderigo has been earlier, and disastrously so. To his mind, the murder is not the act of a deluded man—as we see it—but rather a sacrifice justified in that it prevents Desdemona from betraying more men. Yet as he kneels over his sleeping wife, it is her "balmy breath" (16) that almost persuades him to drop his sword, and this same breath signals the restoration of language in *Othello*. Roused by Desdemona's voice issuing almost miraculously from her mouth after the strangulation, Emilia, the very woman whose tongue Iago would "charm" (5.2.183), now describes herself as "bound to speak" (184), and she does so in direct proportion to the silencing of Iago. When Othello demands of Iago the very thing we as audience would demand—"Why he hath thus ensnar'd my soul and body?"—Iago ends his role in the play with the petulant "I never will speak word" (302). Faithless as he may be elsewhere, here he keeps this promise—to the *letter*, I am tempted to add. The master of language silences himself; his final word is *word* itself. Though Gratiano promises that "torments will ope [his] lips" (305), we never see, or hear, of this within the confines of the present play. Rude of speech, Othello in his final speech is also concerned with language: he asks for "a word or two before you go" (338), and I like to imagine that he also refers to the audience about to exit the theater. His concern in that final speech is that his story be told accurately, that one "speak" of him as he is (343).

Like speech, spectacle, so long distorted in the play, is itself restored. Othello opens the final scene intent on putting out Desdemona's "light," but with Iago's exposure he realizes that her spiritual light, that essence Iago would deny even as Othello would when he "becomes" Iago, cannot be so extinguished. It is "this look" of hers, her eyes, "this heavenly sight," that will hurl him from heaven to hell (274–78), and as he looks down at Iago's feet, Othello sees Iago as he is, not as a devil with cloven hoofs, but as a fellow human, not as some supernatural agent but as a potential image of Othello himself (286–87). Having told Roderigo in the first scene that in "following" Othello he "follow[s]" but himself (1.1.58), Iago has indeed inhabited Othello for most of the play. If a militarist like Othello feels embarrassed at a "woman's" tears when his eyes, "albeit unused to the melting mood," drop "tears as fast as the Arabian trees / Their medicinable gum" (348–51), this same weeping also signals a literal and figurative cleansing of his vision.

Beyond the differences in their themes, their status as comedy or tragedy, both *A Midsummer Night's Dream* and *Othello* thus employ that wide gamut of responses to the language and vision prerequisite for the theater. The nightmarish experience of the lovers, the exposure to confusion that skirts tragedy, actually seems tragic to the characters: witness Hermia's dream of her heart being devoured by a snake while Lysander watched, audiencelike, laughing at her (2.7.145–56).[2] Such experience, whether it be that of audience or character, requires a disruption of the play's visual and verbal halves. Hermia may be right in terms of the common assumption that a loss of one sense enhances another, yet, in point of fact, within the forest the "dark night" in "impair[ing]" the seeing sense has abused the ear as well (3.2.177–83): seconds after she rejoices that her "ear" (183) has led her to Lysander's sound, she is jolted when Lysander proclaims his love for Helena. And when Othello is most under Iago's control, Desdemona observes that his "eyes roll" and that he "gnaw[s]" his "nether lip" (5.2.38–43).

Still, the tragedy in such misalliance of the verbal and visual is offset by the comedy of their alliance. Helena praises Hermia's eyes as "lodestars" and her speech as a "tongue's sweet air / More tuneable than lark to shepherd's ear" (1.1.183–84). It is Iago, of all people, who best defines, beyond his sarcasm, the perfection of the visual and verbal embodied in Desdemona: "What an eye she has! . . . And when she speaks, is it not an alarum to love?" (2.2.21–26). That eye and that speech have been meant only for Othello—as audience we can never doubt this—and when he sees and hears her properly, then he can love her, and the marital comedy, so long aborted by Iago, can reassert itself. Despite the tremendous cost, it is an achievement—better late than never—as Othello sacrifices his own life to win his right to a final kiss on the lips of a chaste wife.

ii

I can now, I trust, reintroduce the nine plays discussed earlier as a way of resolving what is at present the penultimate—and unfinished because it *is* penultimate—chord of this coda. Those plays have led to a single composition built on several strains: the comic results of inadequate vision in *The Comedy of Errors*; the tragic gap between linguistic abstraction and a finite, sordid reality in *Troilus and Cressida*; the struggle through time in *The Winter's Tale* to harmonize language and spectacle; an extension of vision through ghosts and the supernatural that is at one with the existentially complex world of *Julius Caesar* and is a sign of the central character's unique but fatal status in *Macbeth*; the demonic manipulation of language in *Richard III* and the affirmative, politically practical speech informing *Henry V*; the productive relation between language and spectacle in *The Merchant of Venice*; and their extrapolation in *King Lear* toward our real life offstage that stage enactment itself is designed to mirror. This same gamut reflecting Shakespeare's productive employment of the four dimensions of the theater that have been my concern here—language, spectacle, presence, and the audience—is embodied in the endings of the very two plays that form the coda in this final chapter, in this last act of my own "play."

Speaking only for the onstage audience, for those who have experienced the "presence" of *Othello* while ignorant of their "real" status as fictive characters, Gratiano in reacting to Lodovico's description of Othello's suicide as a "bloody period" finds that "all that [Othello has] spoke[n] is marr'd" (357–58). Lodovico, also looking audiencelike at the dead husband and wife, observes that "the object poisons sight" (364). From the confines of their world, a reality that, to us, is only play, they are accurate: the scene *is* repulsive, and Iago's handiwork sickens the onlookers. However, aware of our special status as offstage audience, we know that what we see has served a design far greater than Iago's, that Iago himself serves Shakespeare's larger purpose in underscoring our human need to see and to hear with clarity, with reason, and with love. The visual and verbal thematic failure for the onstage audience is, conversely, a metadramatic achievement for those offstage. Though brought together as audiences by this same presence, our responses are at loggerheads.

Our disengagement in the tragedy is balanced by our engagement in the comedy. In his epilogue, Puck suggests that if "these visions" and "this weak and idle theme" have offended us, we may find an excuse by denying our own consciousness, by pretending that we, no less than the characters in the forest, "have but slumber'd here." Puck *seems* to invite us to dismiss the play as a trifle—as *A Midsummer Night's Dream*, as *Much Ado about Nothing*, *As You Like It*, as a mere *Winter's Tale*, or *Comedy of Errors*—but we know that we have been conscious, that we have not slumbered, and, therefore, by a sort of reverse inference we cannot disassociate ourselves from the apparently insignificant experience onstage. We were part of the equation; we *made it happen* just as Theseus and the aristocrats were responsible for choosing Bottom's *Pyramus and Thisby*, a tragic love story, a *Romeo and Juliet*. If those courtly lovers took the theater more seriously, if they could have resisted Theseus's cynical equation of poets or playwrights with madmen and irrational lovers, they would have found an invaluable perspective on their "real" world as it exists in that opening scene, where instead of a comedy there was promised only a tragedy if Hermia failed to obey a father's wishes.

In effect, if we are disengaged in the tragedy (no less than we are engaged, for surely Othello's problems of belief are our own), we are engaged in the comedy, even as we have spent most of the play disengaged from absurd lovers running madly through the forest. As the playwright's verbal and visual stage is recorded, ratified through our own ears and eyes, we are present for that language and spectacle presently enacted before us, and *for* us. We know that Shakespeare's theater of presence is our own.[3]

Notes and Pertinent Sources

(Note: In the "See Also" section following the notes for each chapter I include those works which I found valuable even though I did not make specific mention of them in either the text or the commentary in the notes. Indeed, many of these works so listed had a most pervasive, albeit general influence. In addition, the "See Also" section includes works that came to me, for a variety of reasons, late in my writing, often after my thoughts and prose had already hardened. I have had a chance, however, to comment on those which were published most recently in "Recent Studies in Elizabethan and Jacobean Drama," *Studies in English Literature* 25 (1985): 439–89.

Preface. On a Book's Title

1. Anne Barton (née Righter), *Shakespeare and the Idea of the Play* (Baltimore, Md.: Penguin Books, 1967).

2. James L. Calderwood, *Shakespearean Metadrama: The Argument of the Play in "Titus Andronicus," "Love's Labour's Lost," "Romeo and Juliet," "A Midsummer Night's Dream," and "Richard II"* (Minneapolis: University of Minnesota Press, 1971); idem, *To Be and Not To Be: Negation and Metadrama in "Hamlet"* (New York: Columbia University Press, 1983).

3. Murray Krieger, *A Window to Criticism: Shakespeare's Sonnets and Modern Poetics* (Princeton, N.J.: Princeton University Press, 1964).

4. "When the Theater Turns to Itself," *New Literary History* 2 (1971): 407–17; and I list my "explorations" through articles in the acknowledgments section (p. 27) of my *When the Theater Turns to Itself: The Aesthetic Metaphor in Shakespeare* (Lewisburg, Pa.: Bucknell University Press, 1981).

5. Alain Robbe-Grillet, "Samuel Beckett, or 'Presence' in the Theatre" (original title: "Samuel Beckett ou La présence sur la scène"), in *Pour un nouveau roman* (Paris: Les Edition de Minuit, 1963).

6. Peter Shaffer, *"Black Comedy," including "White Lies": Two Plays* (New York: Stein and Day, 1967).

7. Mark Howard Medoff, *Children of a Lesser God* (New York: Westmark Productions, Inc., 1980).

Chapter 1. *The Comedy of Errors*

1. My text for *The Comedy of Errors*, and all of Shakespeare's plays considered here, is *The Riverside Shakespeare*, ed. G. Blakemore Evans (Boston, Mass.: Houghton Mifflin Company, 1974).

2. See John Arthos, "Shakespeare's Transformation of Plautus," *Comparative Drama* 1 (Winter 1967–68): 239–53.

3. See John Russell Brown, *Shakespeare and His Comedies* (London: Methuen and Company, 1964, reprint), pp. 54–57; and Richard Henze, "The Comedy of Errors: A Freely Binding Chain," *Shakespeare Quarterly* 22 (1971): 35–41.

4. Anne Barton summarizes this debate nicely in her introduction to the play in *The Riverside Shakespeare*, pp. 79–80. For some provocative comments on the staging, and other matters in the play, see Harry Levin, "Introduction to *The Comedy of Errors*," The Signet Classic Shakespeare, gen. ed. Sylvan Barnet (New York: New American Library, 1965), pp. xxiii–xxxviii.

5. The notion that this is a superficial play, its characters only types, is epitomized in Francis Fergusson's "*The Comedy of Errors* and *Much Ado about Nothing*," *Sewanee Review* 62 (1954): 24–37. Larry Champion finds Adriana alone having something of a "psychology," and hence a subsequent character change, in *The Evolution of Shakespeare's Comedy: A Study in Dramatic Perspective* (Cambridge, Mass.: Harvard University Press, 1970), pp. 13–24. However, Barbara Freedman, in two very insightful pieces, finds much more in the play. See her "Egeon's Debt: Self-Division and Self-Redemption in *The Comedy of Errors*," *English Literary Renaissance* 10 (1980): 360–83; and idem, "Errors in Comedy: A Psychoanalytic Theory of Farce," in the special edition on *Shakespearean Comedy* in *New York Literary Forum*, ed. Maurice Charney, 5–6 (1980): 233–43. In that same issue see Catherine M. Shaw, "The Conscious Art of *The Comedy of Errors*," pp. 17–28. And Ruth Nevo, "My Glass and Not My Brother," in *Comic Transformations in Shakespeare* (London: Methuen and Company, Ltd., 1980), pp. 22–36.

6. See Ralph Berry, *Shakespeare's Comedies: Explorations in Form* (Princeton, N.J.: Princeton University Press, 1972), p. 32.

7. I am especially indebted here to J. Dennis Huston's commentary on Egeon and the play's "induction" scene. *Shakespeare's Comedies of Play* (New York: Columbia University Press, 1981), pp. 14–34.

8. See R. A. Foakes's introduction to the Arden edition, *The Arden Shakespeare*, gen. eds. Harold Brooks and Harold Jenkins (London: Methuen and Company, Ltd., 1963), p. 12.

9. Gamini Salgado, "'Time's Deformed Hand': Sequence, Consequence, and Inconsequence in *The Comedy of Errors*," *Shakespeare Survey* 25 (1972): 81–91.

10. See Michel Grivelet's excellent "Shakespeare, Moliere, and the Comedy of Ambiguity," *Shakespeare Survey* 22 (1969): 15–26.

11. Huston, *Comedies of Play*, pp. 32–33.

12. For the significance of this phrase I am indebted to David Young, *Something of Great Constancy: The Art of "A Midsummer Night's Dream"* (New Haven, Conn.: Yale University Press, 1966).

See also:

1. Harold Brooks, "Themes and Structures in *The Comedy of Errors*," *Early Shakespeare*, Stratford-Upon-Avon Studies 3 (New York: St. Martin's Press, 1961): 55–71.

2. Maurice Charney, *Comedy High and Low: An Introduction to the Experience of Comedy* (New York: Oxford University Press, 1978).

3. Thomas Clayton, "The Text, Imagery, and Sense of the Abbess's Final Speech in *The Comedy of Errors*," *Anglia* 91 (1973): 479–84.

4. Louise George Clubb, "Italian Comedy and *The Comedy of Errors*," *Comparative Literature* 9 (1967): 240–51.

5. Jonathan V. Crewe, "God or the Good Physician: The Rational Playwright in *The Comedy of Errors*," *Genre* 15 (1982): 203–33.

6. John P. Cutts, *The Shattered Glass: A Dramatic Pattern in Shakespeare's Early Plays* (Detroit, Mich.: Wayne State University Press, 1968), pp. 13–22.

7. G. R. Elliott, "Weirdness in *The Comedy of Errors*," in *Shakespeare's Comedies: An Anthology of Modern Criticism*, ed. Laurence Lerner (Baltimore, Md.: Penguin Books, 1967), pp. 19–31.

8. Bertrand Evans, *Shakespeare's Comedies* (Oxford: Clarendon Press, 1960), pp. 1–9.

9. A. C. Hamilton, *The Early Shakespeare* (San Marino, Calif.: The Huntington Library, 1967), pp. 99–108.

10. R. Chris Hassel, Jr. *Faith and Folly in Shakespeare's Romantic Comedies* (Athens: University of Georgia Press, 1980).

11. Robert B. Heilman, "Farce Transformed: Plautus, Shakespeare, and Unamuno," *Comparative Literature* 31 (1979): 113–23.

12. Robert B. Heilman, *The Ways of the World: Comedy and Society* (Seattle and London: University of Washington Press, 1978).

13. G. Wilson Knight, *The Shakespearian Tempest* (London: Methuen and Company, 1953), pp. 113–18.

14. W. Thomas MacCary, "*The Comedy of Errors*: A Different Kind of Comedy," *New Literary History* 9 (1978): 525–36.

15. Vincent F. Petronella, "Structure and Theme Through Separation and Union in Shakespeare's *The Comedy of Errors*," *Modern Language Review* 9 (1974): 481–88.

16. A. P. Riemer, *Antic Fables: Patterns of Evasion in Shakespeare's Comedies* (New York: St. Martin's Press, 1980).

17. Leo Salingar, *Shakespeare and the Traditions of Comedy* (Cambridge: At the University Press, 1974), pp. 59–67.

18. James L. Sanderson, "Patience in *The Comedy of Errors*," *Texas Studies in Language and Literature* 16 (1975): 603–18.

19. Michael Scott, *Renaissance Drama and a Modern Audience* (Atlantic Highlands, N.J.: Humanities Press, 1982), pp. 1–17.

20. William O. Scott, *The God of Arts: Ruling Ideas in Shakespeare's Comedies* (Lawrence: University of Kansas Publications, 1977).

21. Thomas F. Van Laan, *Role-Playing in Shakespeare* (Toronto: University of Toronto Press, 1978), pp. 22–25.

22. Barry Weller, "Identity and Representation in Shakespeare," *English Literary History* 49 (1982): 339–62.

23. Richard P. Wheeler, *Shakespeare's Development and the Problem Comedies. Turn and Counter-Turn* (Berkeley and Los Angeles: University of California Press, 1981).

24. Gwyn Williams, "*The Comedy of Errors* Rescued from Tragedy," *Review of English Literature* 5 (1964): 63–71.

25. Deborah Baker Wyrick, "The Ass Motif in *The Comedy of Errors* and *A Midsummer Night's Dream*," *Shakespeare Quarterly* 33 (1982): 432–48.

Chapter 2. *Troilus and Cressida*

1. *Coleridge's Shakespearean Criticism*, ed. T. M. Raysor (Cambridge, Mass.: Harvard University Press, 1930): 1 : 108.

2. David M. Jago, "The Uniqueness of *Troilus and Cressida*," *Shakespeare Quarterly* 29 (1978): 20.

3. Richard D. Fly, "'I cannot come to Cressid but by Pandar': Mediation in the Theme and Structure of *Troilus and Cressida*," *English Literary Renaissance* 3 (1973): 145–65.

4. D. A. Traversi, "*Troilus and Cressida*," *Scrutiny* 7 (1930): 301.

5. Frederick S. Boas, *Shakespeare and His Predecessors* (New York: Charles Scribner's Sons, 1908), p. 384.

6. Jarold W. Ramsey, "The Provenance of *Troilus and Cressida*," *Shakespeare Quarterly* 21 (1970): 240.

7. R. J. Kaufmann, "'Ceremonies for Chaos': The Status of *Troilus and Cressida*," *English Literary History* 32 (1965): 140.

8. Katherine Stockholder, "Power and Pleasure in *Troilus and Cressida*, or Rhetoric and Structure of the Anti-Tragic," *College English* 30 (1969): 549.

9. See Oscar James Campbell, *Comicall Satyre and Shakespeare's "Troilus and Cressida"* (San Marino, Calif.: The Huntington Library, 1938).

10. Douglas Cole, "Myth and Anti-Myth: The Case of *Troilus and Cressida*," *Shakespeare Quarterly* 31 (1980): 76–84.

11. E. M. W. Tillyard, *Shakespeare's Problem Plays* (Toronto: University of Toronto Press, 1968), p. 65.

12. *Shaw on Shakespeare*, ed. Edwin Wilson (New York: E. P. Dutton, 1961), p. 261.

13. Robert Kimbrough, *Shakespeare's "Troilus and Cressida" and Its Setting* (Cambridge, Mass.: Harvard University Press, 1964).

14. G. Wilson Knight, *The Wheel of Fire* (London: Methuen and Co. Ltd., 1949), p. 62.

15. Alice Shavli, "'Honor' in *Troilus and Cressida*," *Studies in English Literature* 5 (1965): 283–302.

16. Mary Ellen Rickey, "'Twixt the Dangerous Shores: *Troilus and Cressida* Again," *Shakespeare Quarterly* 15 (1964): 3–13.

17. Kenneth Muir, "*Troilus and Cressida*," *Shakespeare Survey* 8 (1955): 36–38.

18. R. A. Yoder, "'Sons and Daughters of the Game': An Essay on Shakespeare's *Troilus and Cressida*," *Shakespeare Survey* 25 (1972): 11–25.

19. William Empson, *Some Versions of Pastoral* (London: Chatto and Windus, 1935): pp. 35–84.

20. See R. C. Harrier, "Troilus Divided," *Studies in English Renaissance Drama in Memory of Karl Julius Holzknecht*, ed. Josephine W. Bennett et al. (New York: New York University Press, 1959), pp. 147–56; and David Kaula, "Will and Reason in *Troilus and Cressida*," *Shakespeare Quarterly* 12 (1961): 271–83.

21. Robert Ornstein, *The Moral Vision of Jacobean Tragedy* (Madison: University of Wisconsin Press, 1960), pp. 240–49; and W. W. Lawrence, *Shakespeare's Problem Comedies* (New York and London: The Macmillan Company, 1931), pp. 122–74.

22. M. T. Jones-Davies, "Discord in Shakespeare's *Troilus and Cressida*; or, The Conflict between 'Angry Mars and Venus Queen of Love,'" *Shakespeare Quarterly* 25 (1974): 33–41.

23. Norman Rabkin, "*Troilus and Cressida*: the Use of the Double Plot," *Shakespeare Studies* 1 (1965): 271.

24. See Winifred M. T. Nowottny, "'Opinion' and 'Value' in *Troilus and Cressida*," *Shakespeare Survey* 4 (1954): 282–96; Camille Slights, "The Parallel Structure of *Troilus and Cressida*," *Shakespeare Quarterly* 25 (1974): 42–51; Wylie Sypher, *The Ethic of Time: Structure and Experience in Shakespeare* (New York: The Seabury Press, 1976), pp. 129–55; and Eileen Jorge Allman, *Player-king and*

Adversary: Two Faces of Play in Shakespeare (Baton Rouge: Louisiana State University Press, 1980), pp. 156–83.

25. Una Ellis-Fermor, *The Frontiers of Drama* (London: Methuen and Company, 1964), pp. 56–76 ("'Discord in the Spheres': The Universe of *Troilus and Cressida*").

26. Tinsley Helton, "Paradox and Hypothesis in *Troilus and Cressida*," *Shakespeare Studies* 10 (1977): 115–32.

27. David Horowitz, *Shakespeare, An Existential View* (London: Hill and Wang, 1965), pp. 103–9.

28. John D. Cox, "The Error of Our Eye in *Troilus and Cressida*," *Comparative Drama* 10 (1976): 147–71.

29. Harry Berger, Jr., "*Troilus and Cressida*: The Observer as Basilisk," *Comparative Drama* 2 (1968): 125–27.

30. Philip Edwards, *Shakespeare and the Confines of Art* (London: Methuen and Company, 1968), p. 97.

31. R. A. Foakes, *Shakespeare: The Dark Comedies to the Last Plays: From Satire to Celebration* (Charlottesville: University of Virginia Press, 1971), p. 45.

32. Albert Gerard, "Meaning and Structure in *Troilus and Cressida*," *English Studies* 40 (1959): 153.

33. L. C. Knights, *Some Shakespearean Themes* (Stanford, Calif.: Stanford University Press, 1959), p. 78.

34. S. L. Bethell, *Shakespeare and the Popular Dramatic Tradition* (Westminster: P. S. King and Staples Ltd., 1944), p. 105.

35. Neil Powell, "Hero and Human: The Problem of Achilles," *Critical Quarterly* 21 (1979): 17–28.

36. Derick R. C. Marsh, "Interpretation and Misinterpretation: the Problem of *Troilus and Cressida*," *Shakespeare Studies* 1 (1965): 186.

37. Rolf P. Lessenich, "Shakespeare's *Troilus and Cressida*: the Vision of Decadence," *Studia Neophilologica* 49 (1977): 230.

38. Nancy S. Leonard, "Substitution in Shakespeare's Problem Comedies," *English Literary Renaissance* 9 (1979): 281–301.

39. Clifford Leech, *The Dramatist's Experience, with Other Essays in Literary Theory* (New York: Barnes and Noble, 1970), p. 165.

40. See Mark Sacharoff, "The Traditions of the Troy-Story Heroes and the Problem of Satire in *Troilus and Cressida*," *Shakespeare Studies* 6 (1970): 125–35; and R. K. Presson, *Shakespeare's "Troilus and Cressida" and the Legends of Troy* (Madison: University of Wisconsin Press, 1953).

41. Again, see Presson, *Shakespeare's "Troilus and Cressida."*

42. D. W. Robertson, *A Preface to Chaucer: Studies in Medieval Perspectives* (Princeton, N.J.: Princeton University Press, 1963), pp. 477–502.

43. S. L. Bethell, *Shakespeare and the Popular Dramatic Tradition* (Westminster: P. S. King and Staples Ltd., 1944), p. 102; and M. M. Mahood, *Shakespeare's Wordplay* (London: Methuen and Company, 1965), p. 127.

44. P. M. Kendall, "Inaction and Ambivalence in *Troilus and Cressida*," *English Studies in Honor of James Southall Wilson*, ed. Fredson Bowers (Charlottesville: University of Virginia Press, 1951), pp. 131–45.

45. L. C. Knights, *Some Shakespearean Themes* (Stanford, Calif.: Stanford University Press, 1959), p. 113.

46. J. Oates Smith, "Essence and Existence in Shakespeare's *Troilus and Cressida*," *Philological Quarterly* 46 (1967): 167–85.

47. Carolyn Asp, "Transcendence Denied: The Failure of Role Assumption

in *Troilus and Cressida*," *Studies in English Literature* 18 (1978): 274.

48. Arnold Stein, "*Troilus and Cressida*: The Disjunctive Imagination," *English Literary History* 36 (1969): 163–64.

49. A point made by Marshall McLuhan in "Roles, Masks, and Performances," *New Literary History* 2 (1971): 221: "We are the text of any performance," and echoed by Jacques Derrida in a lecture on Kafka's *The Trial*, University of Florida, April 19, 1982, where he suggests that we are the man before the Law of the Text and that it is we, not the gatekeeper (the author), who must "open" that text and for whom it was ultimately intended.

50. Morris Weitz in his closing remarks in *Hamlet and the Philosophy of Literary Criticism* (Chicago: University of Chicago Press, 1964), pp. 316–19.

51. From the title of an article on Beckett by Mark J. Sachner, "The Artist as Fiction: An Aesthetics of Failure in Samuel Beckett's Trilogy," *Midwest Quarterly* 18 (1977): 144–55.

52. Richard Fly, " 'Suited in Like Conditions as Our Argument': Imitative Form in Shakespeare's *Troilus and Cressida*," *Studies in English Literature* 15 (1975): 287.

53. See J. O. Smith, "Essence and Existence," p. 167–85.

54. Shavli, " 'Honor' in *Troilus and Cressida*," pp. 283–302.

55. I. A. Richards, *Speculative Instruments* (Chicago: University of Chicago Press, 1955), pp. 198–213. For some practical commentary on the scene's staging see Douglas C. Sprigg, "Shakespeare's Visual Stagecraft: The Seduction of Cressida," *Shakespeare: The Theatrical Dimension*, ed. Philip C. McGuire and David A. Samuelson (New York: AMS Press, 1979), pp. 149–63.

56. See, for example, Brian Morris, "The Tragic Structure of *Troilus and Cressida*," *Shakespeare Quarterly* 10 (1959): 488.

57. See Stockholder, "Power and Pleasure in *Troilus and Cressida*," pp. 547–54.

58. See Carolyn Asp, "In Defense of Cressida," *Studies in Philology* 74 (1977): 406–17.

59. See Cole, "Myth and Anti-Myth," p. 82.

60. Marsh, "Interpretation and Misinterpretation," p. 189.

61. Campbell, *Comicall Satyre*, p. 216.

62. Cole, "Myth and Anti-Myth," p. 82.

63. J. Hillis Miller, "Ariachne's Broken Woof," *Georgia Review* 31 (1977): 44–60.

64. Kaufmann, " 'Ceremonies for Chaos,' " p. 157.

65. Again, see Miller, "Ariachne's Broken Woof," pp. 44–60.

66. Asp, "Transcendence Denied," p. 260.

67. Richard Fly, "Cassandra and the Language of Prophecy in *Troilus and Cressida*," *Shakespeare Quarterly* 26 (1975): 158.

68. In *The Victorian Age of German Literature: Eight Essays* (University Park: Pennsylvania State University Press, 1966), p. 25, Norbert Fuerst comments that even tragedy, the epitome of dramatic art, is not about death but is, instead, "a hymn to life," that it is the artist's way of saying that the universe is not totally absurd, not so formless or meaningless as to be unworthy of being given the fictive form of the drama itself.

69. Berger, "The Observer as Basilisk," p. 125.

70. Ibid., p. 128.

71. Nowottny, " 'Opinion' and 'Value,' " pp. 282–96.

72. Fly, " 'I cannot come to Cressid,' " p. 162.

73. Ellis-Fermor, *Frontiers of Drama*, p. 59.

74. The term used by T. S. Eliot in "Hamlet and His Problems," *Selected Essays: 1917–1932* (New York: Harcourt, Brace and Co., 1932), p. 125.

75. See the good review of such speculations by Anne Barton in her preface to the play in *The Riverside Shakespeare*, p. 444.

76. Leech, *The Dramatist's Experience*, p. 163.

77. Knights, *Some Shakespearean Themes*, p. 81.

See also:

1. L. A. Beaurline, *Jonson and Elizabethan Comedy: Essays in Dramatic Rhetoric* (San Marino, Calif: The Huntington Library, 1978).

2. M. M. Burns, "*Troilus and Cressida*: The Worst of Both Worlds," *Shakespeare Studies* 13 (1980): 105–30.

3. Barbara Everett, "The Inaction of *Troilus and Cressida*," *Essays in Criticism* 32 (1982): 119–39.

4. Gayle Greene, "Language and Value in Shakespeare's *Troilus and Cressida*," *Studies in English Literature* 21 (1981): 271–85.

5. Gayle Greene, "Shakespeare's Cressida: 'A kind of self,'" in *The Woman's Part: Feminist Criticism of Shakespeare*, ed. Carolyn R. S. Lenz, Gayle Greene, and Carol Thomas Neely (Urbana: University of Illinois Press, 1980), pp. 133–49.

6. Colin N. Manlove, *The Gap in Shakespeare: The Motif of Division from "Richard II" to "The Tempest,"* Critical Studies Series (London: Vision Press, and Totowa, N.J.: Barnes and Noble, 1981), pp. 50–55.

7. Arlene N. Oberlund, "In Defense of Cressida: Character as Metaphor," *Women's Studies* 7 (1980): 1–17.

8. Roger Owens, "The Seven Deadly Sins in the Prologue to *Troilus and Cressida*," *Shakespeare Jahrbuch* (Weimer) 116 (1980): 85–92.

9. Neil Powell, "Hero and Human: The Problem of Achilles," *Critical Quarterly* 21 (1979): 17–28.

10. A. J. Smith, *Literary Love: The Role of Passion in English Poems and Plays of the Seventeenth Century* (London and Baltimore: Edward Arnold, 1983), pp. 10–34.

Chapter 3. *The Winter's Tale*

1. *Bartholomew Fair*, induction, ll. 115–17, in Eugene Waith's edition (New Haven, Conn.: Yale University Press, 1963).

2. This organizing principal has been variously expressed as: GRACE VERSUS JUSTICE; in Eben Bass, "*The Winter's Tale*: Great Difference between Bohemia and Sicilia," *Massachusetts Studies in English* 6 (1978/79): 15–24; as KNOWLEDGE VERSUS WONDER, Richard L. Harp, "*The Winter's Tale*: An 'Old Tale' Begetting Wonder," *Dalhousie Review* 58 (1978): 303; as IDOLATRY VERSUS ADORATION, David Kaula, "Autolycus' Trumpery," *Studies in English Literature* 16 (1976): 287–303; as YOUTH VERSUS MATURITY, Peter Lindenbaum, "Time, Sexual Love, and the Uses of Pastoral in *The Winter's Tale*," *Modern Language Quarterly* 33 (1972): 13; as DIPLOMACY VERSUS PROVIDENCE, James Smith, *Shakespearian and Other Essays*, ed. Edward M. Wilson (Cambridge: At the University Press, 1974), pp. 125–58; as COURT VERSUS COUNTRY, F. C. Tinkler, "*The Winter's Tale*," *Scrutiny* 55 (1937): 359; as SECULAR VERSUS SACRED, Brian Cosgrove, "*The Winter's Tale* and the

Limits of Criticism," *Studies* (Dublin) 66 (1977): 176–87. Other, less dichotomous approaches include: STRUCTURAL, Adrien Bonjour, "Polixenes and the Winter of His Discontent," *English Studies* 50 (1969), 206–12; James Edward Siemon, "'But It Appears She Lives': Iteration in *The Winter's Tale*," *PMLA* 89 (1974): 10–16; Marion Trousdale, "Style in *The Winter's Tale*," *Critical Quarterly* 18 (1976): 30; Richard Proudfoot, "Directing the Romances: 2. Verbal Reminiscence and the Two-Part Structure of *The Winter's Tale*," *Shakespeare Survey* 29 (1976): 68; THEO-LOGICAL, J. A. Bryant, "Shakespeare's Allegory: *The Winter's Tale*," *Sewanee Review* 63 (1955): 202–22; HISTORICAL, Glynne Wickham, "Romance and Emblem: A Study in the Dramatic Structure of *The Winter's Tale*," *Elizabethan Theater III*, ed. David Galloway (Toronto: Macmillan, 1973), pp. 82–99; in terms of PARALLELS AMONG THE CHARACTERS, Joan Hartwig, Shakespeare's *Tragicomic Vision* (Baton Rouge: Louisiana State University Press, 1972), pp. 104–36; as AN EXTENSION OF THE OTHER THREE ROMANCES, Derek Traversi, *Shakespeare: The Last Phase* (Stanford, Calif.: Stanford University Press, 1965), pp. 105–92; Walter F. Eggers, Jr., "'Bring Forth a Wonder': Presentation in Shakespeare's Romances," *Texas Studies in Language and Literature* 21 (1978): 455–77; Clifford Leech, "The Structure of the Last Plays," *Shakespeare Survey* 11 (1958): 19–30; Barbara Adams Mowat, "A Tale of Sprights and Goblins," *Shakespeare Quarterly* 20 (1969): 37–46, and in her *The Dramaturgy of Shakespeare's Romances* (Athens: University of Georgia Press, 1976); and E. C. Pettet, *Shakespeare and the Romance Tradition* (London: Staples Press, 1949), pp. 161–99. Also see F. David Hoeniger's pioneering article, "The Meaning of *The Winter's Tale*," *University of Toronto Quarterly* 20 (1950): 11–26.

3. S. L. Bethell, *"The Winter's Tale": A Study* (London: Staples Press, 1947).

4. On the issue of the play and art see: Robert Egan, *Drama Within Drama: Shakespeare's Sense of His Art in "King Lear," "The Winter's Tale," and "The Tempest"* (New York: Columbia University Press, 1975); Howard Felperin, *Shakespearean Romance* (Princeton, N.J.: Princeton University Press, 1972); Mary L. Livingston, "The Natural Art of *The Winter's Tale*," *Modern Language Quarterly* 30 (1969): 340–55; William H. Matchett, "Some Dramatic Techniques in *The Winter's Tale*," *Shakespeare Survey* 22 (1969): 106; L. G. Salingar, "Time and Art in Shakespeare's Romances," *Renaissance Drama* 9 (1966): 30; Harold E. Toliver, *Pastoral Forms and Attitudes* (Berkeley and Los Angeles: University of California Press, 1971), p. 99.

5. On the play's commentary about art and time see: William Blisset, "The Wide Gap of Time: *The Winter's Tale*," *English Literary Renaissance* 1 (1971): 52–70; Inga-Stina Ewbank, "The Triumph of Time in *The Winter's Tale*," *Review of English Literature* 5 (1964): 83–100; Charles Lloyd Holt, "Notes on the Dramaturgy of *The Winter's Tale*," *Shakespeare Quarterly* 20 (1969): 47–51; P. M. Weinstein, "An Interpretation of Pastoral in *The Winter's Tale*," *Shakespeare Quarterly* 22 (1971): 97–109; and David P. Young, *The Heart's Forest: A Study of Shakespeare's Pastoral Plays* (New Haven, Conn.: Yale University Press, 1972), p. 134.

6. On the play and women see, especially, Norman Holland, *The Shakespearean Imagination* (New York: Macmillan, 1964), p. 299; Patricia Southard Gourlay, "'O my most sacred lady': Female Metaphor in *The Winter's Tale*," *English Literary Renaissance* 5 (1975): 375–95; and Carol Thomas Neely, "Women and Issue in *The Winter's Tale*," *Philological Quarterly* 57 (1978): 181–94.

7. On the play and language see: A. F. Bellette, "Truth and Untruth in *The Winter's Tale*," *Shakespeare Survey* 31 (1978): 66; Charles Frey, *Shakespeare's Vast Romance: A Study of "The Winter's Tale"* (Columbia: University of Missouri Press, 1980), p. 127 especially; and Carol Thomas Neely, *"The Winter's Tale*: The Triumph of Speech," *Studies in English Literature* 15 (1975): 321–38.

8. Nevill Coghill, "Six Points of Stage-Craft in *The Winter's Tale*," *Shakespeare Survey* 11 (1958): 31–41.

9. See C. L. Barber's provocative comments about the difficulty that both Leontes and Polixenes have in making the transition from their boyhood love to adulthood and heterosexuality, in "'Thou That Beget'st Him Did Thee Beget': Transformation in *Pericles* and *The Winter's Tale*," *Shakespeare Survey* 22 (1969): 59–67. Marjorie Garber observes that individuation is linked to sexual maturity, the opposite pole from the nonindividual twinning of childhood, in "Coming of Age in Shakespeare," *Yale Review* 66 (1977): 517–33.

10. See again Barber, "'Thou That Beget'st,'" pp. 59–67, and Garber, "Coming of Age," pp. 517–33. Charles Frey in *Vast Romance* finds the conversation among Leontes, Polixenes, and Hermione in Act 1, scene 2 poised among grace, balance, and alienation (p. 121).

11. On the issue of Leontes' speech see Anne Barton, "Leontes and the Spider: Language and Speaking in Shakespeare's Last Plays," *Shakespeare's Styles: Essays in Honour of Kenneth Muir*, ed. Philip Edwards, Inga-Stina Ewbank, and G. K. Hunter (Cambridge: At the University Press, 1980), pp. 131–50.

12. Hartwig, *Tragicomic Vision*, pp. 104–36.

13. Ellen F. Wright speaks of a divided response to the theater in "'We Are Mock'd with Art': Shakespeare's Wintry Tale," *Essays in Literature* 6 (1979): 147–59.

14. Livingston observes that in such destructive court language Hermione seems "lost". "The Natural Art," pp. 340–55.

15. Samuel Taylor Coleridge, *Shakespearean Criticism*, ed. Thomas Middleton Raysor, 2d ed. (London: Dent, 1960), 1:110–11.

16. Again, the distinction between corrupt male language and wholesome female sight made by Holland, *Shakespearean Imagination*, p. 299.

17. Matchett, "Some Dramatic Techniques," p. 104.

18. I have looked at this speech and the play's own divided attitude toward art—as well as that of the Romances generally—in "*The Tempest* and Shakespeare's Last Plays: The Aesthetic Dimensions," *Shakespeare Quarterly* 24 (1973): 69–76.

19. See Guy Boas, "Exit Antigonus," *Drama* 70 (1963): 34–35.

20. Bernard Beckerman surveys the transition from the verbal to the visual, and the parallels between Shakespeare's plea that the audience employ imaginary vision and the audience's sense of itself in "Shakespearean Playgoing: Then and Now," in *Shakespeare's "More Than Words Can Witness": Essays on Visual and Nonverbal Enactment in the Plays*, ed. Sidney Homan (Lewisburg, Pa.: Bucknell University Press, 1980), pp. 142–59.

21. On the visible presence of Time see Coghill, "Six Points of Stage-Craft," pp. 31–41.

22. Kenneth Muir calls Act 4 "Shakespeare's answer to the corruption of man's heart." *The Last Periods of Shakespeare, Racine, Ibsen* (Detroit, Mich.: Wayne State University Press, 1961), p. 50. Frey finds in its "new" character, Autolycus, the "third beat" to the play's earlier dichotomies, in *Vast Romance*, pp. 148–50.

23. Barton notes that Autolycus's association is with fiction and not evil, in "Leontes and the Spider," p. 149.

24. Theodore Spencer argues that the issue, flourishing most fully in Act 4, is to see "things as they are, but with glory around them." "Appearance and Reality in Shakespeare's Last Plays," *Modern Philology* 39 (1942): 269.

25. John Armstrong, *The Paradise Myth* (New York: Oxford University Press, 1969), pp. 73–74.

26. John Danby comments on the "intelligent manipulation" in the plays, in *Poets on Fortune's Hill: Studies in Sidney, Shakespeare, Beaumont and Fletcher* (Port Washington, N.Y.: Kennikat Press, 1966 reissue), p. 106.

27. For Autolycus's theatrics see Lee Sheridan Cox, "The Role of Autolycus in *The Winter's Tale*," *Studies in English Literature* 9 (1969): 283–301.

28. Robert W. Uphaus, "The 'Comic' Mode of *The Winter's Tale*," *Genre* 3 (1970): 40–54.

29. For commentary on this debate see, particularly, Northrop Frye, "Recognition in *The Winter's Tale*," in *Essays on Shakespeare and Elizabethan Drama in Honor of Hardin Craig*, ed. Richard Hosley (Columbia: University of Missouri Press, 1962), pp. 234–46; and Harold S. Wilson, "Nature and Art in *The Winter's Tale*," *Shakespeare Association Bulletin* 18 (1943): 114–20.

30. Norman Rabkin, "The Holy Sinner and the Confidence Man: Illusion in Shakespeare's Romances," in *Four Essays on Romance*, ed. Herschel Baker (Cambridge, Mass.: Harvard University Press, 1971), p. 53.

31. There has been, of course, much commentary on the play's final scene. I have found particularly useful the following: David M. Bergeron, "The Restoration of Hermione in *The Winter's Tale*," in *Shakespeare's Romances Reconsidered*, ed. Carol McGinnis Kay and Henry E. Jacobs (Lincoln: University of Nebraska Press, 1978), pp. 125–33; S. L. Bethell, *"The Winter's Tale": A Study* (London: Staples Press, 1947); Adrien Bonjour, "The Final Scene of *The Winter's Tale*," *English Studies* 33 (1952): 193–208; Coghill, "Six Points of Stage-Craft," pp. 31–41; Felperin, *Shakespearean Romance*, pp. 211–45; H. Carrington Lancaster, "Hermione's Statue," *Studies in Philology* 29 (1932): 233–38; F. H. Langman, "*The Winter's Tale*," *Southern Review* 9 (1976): 195–204; Terence J. B. Spencer, "The Statue of Hermione," *Essays and Studies* 30 (1977): 39–49; Richard Studing, "'That rare Italian master'—Shakespeare's Julio Romano," *Humanities Association Bulletin* 22 (1971): 22–26.

32. See the comments on Shakespeare's purposes in Act 5, scene 2 by Joan Rees, "Revenge, Retribution, and Reconciliation," *Shakespeare Survey* 24 (1971): 31–35.

33. Bethell, *"The Winter's Tale": A Study*.

34. R. A. Foakes, *Shakespeare: The Dark Comedies to the Last Plays: From Satire to Celebration* (Charlottesville: University of Virginia Press, 1971), p. 144.

35. In "The Holy Sinner and the Confidence Man" (p. 53), Norman Rabkin speaks eloquently to this issue: "Every motion of the spirit, every event of life, is infinitely serious, yet, as such stuff as dreams are made on is an inconsequential ripple on the flux of time, infinitely trivial, the subject of an entertainment for a play's audience constantly reminded it is an audience, and for the gods."

See also:

1. Richard H. Abrams, "*The Winter's Tale*: Problems of Iconoclasm and Dramatic Agency," in *Literature and Iconoclasm: Shakespeare*, Occasional Papers II: By Members of the Program of Literature and Philosophy, State University of New York at Buffalo, ed. Brian Caraker and Irving Massey (Buffalo, N.Y.: Department of English, 1976), pp. 29–41.

2. Leonard Barkan, "'Living Sculptures': Ovid, Michelangelo, and *The Winter's Tale*," *English Literary History* 48 (1981): 639–67.

3. Dennis Bartholomeusz, *"The Winter's Tale" in Performance in England and America 1611–1976* (Cambridge: At the University Press, 1982).

4. Roy Battenhouse, "Theme and Structure in *The Winter's Tale*," *Shakespeare Survey* 33 (1980): 123–38.

5. Stephen Booth, "Exit, Pursued by Gentlemen Born," in *Shakespeare's Art from a Comparative Perspective*, Proceedings: Comparative Literature Symposium, Texas Technological University, vol. 12, ed. Wendell M. Aycock (Lubbock, Tex.: Texas Technological University Press, 1981), pp. 51–66.

6. Stanley Cavell, *The Claim of Reason* (New York: Oxford University Press, 1979), pp. 481–82.

7. Wilson F. Engel, III, "Sculpture and the Art of Memory in Elizabethan and Jacobean Drama," *Modern Language Studies* 10 (1980): 3–9.

8. Peter B. Erickson, "Patriarchal Structures in *The Winter's Tale*," *PMLA* 97 (1982): 819–29.

9. Theresa M. Krier, "The Triumph of Time: Paradoxes in *The Winter's Tale*," *Centennial Review* 26 (1982): 341–53.

10. Louis L. Martz, "Shakespeare's Humanistic Enterprise: *The Winter's Tale*," in *English Renaissance Studies Presented to Dame Helen Gardner in Honour of Her Seventieth Birthday*, ed. John Carey (Oxford: Clarendon Press, 1980), pp. 114–31.

11. Murray M. Schwartz, "Leontes' Jeolousy in *The Winter's Tale*," in *The Practice of Psychoanalytic Criticism*, ed. Leonard Tennenhouse (Detroit, Mich.: Wayne State University Press, 1976), pp. 202–25.

12. Garrett Stewart, "Shakespearean Dreamplay," *English Literary Renaissance* 11 (1981): 44–69.

13. Richard Studing, "Shakespeare's Bohemia Revisited: A Caveat," *Shakespeare Studies* 15 (1982): 217–26.

14. Michael Taylor, "Increase in *The Winter's Tale*," *Shakespeare Studies* 15 (1982): 227–42.

15. Robert W. Uphaus, *Beyond Tragedy: Structure and Experience in Shakespeare's Romances* (Lexington: University of Kentucky Press, 1982), pp. 69–91.

16. Robert N. Watson, *Shakespeare and the Hazards of Ambition* (Cambridge, Mass.: Harvard University Press, 1984), pp. 222–79.

Chapter 4. *Julius Caesar*

1. For example. Bernard Breyer, dismayed by the "few meager lines" given to the ghost's appearance, observes that it is "mighty unimpressive for a stellar role." "A New Look at *Julius Caesar*," *Essays in Honor of Walter Clyde Curry*, ed. Richmond C. Beatty et al. (Nashville, Tenn.: Vanderbilt University Press, 1954), p. 162. It has been called "a dramatic condensation of the immortality" achieved by Caesar during his life (Brigid Brophy, *Black Ship to Hell* [New York: Harcourt, Brace, and World, 1962], p. 77), a manifestation of "the Caesar-principle" (Kenneth Burke, *The Philosophy of Literary Form* [New York: Vintage, 1957], p. 281), and thereby a "visible symbol" of his power and significance (Edward Dowden, *Shakespeare: A Critical Study of His Mind and Art* [New York: Harper and Brothers Publishers, 1881], p. 256). A reminder that "Caesar is never for a moment absent" (John Palmer, *Political and Comic Characters in Shakespeare* [London: Macmillan, 1962], p. 58), the ghost is the "reaffirmation of the monarchic principle" (J. E. Phillips, *The State in Shakespeare's Greek and Roman Plays*, Columbia University Studies in English and Comparative Literature 149 [New York: Columbia University Press, 1940], p. 187), the personification of a great man (Virgil Whitaker, *Shakespeare's Use of Learning* [San Marino, Calif.: Huntington Library, 1964], p. 230), the Northern Star (Roy Walker, "Unto Caesar: A Review of

Recent Productions," *Shakespeare Survey* 11 [1958]: 132–35). Conversely, the ghost has been seen as a premonition of the ill that the conspirators have failed to eradicate (Derek Traversi, *Shakespeare: The Roman Plays* [Stanford, Calif.: Stanford University Press, 1963], p. 70), or the unwanted, repudiated parts of Brutus's personality that break through despite his attempts to deny them (Lynn de Gerenday, "Play, Ritualism, and Ambivalence in *Julius Caesar,*" *Literature and Psychology* 24 [1974]: 30). It has been called Brutus's evil spirit and thus an ironic counterpart to his earlier reputation as Caesar's "angel" (David C. Green, *"Julius Caesar" and Its Sources,* Salzburg Studies in English Literature [Salzburg, Austria: University of Salzburg Press, 1979], pp. 269–70), or, at very least, the "over-reacher side of Brutus" (R. J. Kaufmann and Clifford J. Ronan, "Shakespeare's *Julius Caesar:* An Apollonian and Comparative Reading," *Comparative Drama* 4 [1970]: 45). In fact, that critical response, often ignoring the fact that it is indeed a hybrid ghost, has tended to read it as Caesar's positive or Brutus's negative side. However, E. E. Stoll would take the ghost "not intellectually or philosophically, but as a matter of art." *Shakespeare Studies Historical and Comparative in Method* (New York: The Macmillan Co., 1927), p. 209.

2. Perhaps Coleridge initiates the debate with his question, "What character does Shakespeare mean his Brutus to be?" See *Coleridge's Shakespearean Criticism,* ed. T. M. Raysor (Cambridge, Mass.: Harvard University Press, 1930), 1:16. For William R. Bowden, Brutus is well-intentioned but lacking any real vision ("The Mind of Brutus," *Shakespeare Quarterly* 17 [1966]: 57–67); Moody E. Prior doubts "whether the most fruitful way to approach *Julius Caesar* is as the tragedy of Brutus ("The Search for a Hero in *Julius Caesar,*" *Renaissance Drama,* N.S. 2 [1969]: 81–101). For Phyllis Rackin, Brutus dies "unconvinced," still believing that all men were true to him, never fully understanding the realities of political life ("The Pride of Shakespeare's Brutus," *Library Chronicle* 32 [1966]: 18–30), while Gordon Ross Smith sees him as an inflexible character, self-righteous, alternating between an imperious will and childish impulsiveness ("Brutus, Virtue, and Will," *Shakespeare Quarterly* 10 [1959]: 367–79). Margaret Greaves presents a more divided Brutus, his self-reliance being a positive, but inseparable from his self-satisfaction, a negative (*The Blazon of Honour: A Study of Renaissance Magnanimity* [London: Methuen, 1964], pp. 121–22); for Ruth M. Levitsky, Brutus, despite his Stoic flaw of pride, is still the noblest Roman of them all (" 'The Elements Were So Mix'd . . . ,' " *PMLA* 88 [1973]: 240–45. We will recall that in Orson Welles's modern-dress production in 1937 Brutus, played by Welles, was the unqualified hero, symbolic of the Allies fighting a modern dictator embodied in Caesar. Mildred O. Durham finds Caesar of the "semi-divine species" ("Drama of the Dying God in *Julius Caesar,*" *University of Hartford Studies in Literature* 11 [1979]: 49–57), and for M. W. MacCallum the assassination proves that the "rule of the single master-mind is the only admissible solution for the problems of the time" (*Shakespeare's Roman Plays and Their Backgrounds* [New York: Russell and Russell, 1967, reissue], p. 214). Douglas L. Peterson links Caesar and Brutus in their rigid belief in their own invulnerability (" 'Wisdom Consumed in Confidence': An Examination of Shakespeare's *Julius Caesar,*" *Shakespeare Quarterly* 16 [1965]: 19–28, while Andrew M. Wilkinson examines what he calls Caesar's paranoia ("A Psychoanalytic Approach to *Julius Caesar,*" *Review of English Literature* 7 [1966]: 65–78). In a very insightful article Michael Payne argues that the conscious motives of the conspirators only cover a psychological conflict in which fraternal and paternal loyalties clash ("Political Myth and Rhetoric in *Julius Caesar,*" *Bucknell Review* 19 [1971]: 85–106). This taking sides, in which a positive assessment of Brutus or Caesar leads to a negative assessment

of the other, has given way to a more divided view of both characters, and of the assassination itself. Robert Ornstein, for example, reads the play through Seneca's *De Beneficiis*, which offers a divided response to Brutus's motives ("Seneca and the Political Drama of *Julius Caesar*," *Journal of English and Germanic Philology* 57 [1958]: 51–56), and Schanzer presents a Pirandello-like Caesar, who is what the characters variously see him to be (*The Problem Plays of Shakespeare*, p. 32). A very excellent review of the conflicting readings of the play, at least up to 1966, is provided by Mildred E. Hartsock, "The Complexity of *Julius Caesar*," *PMLA* 81 (1966): 56–62.

3. Ernest Schanzer, *The Problem Plays of Shakespeare: A Study of "Julius Caesar," "Measure for Measure," "Antony and Cleopatra"* (New York: Schocken Books, 1963), p. 34.

4. On this episode see David L. Carson, "The Dramatic Importance of Prodigies in *Julius Caesar*, Act II, Scene I," *English Language Notes* 2 (1965): 177–80. And the reply by Michael G. Southwell, "Dawn in Brutus' Orchard," *English Language Notes* 5 (1967): 91–98.

5. On the Cinna episode see Norman H. Holland, "The 'Cinna' and 'Cynicke' Episodes in *Julius Caesar*," *Shakespeare Quarterly* 11 (1960): 439–44; and John W. Velz, " 'If I Were Brutus Now': Role-Playing in *Julius Caesar*," *Shakespeare Studies* 4 (1969): 149–59.

6. Barbara L. Parker elaborates on this point in " 'This Monstrous Apparition': The Role of Perception in *Julius Caesar*," *Ball State University Forum* 16 (1975): 70–77.

7. John W. Velz, "Cassius as a 'Great Observer,' " *Modern Language Review* 68 (1973): 256–59.

8. On the issue about Caesar's ear see, among other pieces, John W. Velz, "Caesar's Deafness," *Shakespeare Quarterly* 22 (1971): 400–401); and Sidney R. Homan, "Dion, Alexander, and Demetrius—Plutarch's Forgotten Parallel Lives—as Mirrors for Shakespeare's *Julius Caesar*," *Shakespeare Studies* 8 (1976): 207.

9. Kaufmann and Ronan, "An Apollonian and Comparative Reading," p. 22.

10. L. C. Knights, "Shakespeare and Political Wisdom: A Note on the Personalism of *Julius Caesar* and *Coriolanus*," *Sewanee Review* 61 (1953): 47.

11. R. E. Spakowski, "Deification and Myth-Making in the Play *Julius Caesar*," *University Review* 36 (1969): 135–40.

12. J. L. Simmons, *Shakespeare's Pagan World: The Roman Tragedies* (Charlottesville: University of Virginia Press, 1973): p. 67.

13. John W. Velz, "Undular Structure in *Julius Caesar*," *Modern Language Review* 66 (1971): 21–30.

14. Julian C. Rice suggests that the play shows the inadequacy of both Cassius's Epicureanism and Brutus's Stoicism, in "*Julius Caesar* and the Judgment of the Senses," *Studies in English Literature* 13 (1973): 238–55.

15. Maynard Mack, *Killing the King: Three Studies in Shakespeare's Tragic Structure*, Yale Studies in English 180 (New Haven, Conn.: Yale University Press, 1973), p. 72. And see J. Leeds Barroll, "Shakespeare's Idea of Roman History," *Modern Language Review* 53 (1958): 327–43.

16. On this issue see the brilliant article by Peter S. Anderson, "Shakespeare's *Caesar*: The Language of Sacrifice," *Comparative Drama* 3 (1969): 3–26). Anderson speaks of the "exchangeability among the elements" (p. 13). I have been very much influenced by his study. Also, see Manfred Weidhorn, "The Rose and Its Name: On Denomination in *Othello*, *Romeo and Juliet*, and *Julius Caesar*," *Texas*

Studies in Language and Literature 11 (1969): 671–86; and R. A. Yoder, "History and the Histories in *Julius Caesar*," *Shakespeare Quarterly* 24 (1973): 309–27.

17. Myron Taylor, "Shakespeare's *Julius Caesar* and the Irony of History," *Shakespeare Quarterly* 24 (1973): 301–8. And see Joseph M. S. J. Chang, "*Julius Caesar* in the Light of Renaissance Historiography," *Journal of English and Germanic Philology* 69 (1970): 63–71, where he comments on the warning from Montaigne against seeking coherence in a man's life: "*Julius Caesar* is not the first instance of events shaping themselves in spite of conscious human intention" (p. 71).

18. T. J. B. Spencer, "Shakespeare and the Elizabethan Romans," *Shakespeare Studies* 10 (1957): 27–38.

19. Sigurd Burckhardt, "How Not to Murder Caesar," *Centennial Review* 11 (1967): 141–56. Schanzer suggests that Brutus is tortured not so much by what he has lost as by what he has "gained," by "the kind of world which he has helped bring into existence" (*Problem Plays*, p. 63).

20. See particularly the fine article by John S. Anson, "*Julius Caesar*: The Politics of the Hardened Heart," *Shakespeare Studies* 2 (1966): 11–33.

21. Brents Stirling, "Or Else This Were a Savage Spectacle," *PMLA* 66 (1951): 765–74; and reprinted in his *Unity in Shakespearian Tragedy* (New York: Columbia University Press, 1956), pp. 40–54.

22. G. Wilson Knight, "The Eroticism of *Julius Caesar*," in *The Imperial Theme* (London: Methuen and Company, 1954), pp. 63–95.

23. On this issue of characters being like playwrights shaping or attempting to shape reality, see William B. Toole, "The Metaphor of Alchemy in *Julius Caesar*," *Costerus* 5 (1972): 135–51.

24. Hartsock, "The Complexity of *Julius Caesar*," p. 62.

25. Sidney Homan, *When the Theater Turns to Itself: The Aesthetic Metaphor in Shakespeare* (Lewisburg, Pa.: Bucknell University Press, 1981), pp. 11–12.

26. Albert Kearney, "The Nature of an Insurrection: Shakespeare's *Julius Caesar*," *Studies* (Dublin) 63 (1974): 141–52.

27. MacCallum, *Roman Plays*, p. 269.

28. Rackin, "Pride of Brutus," p. 28.

29. Simmons, *Pagan World*, p. 107.

30. John W. Crawford, "The Religious Question in *Julius Caesar*," *Southern Quarterly* 15 (1977): 297–302.

31. See T. Walter Herbert, "Shakespeare Announces a Ghost," *Shakespeare Quarterly* 1 (1950): 247–54.

32. In *The Structure of "Julius Caesar"* (Liverpool: Liverpool University Press, 1958), p. 48, Adrien Bonjour observes that "for the first time in the play Brutus is clearly led to contemplate acting himself in flagrant opposition to his own philosophical ideal. . . ."

33. On this issue of the necessity of entertaining doubles see René Girard, "Lévi-Strauss, Frye, Derrida, and Shakespearean Criticism," *Diacritics* 3 (1973): 34–38.

34. Maurice Charney, *Shakespeare's Roman Play: The Function of Imagery in the Drama* (Cambridge, Mass.: Harvard University Press, 1961), p. 70.

35. See Vincent F. Petronella, "Dramatic Conjuring in Shakespeare's *Julius Caesar*," *Dalhousie Review* 57 (1977): 130–40.

36. See John Hollander, *The Untuning of the Sky* (Princeton, N.J.: Princeton University Press, 1961), p. 150, where he suggests that the reference to false strings shows "the discordant conspirators, now jangling and out of tune even

among themselves." And F. W. Sternfeld, *Music in Shakespearean Tragedy* (London: Routledge and Kegan Paul, 1963), pp. 80–81.

37. A. W. Bellringer, "*Julius Caesar*: Room Enough," *Critical Quarterly* 12 (1970): 46.

38. Anderson, "Language of Sacrifice," p. 20.

39. Bellringer, "Room Enough," p. 46.

40. Ruth Nevo, *Tragic Form in Shakespeare* (Princeton, N.J.: Princeton University Press, 1972), p. 46.

41. John Russell Brown, "Shakespeare's Subtext: I," *Tulane Drama Review* 8 (1963): 90.

42. Norman Rabkin, "Structure, Convention, and Meaning in *Julius Caesar*," *Journal of English and Germanic Philology* 63 (1964): 253.

43. Harriet Hawkins, *Likeness of Truth in Elizabethan and Restoration Drama* (Oxford: Clarendon Press, 1972), pp. 146, 151.

See also:

1. Thomas Clayton, "'Should Brutus Never Taste of Portia's Defeat But Once?': Text and Performance in *Julius Caesar*," *Studies in English Literature* 23 (1983): 237–55.

2. Jonathan Goldberg, *James I and the Politics of Literature: Jonson, Shakespeare, Donne, and Their Contemporaries* (Baltimore, Md.: Johns Hopkins University Press, 1983), pp. 164–76.

3. Frederick Kiefer, *Fortune and Elizabethan Tragedy* (San Marino, Calif.: Huntington Library, 1983), pp. 244–51.

4. Michael Payne, *Irony in Shakespeare's Roman Plays*. Institute for English Language and Literature (Salzburg, Austria: University of Salzburg Press, 1974), pp. 29–55.

5. Marion Trousdale, *Shakespeare and the Rhetoricians* (Chapel Hill: University of North Carolina Press, 1982), pp. 135–36.

6. John W. Velz, "*Orator* and *Imperator* in *Julius Caesar*: Style and the Process of Roman History," *Shakespeare Studies* 15 (1982): 55–75.

Chapter 5. *Macbeth*

1. A. C. Bradley, *Shakespearean Tragedy: Lectures on "Hamlet," "Othello," "King Lear," "Macbeth"* (London: Macmillan and Co., 1960 reissue), pp. 358–76.

2. James Kirsch, *Shakespeare's Royal Self* (New York: C. G. Jung Foundation for Analytical Psychology, 1966), p. 324.

3. William Empson suggests that the idea of the assassination exists symbolically in Macbeth's mind from the start. "Dover Wilson on *Macbeth*," *Kenyon Review* 14 (1952): 84–102. And on the witches, though his view has been challenged, see Walter Clyde Curry, *Shakespeare's Philosophical Patterns* (Baton Rouge: Louisiana State University Press, 1937), "Demonic Metaphysics," pp. 53–93.

4. On this notion and for a divided reading of Banquo's character see Harry Berger's "The Early Scenes of *Macbeth*: Preface to a New Interpretation," *English Literary History* 47 (1980): 1–31.

5. See Laurence Michel, *The Thing Contained: Theory of the Tragic* (Bloomington: Indiana University Press, 1970), pp. 53–58.

6. Marvin Rosenberg, *The Masks of Macbeth* (Berkeley and Los Angeles: University of California Press, 1978), p. 1.

7. On the value of such playing in Shakespeare see J. Dennis Huston, *Shakespeare's Comedies of Play* (New York: Columbia University Press, 1981).

8. On the play in its historical and political context see Henry N. Paul, *The Royal Play of Macbeth* (New York: Octagon Books, 1971).

9. Robert B. Heilman in "The Criminal as Tragic Hero: Dramatic Methods," *Shakespeare Quarterly* 19 (1966), 12–24, comments that as audience we feel "murderousness to be as powerful as a host of motives more familiar to consciousness" (p. 15), that the complexities and consequent uncertainties we thus experience are aroused by the play's first-half tragedy and then released, absolved by its second-half melodrama.

10. See Richard J. Jaarsma, "The Tragedy of Banquo," *Literature and Psychology* 17 (1967): 87–94.

11. On the parallels between leaving home and the family by Macduff and Macbeth see William B. Bach, "Hamlet, Macbeth, and Lear Offstage: The Significance of Absence," *Dalhousie Review* 59 (1979): 317.

12. See S. Nagarajan, "A Note on Banquo," *Shakespeare Quarterly* 7 (1956): 371–76.

13. In *Our Naked Frailties: Sensational Art and Meaning in "Macbeth"* (Berkeley and Los Angeles: University of California Press, 1971), Paul A. Jorgensen speaks of the play's "amazement of eyes and ears" (p. 10).

14. Frederic Tromly in "Macbeth and His Porter," *Shakespeare Quarterly* 26 (1975), focuses on "Macbeth's frequent ocular and auditory hallucinations" (p. 155).

15. G. R. Elliott, *Dramatic Providence in "Macbeth": A Study of Shakespere's Tragic Theme of Humanity and Grace* (Princeton, N.J.: Princeton University Press, 1958), p. 45.

16. Margreta de Grazia in "Shakespeare's View of Language: An Historical Perspective," *Shakespeare Quarterly* 29 (1978): 374–88, traces a change in the Renaissance from an earlier belief that language was perfect but could be marred by the speaker to a later belief that language itself, despite the speaker, was imperfect. Arnold Stein in "Macbeth and Word-Magic," *Sewanee Review* 59 (1951): 271–84, argues that Macbeth moves from an attempt to talk himself back into a state of innocence to a later contempt for language, and for incantation in particular.

17. Arthur R. McGee, "Macbeth and the Furies," *Shakespeare Survey* 19 (1966): 55–67, describes this inner world as "the language of conscience" (p. 59); and Maynard Mack, "The Jacobean Theater," *Jacobean Theater*, Stratford-Upon-Avon Studies 1 (1960): 11–42, finds Lady Macbeth's sleep-walking scene an internal play reenacting Macbeth's own inner world.

18. I take the terms from Murray Krieger's *A Window to Criticism: Shakespeare's Sonnets and Modern Poetics* (Princeton, N.J.: Princeton University Press, 1964).

19. On the word "amphibology, or an equivocation that lies like the truth," see Steven Mullaney, "Lying Like Truth: Riddle, Representation and Treason in Renaissance England," *English Literary History* 47 (1980): 32–47; and also Harriet Hawkins, *Likeness of Truth in Elizabethan and Restoration Drama* (Oxford: Clarendon Press, 1972), pp. 151–60. In "This Goodly Frame, the Stage: the Interior Theater of Imagination in English Renaissance Drama," *Shakespeare Quarterly* 25 (1974), Alvin Kernan calls the theater "an image of fear, transiency, of insubstan-

tiality and endless mutability" (p. 4). Edith Kern in "Ionesco and Shakespeare's *Macbeth* on the Modern Stage," *South Atlantic Bulletin* 39 (1974), finds the task of the central character of both plays that of seeing "the role he plays in the tragic farce of a life he has created": (p. 16).

20. In *Fools of Time: Studies in Shakespearean Tragedy* (Toronto: University of Toronto Press, 1967), Northrop Frye holds that "in tragedy the personality takes precedence over whatever is conceptual or moral" (p. 32), that tragedy is existential, beyond religious or ethical categories. H. C. Goddard sustains the paradox generated by a theatrical and ethical response when he calls Macbeth a "tragic criminal" (*The Meaning of Shakespeare* [Chicago: University of Chicago Press, 1951], p. 500). Phyllis Gorfain in "Riddles and Tragic Structure in *Macbeth*," *Mississippi Folklore Register* 10 (1976): 187–209, argues that alongside our ethical judgment of Macbeth "we participate in his error" even as "we can judge his inability to recognize the ambiguity" (p. 192). Patrick Murray in *The Shakespearean Scene: Some Twentieth-Century Perspectives* (London and Harlow: Longmans, 1967), points out that *Hamlet*'s "moral pattern can never be as clear as that of *Macbeth*" (p. 125); and this, to me, seems precisely one-half the issue.

21. Emrys Jones, *Scenic Form in Shakespeare* (Oxford: Clarendon Press, 1971), p. 195. In "Macbeth and the Metaphysics of Evil," *The Wheel of Fire* (Oxford: Clarendon Press, 1930), G. Wilson Knight calls this inner world one of "dream-consciousness" (p. 161).

22. Bertram L. Joseph, in "Character and Plot. Towards Standards of Criticism for Elizabethan Drama: 2," *Drama Survey* 3 (1964): 541–54, arguing against naturalism and the play as being essentially its plot, calls dialogue "the expression of the inner life of the character" (p. 542); and L. C. Knights, in his well-known essay, would see the play as essentially its language, as a dramatic poem. *How Many Children Had Lady Macbeth? An Essay in the Theory and Practice of Shakespearean Criticism* (New York: Haskel House, 1973).

23. Alex Aronson, "Shakespeare and the Ocular Proof," *Shakespeare Quarterly* 21 (1970): 411–29.

24. Roy Walker, *The Time Is Free: A Study of "Macbeth"* (London: Andrew Dakers Ltd, 1949), p. 13.

25. Nicholas Brooke distinguishes between the realms of conscious thought and unconscious image in "Language Most Shows a Man. . . . ? Language and Speaker in *Macbeth*," *Essays in Honour of Kenneth Muir*, ed. Phillip Edwards et al. (Cambridge: At the University Press, 1980), pp. 67–77.

26. Anthony Harris in *Night's Black Agents: Witchcraft and Magic in Seventeenth Century English Drama* (Manchester: Manchester University Press, 1980) speaks of Macbeth's increasing identification with Satanic forces (pp. 46–63). Stein in "Macbeth and Word-Magic" sees him as invoking his own dark self (p. 275) On Lady Macbeth, Alan Hughes calls her dispossessed of supernatural forces by Act 3, sadder, wiser, resigned ("Lady Macbeth: A Fiend Indeed," *Southern Review* 11 [1978]: 107–12), while R. G. Moulton, in *Shakespeare as a Dramatic Artist: A Popular Illustration of the Principles of Scientific Criticism* (New York: Dover Publications, 1966, reissue), distinguishes between Lady Macbeth's inner life, evoked by her complete identification with supernatural forces, and her husband's practical, outer world; he observes that practical action is rendered inferior if the inner life is not sustained and served (p. 154). Jovan Hristic in "On the Interpretation of Drama," *New Literary History* 3 (1972): 345–54, calls on the audience as well to invoke the spirit of the play, asking for "evocation" rather than "interpretation" (p. 354).

27. On "acting" in the play see Robert Egan, "His Hour upon the Stage: Role-Playing in *Macbeth*," *Centennial Review* 22 (1978): 327–45. Curiously, real-life theater problems may have made their way into the play. In "The Hecate Scenes in *Macbeth*," *Review of English Studies* 24 (1948): 138–39, J. M. Nosworthy suggests that Hecate's "was never call'd to bear my part" (3.5.8) refers to her exclusion from previous performances, that is, in an earlier version of the text.

28. See Franco Ferrucci, *Poetics of Disguise: The Autobiography of the Work of Homer, Dante, and Shakespeare*, trans. Ann Dunnigan (Ithaca, N.Y.: Cornell University Press, 1980), pp. 132–58. Richard Horwich in "Integrity in *Macbeth*: The Search for the 'Single State of Man,'" *Shakespeare Quarterly* 29 (1978): 367–73, calls Malcolm "a Macbeth in embryo" (371). In "The Role of Macduff in *Macbeth*," *Etudes Anglaises* 32 (1979): 11–19, Vincent Petronella finds Macduff a parallel figure to Macbeth, one "participating at the center of horror" (p. 17), violating the home as Macbeth does, but one who can still perceive "central truths" (p. 17) and hence win the status, finally, as Macbeth's adversary.

29. For Richard S. Ide, "The Theatre of the Mind: An Essay on *Macbeth*," *English Literary History* 42 (1975): 338–61, Macbeth carries out "self-deception by creating his own equivocal stage in the psychological theater of the mind" (p. 347).

30. Clifford Leech, "The Incredible in Jacobean Tragedy," *Rice University Studies* 60 (1974): 109–12.

31. Harold Toliver, "Shakespeare and the Abyss of Time," *Journal of English and Germanic Philology* 64 (1965): 249.

32. On the word *rapt* see Brents Stirling, *Unity in Shakespearian Tragedy* (New York: Columbia University Press, 1956), pp. 139–56.

33. See V. Y. Kantak, "An Approach to Shakespearian Tragedy: The 'Actor' Image in *Macbeth*," *Shakespeare Survey* 16 (1963): 45–52.

34. John Lawlor, "Mind and Hand: Some Reflections on the Study of Shakespeare's Imagery," *Shakespeare Quarterly* 8 (1957): 188.

35. The phrase is that of William Rosen, *Shakespeare and the Craft of Tragedy* (Cambridge, Mass.: Harvard University Press, 1960), p. 83.

36. Edwin Everitt Williams, *Tragedies of Destiny: "Oedipus Tyrannus," "Macbeth," "Atalie"* (Cambridge, Mass.: University Press Editions, 1940), p. 32.

37. G. I. Duthie, "Antithesis in *Macbeth*," *Shakespeare Survey* 19 (1966): 30.

38. H. L. Rogers, *"Double Profit" in Macbeth* (Melbourne: Melbourne University Press, 1964), p. 65.

39. Curry, *Philosophical Patterns*, p. 132.

40. In "*Macbeth*: The Great Illusion," *Sewanee Review* 78 (1970): 476–87, Barbara L. Parker comments that "Illusion, then, is the bedrock on which the thematic structure of the play rests and from which the underlying principle of duality derives" (p. 487).

41. Terence Hawkes, *Shakespeare and the Reason: A Study of His Tragedies and the Problem Plays* (New York: The Humanities Press, 1965), pp. 124–59.

42. Again, see Heilman's discussion of the movement from tragedy to melodrama in "The Criminal as Tragic Hero."

43. J. A. Bryant, *Hippolyta's View* (Lexington: University of Kentucky Press, 1961), p. 156.

44. See the fine article by Karl F. Zender in which he qualifies the optimism brought by Macbeth's defeat, arguing that "the right reign of nature and providence does not abolish pain, nor eliminate mystery" (p. 422), that the victory of Macbeth's opponents and their dismissal of him as a tyrant does not constitute

the whole truth of the play, certainly not the whole imaginative truth. "The Death of Young Siward: Providential Order and Tragic Loss in *Macbeth*," *Texas Studies in Language and Literature* 17 (1975): 415–25.

45. Hawkes, *Shakespeare and the Reason*, p. 142.

46. Francis Fergusson, "Macbeth as the Imitation of an Action," in *The Human Image in Dramatic Literature* (Garden City, N.Y.: Doubleday and Co., 1957), p. 121.

47. Emrys Jones, *Scenic Form in Shakespeare*, p. 207.

48. On this issue in the Porter's scene see, especially, John Harcourt, "I Pray You, Remember the Porter," *Shakespeare Quarterly* 12 (1961): 393–402.

49. Cleanth Brooks, *The Well-Wrought Urn: Studies in the Structure of Poetry* (New York: Reynal and Hitchcock, 1947), p. 42.

50. In "Macbeth the Player King: The Banquet Scene as Frustrated Play Within the Play," *Shakespeare-Jahrbuch* (Weimar) 114 (1978): 107–14, Robert F. Wilson observes that after Act 3, scene 4 Macbeth will "wake" into a reality characterized by sleeplessness, terror, and suffering (p. 114).

See also:

1. Harry Berger, Jr., "Text Against Performance in Shakespeare: The Example of *Macbeth*," *Genre* 15 (1982): 49–79.

2. R. A. Foakes, "Images of Death: Ambition in *Macbeth*," in *Focus on Macbeth*, ed. John Russell Brown (London and Boston: Routledge and Kegan Paul, 1982), pp. 7–29.

3. Robin Grove, "'Multiplying villanies of nature,'" in Brown, *Focus on Macbeth*, pp. 113–39.

4. Michael Goldman, "Language and Action in *Macbeth*," in Brown, *Focus on Macbeth*, pp. 140–51.

5. Joan Hartwig, *Shakespeare's Analogical Scene: Parody as Structural Syntax* (Lincoln: University of Nebraska Press, 1983), pp. 43–65.

6. Derick R. C. Marsh, "*Macbeth*: Easy Question, Difficult Answers," *Sydney Studies in English* 8 (1982–83): 3–15.

7. D. J. Palmer, "'A New Gorgon': Visual Effects in *Macbeth*," in Brown, *Focus on Macbeth*, pp. 54–69.

8. Bernard J. Paris, "Bargains with Fate: The Case of *Macbeth*," *American Journal of Psychoanalysis* 42 (1982): 7–20.

9. Robert Rentoul Reed, Jr., *Crime and God's Judgment in Shakespeare* (Lexington: The University Press of Kentucky, 1984), pp. 165–98.

10. Peter Stalbybrass, "*Macbeth* and Witchcraft," in Brown, *Focus on Macbeth*, pp. 189–209.

Chapter 6. *Richard III*

1. Nicholas Brooke, "Reflecting Gems and Dead Bones: Tragedy versus History in *Richard III*," *Critical Quarterly* 7 (1965): 127.

2. Wolfgang Clemen, "Tragedy and Originality in Shakespeare's *Richard III*," *Shakespeare Quarterly* 5 (1954): 225.

3. See Bernard Spivack, *Shakespeare and the Allegory of Evil: The History of a Metaphor in Relation to His Major Villains* (New York: Columbia University Press, 1958), pp. 386–407.

4. Ibid., *Allegory of Evil*, p. 389.

5. M. M. Reese, *The Cease of Majesty: A Study of Shakespeare's History Plays* (New York: St. Martin's Press, 1961), p. 208.

6. James L. Calderwood, *Shakespearean Metadrama* (Minneapolis: University of Minnesota Press, 1970).

7. Leonard F. Dean, "Shakespeare's *Richard III*," *Studies in Language, Literature, and Culture of the Middle Ages and Later*, ed. E. Bagby Atwood and Archibald A. Hill (Austin: University of Texas Press, 1969), p. 350.

8. Donald R. Shupe in "The Wooing of Lady Anne: A Psychological Inquiry," *Shakespeare Quarterly* 29 (1978), comments that it is the "heightened emotionality" that is the source of Anne's undoing in this scene (p. 33).

9. See Peter Sacchio's account of the historical Richard in *Shakespeare's English Kings: History, Chronicle, and Drama* (New York: Oxford University Press, 1977), pp. 157–86.

10. Wilbur Sanders comments on the change from the silent citizens at the coronation to the concerned citizenry later in the play, in *The Dramatist and the Received Idea: Studies in the Plays of Marlowe and Shakespeare* (Cambridge: At the University Press, 1968), "Providence and Policy in *Richard III*," pp. 72–109.

11. For commentary on Richard's meeting with Elizabeth, see Louis E. Dollarhide, "Two Unassimilated Movements in *Richard III*: An Interpretation," *Mississippi Quarterly* 14 (1960): 40–46; Emrys Jones, "Bosworth Eve," *Essays in Criticism* 25 (1975): 38–54; and Stephen L. Tanner, "Richard III Versus Elizabeth: An Interpretation," *Shakespeare Quarterly* 24 (1973): 468–72. I shall return to this scene in more detail later in the chapter.

12. For contrasting views on the psychological dimension of this scene, particularly on the issue of whether Richard is being directed by psychological forces beyond his knowledge and hence control, see Michael Steig, "The Grotesque and the Aesthetic Response in Shakespeare, Dickens, and Günter Grass," *Comparative Literature Studies* 6 (1969): 170–73; and, for a basically nonpsychological reading, Robert Ornstein, *A Kingdom for a Stage: The Achievement of Shakespeare's History Plays* (Cambridge, Mass.: Harvard University Press, 1972), p. 67 particularly.

13. R. A. Law, "*Richard III*: A Study in Shakespeare's Composition," *PMLA* 60 (1945): 689–96, speculates that the first act may have been conceived after the rest of the play was finished.

14. Murray Krieger, *The Play and Place of Criticism* (Baltimore, Md.: Johns Hopkins University Press, 1967), "The Dark Generation of *Richard III*," pp. 37–52.

15. Bridget Gellert Lyons, "'King Games': Stage Imagery and Political Symbolism in *Richard III*," *Criticism* 20 (1978): 24.

16. A. P. Rossiter, *Angel with Horns, and Other Shakespeare Lectures*, ed. Graham Storey (New York: Theatre Arts Books, 1969), "Angel with Horns: The Unity of *Richard III*," pp. 1–22.

17. Theodore Spencer, *Shakespeare and the Nature of Man* (New York: Macmillan Co., 1942), p. 72; and see Ronald Berman, "Anarchy and Order in *Richard III* and *King John*," *Shakespeare Survey* 20 (1967), where he calls Richard the "natural man" or an example of "a new kind of mind" for the Renaissance (pp. 52–53).

18. Ruth L. Anderson, "The Pattern of Behavior Culminating in *Macbeth*," *Studies in English Literature* 3 (1963): 164; and Ornstein, *Kingdom for a Stage*, p. 62.

19. Moody E. Prior, *The Drama of Power: Studies in Shakespeare's History Plays* (Evanston, Ill.: Northwestern University Press, 1973), p. 56.

20. Steig, "The Grotesque," pp. 167–81, 172.

21. Krieger, *Play and Place of Criticism*, p. 39.

22. On Richard's demonic origins see Anthony J. Lewis, "The Dog, Lion, and Wolf in Shakespeare's Descriptions of Night," *Modern Language Review* 66 (1971): 1–10.

23. I refer again to Spivack's *Shakespeare and the Allegory of Evil*.

24. Hugh M. Richmond, in "Personal Identity and Literary Personae: A Study in Historical Psychology," *PMLA* 90 (1975), speaks of Richard's movement to his private self and of the "flight into subjectivity" (p. 210).

25. Emrys Jones, *The Origins of Shakespeare* (Oxford: Clarendon Press, 1971), p. 201.

26. Christopher Morris, *Political Thought in England. Tyndale to Hooker* (London: Oxford University Press, 1953), p. 98.

27. A point made by Waldo F. McNeir, "The Masks of Richard the Third," *Studies in English Literature* 11 (1971): 180.

28. A. F. French in "The World of *Richard III*," *Shakespeare Studies* 4 (1968): 25–39, speaks of the tight, constricted world of the play, a secular world that, despite the references to Saint Paul, would blot out the larger context afforded by heaven. The "finished perfection" (p. 38) of the play is thus both a structural and a thematic, even a philosophic device.

29. But William E. Sheriff would have it this way in "The Grotesque Comedy of *Richard III*," *Studies in the Literary Imagination* 5 (1972): 51–64.

30. Travis Bogard in "Shakespeare's Second Richard," *PMLA* 70 (1955) speaks of the "vitality of [Richard as] a stage figure" but argues that he is too much the actor and thus prohibits a human response (pp. 196–97). Wolfgang Clemen observes that in earlier plays the prologue was not delivered by a figure so caught up in the main action of the plot and that, as a consequence, Richard has a mysterious personal fascination for us. *A Commentary on Shakespeare's "Richard III,"* trans. Jean Bonheim (London: Methuen and Co., 1968), pp. 9, 22.

31. On Shakespeare's own divided attitude toward the theater see Sidney Homan, *When the Theater Turns to Itself: The Aesthetic Metaphor in Shakespeare* (Lewisburg, Pa.: Bucknell University Press, 1981), "*Hamlet*: the Double Edge of Aesthetics," pp. 152–76, and "Love and the Imagination in *Antony and Cleopatra*," pp. 177–91.

32. I echo here the brilliant analysis of the related plots of the play, where "those who triumph in one nemesis become the victim of the next" (p. 110), in Richard G. Moulton's *Shakespeare as a Dramatic Artist: A Popular Illustration of the Principles of Scientific Criticism* (New York: Dover Publications, 1966, reissue), pp. 107–24.

33. Robert B. Heilman, "Satiety and Conscience: Aspects of *Richard III*," *Antioch Review* 24 (1964): 66.

34. Richard P. Wheeler, "History, Character, and Conscience in *Richard III*," *Comparative Drama* 5 (1971–72): 301–21, particularly pp. 311–12.

35. Jones, "Bosworth Eve," p. 52.

36. For a much more detailed look at this idea of staging one's self see Stephen Greenblatt's *Renaissance Self-Fashioning: From More to Shakespeare* (Chicago: University of Chicago Press, 1980).

37. McNeir, "Mask of Richard," p. 184.

38. Tanner, "Richard III Versus Elizabeth," pp. 468–72.

39. Jones, "Bosworth Eve," pp. 43–44.

40. Dollarhide, "Two Unassimilated Movements," pp. 44–46.

41. David Young speaks of Richard as cracking open, like Volpone, in

"'Myself Myself Confound': The Doctrine of Self in *Richard III*," *Shakespeare Newsletter* 28 (1978): 35 (abstract of a talk given before the Shakespeare Association Meeting, April 8, 1977, in Washington, D.C.). Francis Berry in "Shakespeare's Stage Geometry," *Shakespeare-Jahrbuch* (Heidelberg) (1974): 160–71, focuses on how the three dimensions of the stage—and Shakespeare's use of them both physically and poetically—work toward a more circumspect response to Richard's otherwise seductive character.

42. On these curses see Wolfgang Clemen, "Anticipation and Foreboding in Shakespeare's Early Histories," *Shakespeare Survey* 6 (1953): 25–35; and Moulton, *Shakespeare as a Dramatic Artist*, pp. 107–24.

43. Dean, "Shakespeare's *Richard III*," pp. 349–50.

44. Brooke, "Reflecting Gems," p. 133. And Roy E. Aycock in "Dual Progression in *Richard III*," *South Atlantic Bulletin* 38 (1973), sees the play's "co-protagonists" as "Richard's character and Margaret's curses" (p. 78).

45. Jones, *Origins of Shakespeare*, p. 231. In his study of the play, "The Self Alone," Edward I. Berry concludes that *Richard III* is tied to "the orthodoxies of the Old and New Testament," that the play, along with the first tetralogy, reveals "history in process" (p. 103). See *Patterns of Decay: Shakespeare's Early Histories* (Charlottesville: University of Virginia Press, 1975), pp. 75–103.

46. Clemen, "Tradition and Originality," p. 249.

47. Brooke, "Reflecting Gems," pp. 126, 133–34. And see Joan Rees, "Revenge, Retribution, and Reconciliation," *Shakespeare Survey* 24 (1971): 31–35.

48. Reginald A. Saner, "Shakespeare and the Shape of Civil Strife: 'Myself Upon Myself,'" *Western Humanities Review* 25 (1971): 148.

49. W. A. Armstrong, "The Influence of Seneca and Machiavelli on the Elizabethan Tyrant," *Review of English Studies* 24 (1948): 28.

50. Berman, "Anarchy and Disorder," observes that for Richard time moves from present to future, while in the larger play it moves toward chaos (p. 57). Tom Driver in *The Sense of History in Greek and Shakespearean Drama* (New York: Columbia University Press, 1961), "Nemesis and Judgment: *The Persians* and *Richard III*," pp. 87–115, comments that Richard "operates on a different schedule of time from the ultimately victorious forces" (p. 91) but that "at the proper time, decisive and redemptive action is taken" (p. 103).

51. Heilman, "Satiety and Conscience," p. 61.

52. Raymond O'Dea, "The King of Men in Shakespeare's Early Work: Time," *Discourse* 11 (1968): 142. See Zdeněk Stříbrný, "The Idea and Image of Time in Shakespeare's Early Histories," *Shakespeare-Jahrbuch* (Weimar) 110 (1974): 129–38.

53. See the account of these dates in Jones, "Bosworth Eve," pp. 47–49.

54. Moulton, *Shakespeare as a Dramatic Artist*, pp. 107–24.

55. Sanders, *Received Idea*, p. 81.

56. This is the double perspective argued for by John Jump, "Shakespeare's Ghosts," *Critical Quarterly* 12 (1970): 339–51.

57. See the distinctions between "Two Types of Dreams in the Elizabethan Drama, and Their Heritage: *Somnium Animale* and the Prick-of-Conscience," by Robert K. Presson in *Studies in English Literature* 7 (1967): 239–56.

58. Jones, "Bosworth Eve," speaks of Richmond's name occurring as something of a "leit-motif" (p. 41), and see also Jones's response, in the same article, to the blackening of Richmond's character by Andrew Gurr in "*Richard III* and the Democratic Process," *Essays in Criticism* 24 (1974): 39–47—a correction that, at least within the context of my own analysis, seems proper.

59. The view of Lily B. Campbell, *Shakespeare's Histories: Mirrors of Elizbethan Policy* (San Marino, Calif.: The Huntington Library, 1947), "The Tragical Doings of King Richard III," pp. 306–34.

60. Robert Hapgood, "Shakespeare's Maimed Rites: The Early Tragedies," *Centennial Review* 9 (1965): 494–508; I am indebted to Hapgood's skillful review of the issue of sacrifice, and his distinction between the sacrifices of *Titus Andronicus* and *Romeo and Juliet* and those in *Richard II* and *Julius Caesar*.

61. Phillip Mallet, "Shakespeare's Trickster-kings: Richard III and Henry V," in *The Fool and the Trickster: Studies in Honour of Enid Welsford*, ed. Paul V. A. Williams (Totowa, N.J.: Rowman and Littlefield, 1979), pp. 64–82, and p. 70 for the quotation.

62. William B. Toole, "The Motif of Psychic Division in *Richard III*," *Shakespeare Survey* 27 (1974): 24.

63. See the distinction made by Robert Y. Turner, "Characterization in Shakespeare's Early History Plays," *English Literary History* 31 (1964): 241–58.

64. J. M. R. Margeson, *The Origins of English Tragedy* (Oxford: Clarendon Press, 1967), p. 118.

65. Bogard, "Shakespeare's Second Richard," p. 198.

66. See Turner, "Characterization," p. 257.

67. McNeir, "The Masks of Richard," p. 184.

68. Heilman, "Satiety and Conscience," p. 68.

69. John Velz, "Episodic Structure in Four Tudor Plays: A Virtue of Necessity," *Comparative Drama* 6 (1972): 96.

70. Sanders, *Received Idea*, pp. 107–8.

71. Reese, *Cease of Majesty*, p. 224.

See also.

1. Ralph Berry, "*Richard III:* Bonding the Audience," in *Mirror up to Nature: Essays in Honour of G. R. Hibbard*, ed. J. C. Gray (Toronto: University of Toronto Press, 1984), pp. 114–27.

2. David Scott Kastan, " 'To Set a Form upon that Indigest': Shakespeare's Fictions of History," *Comparative Drama* 17 (1983): 1–16.

3. Robert Rentoul Reed, Jr., *Crime and God's Judgment in Shakespeare* (Lexington: The University Press of Kentkucky, 1984), pp. 113–28.

4. Robert N. Watson, "Horsemanship in Shakespeare's Second Tetralogy," *English Literary Renaissance* 13 (1983): 274–300.

Chapter 7. *Henry V*

1. Of all the commentators on the language of *Henry V*, James Calderwood has influenced me the most. He devotes two chapters to the play ("*Henry V:* The Act of Order," pp. 134–61; and "*Henry V:* English, Rhetoric, Theater," pp. 162–81) in his *Metadrama in Shakespeare's Henriad* (Berkeley and Los Angeles: University of California Press, 1979). Calderwood's first concern is with the "source" (p. 159) of Hal's royalty, the way he rises to the kingship. Once established, Hal, in his control of language, wins Shakespeare's right to have the play "*in* English" (p. 164) by finding a speech that "works" (p. 172), a "verbal efficiency" (p. 180) that coexists with the fragility of language, and of Shakespeare's play itself. Also most influential has been Joseph A. Porter's *The Drama of Speech Acts: Shakespeare's*

Lancastrian Tetralogy (Berkeley and Los Angeles: University of California Press, 1979). I shall return to Porter's study later in the notes.

2. Richard Lanham, *The Motives of Eloquence: Literary Rhetoric in the Renaissance* (New Haven, Conn.: Yale University Press, 1976), p. 198.

3. W. B. Yeats, "At Stratford-on-Avon," *Essays and Introductions* (New York: The Macmillan Co., 1961), reprinted in Ronald Berman's edition of *Twentieth Century Interpretations of "Henry V": A Collection of Critical Essays* (Englewood Cliffs, N.J.: Prentice Hall, 1968), pp. 94–98.

4. Robert Ornstein, *A Kingdom for a Stage: The Achievement of Shakespeare's History Plays* (Cambridge, Mass.: Harvard University Press, 1972), pp. 190–91.

5. The judgment of E. E. Stoll in *Poets and Playwrights* (Minneapolis: University of Minnesota Press, 1930), reprinted in R. J. Dorius, *Discussions of Shakespeare's Histories: "Richard II" to "Henry V"* (Boston, D. C. Heath and Co., 1964), p. 125.

6. Such was the ideal king, whose play has heroism as its theme, of J. Dover Wilson in his edition for the New Cambridge Shakespeare (Cambridge: At the University Press, 1947), pp. vii–xlvii; see particularly pp. xii and xxxii.

7. See, for example, E. M. W. Tillyard, *Shakespeare's History Plays* (New York: Barnes and Noble, 1944), in Berman, *Interpretations*, pp. 37–41. Or Mark Van Doren, *Shakespeare* (New York: Holt, Rinehart and Winston, 1939), also in Berman, *Interpretations*, pp. 106–110.

8. Jonas Barish, "The Turning Away of Prince Hal," *Shakespeare Studies* 1 (1965): 15.

9. Edward I. Berry in " 'True Things and Mock'ries': Epic and History in *Henry V*," *Journal of English and Germanic Philology* 78 (1979), argues that, aided by the Chorus, we realize that the real truth of the play rests in our imagination (p. 4).

10. Anthony Brennan suggests that the Chorus is closer to poetry than to reality. "That Within Which Passes Show: The Function of the Chorus in *Henry V*," *Philological Quarterly* 58 (1979): 43.

11. Eamon Grennan, " 'This Story Shall the Good Man Teach His Son': *Henry V* and the Art of History," *Papers on Language and Literature* 15 (1979): 370–82.

12. See particularly, Robert P. Merrix, "The Alexandrian Allusions in Shakespeare's *Henry V*," *English Literary Renaissance* 2 (1972): 321–33.

13. J. H. Walter, ed., *King Henry V, The Arden Shakespeare* (London: Methuen and Co., Ltd., 1954), p. 11.

14. Lanham, *Motives of Eloquence*, p. 191.

15. Charles Forker, "Shakespeare's Chronicle Plays as Historical-Pastoral," *Shakespeare Studies* 1 (1965): 96.

16. Joanne Altieri, "Romance in *Henry V*," *Studies in English Literature* 21 (1981): 223–40.

17. William Babula, "Whatever Happened to Prince Hal? An Essay on *Henry V*," *Shakespeare Survey* 30 (1977): 47–59, and quotation on p. 51.

18. William Empson, "Falstaff and Mr. Dover Wilson," *Kenyon Review* 15 (1953): 261–62.

19. Emrys Jones, *The Origins of Shakespeare* (Oxford: Clarendon Press, 1977), p. 20.

20. Porter, *Speech Acts*, pp. 116–23.

21. Robert G. Hunter, "Shakespeare's Comic Sense as It Strikes Us Today: Falstaff and the Protestant Ethic," in David Bevington and Jay L. Halio, eds.,

Shakespeare: Pattern of Excelling Nature (Newark: University of Delaware Press, 1978), pp. 125–32.

22. Robert L. Kelly, "Shakespeare's Scroop and the Spirit of Cain," *Shakespeare Quarterly* 20 (1969): 71–80.

23. A. C. Bradley, "The Rejection of Falstaff," *Oxford Lectures on Poetry* (London: Macmillan and Co., Ltd., 1909), in Berman, *Interpretations*, p. 101.

24. Marilyn L. Williamson makes this observation in "The Episode with Williams in *Henry V*," *Studies in English Literature* 9 (1969): 276–77.

25. John Wilders, *The Lost Garden: A View of Shakespeare's English and Roman History Plays* (Totowa, N.J.: Rowman and Littlefield, 1978), p. 60.

26. The classic study of the monarch's two selves is, of course, Ernst Kantorowicz's *The King's Two Bodies* (Princeton, N.J.: Princeton University Press, 1957).

27. Paul Dean, "Chronicle and Romance Mode in *Henry V*," *Shakespeare Quarterly* 32 (1981), points out that, at length, Williams penetrates the myth that the king is like the common man (pp. 23–24).

28. Anne Barton, "The King Disguised: Shakespeare's *Henry V* and Comical History," in Joseph G. Price, ed., *The Triple Bond: Plays Mainly Shakespearean in Performance* (University Park: Penn State University Prss, 1975), p. 107.

29. Berry, "'True Things,'" p. 12.

30. Walter, ed., *Henry V*, p. xxxii.

31. Norman Sanders, in "The True Prince and the False Thief: Prince Hal and the Shift of Identity," *Shakespeare Survey* 30 (1977), suggests that Hal needs to find his "public role and right doing," whereas Hamlet seeks the "discovery of self and true being" (p. 34).

32. Walter, *Henry V*, cites Aldis Wright's note that "the charters of foundations for the two chauntries . . . do not suggest that Henry established the houses so that masses might be sung for Richard's soul" (p. 106).

33. Robert Egan, "A Muse of Fire: *Henry V* in the Light of *Tamburlaine*," *Modern Language Quarterly* 29 (1968): 26.

34. The judgment of John Palmer, *Political and Comic Characters of Shakespeare* (London: Macmillan Co., Ltd., 1962), p. 241.

35. Herbert R. Coursen, Jr., "*Henry V* and the Nature of Kingship," *Discourse* 13 (1970): 297.

36. See L. C. Knights, *Explorations 3* (Pittsburgh: University of Pittsburgh Press, 1976), p. 126.

37. Robert P. Adams in "Transformations in the Late Elizabethan Tragic Sense of Life: New Critical Approaches," *Modern Language Quarterly* 35 (1974), observes that "history and tragedy, in the last days of Elizabeth, were on a collision course" (p. 362) since "both kinds of drama" can be seen as "expressions of a persistent search for justice and human dignity in the power-state" (p. 361). *Henry V*, in its definition of the public, political hero, thus occupies a very special place in this convergence of tragedy and history. Gunnar Boklund, "Henry V—A Hero for Our Time?," *Denver Quarterly* 10 (1975): 83–92, sees the play as asking "under what conditions we live as political creatures" (p. 92). For Peter G. Phialas in "Shakespeare's *Henry V* and the Second Tetralogy," *Studies in Philology* 62 (1965), the playwright's purpose here is "to isolate and underscore those aspects of character which make for success in public life" (p. 173), while for Irving Ribner in *The English History Play in the Age of Shakespeare* (Princeton, N.J.: Princeton University Press, 1957), the play is Shakespeare's "eulogistic portrait of a conquering soldier-king" (p. 183).

38. On the changes in perspective on man and history in the *Henriad* see Alvin Kernan, "*The Henriad*: Shakespeare's Major History Plays," *Yale Review* 59 (1969): 3–32. Kernan traces a general movement from the old to the new, from a more hierarchical, certain, but inflexible notion of man to the "existential condition in which any identity is only a temporary role" (p. 3). Hal is not so much an ideal king as an "ideal man" (p. 23). Moody E. Prior argues that *Henry V* is separate from the other histories and should not necessarily be subject to the political or moral objectives found elsewhere in the tetralogy. *The Drama of Power: Studies in Shakespeare's History Plays* (Evanston, Ill.: Northwestern University Press, 1973), p. 282.

39. Bernard Beckerman in "Shakespearean Playgoing Then and Now," in *Shakespeare's "More Than Words Can Witness": Essays on Visual and Nonverbal Enactment in the Plays*, ed. Sidney Homan (Lewisburg, Pa.: Bucknell University Press, 1980), pp. 151–54.

40. Lanham, *Motives of Eloquence*, p. 195. But see the argument by G. P. Jones that the Chorus was added so that the play, and particularly its staging, could be adapted for a performance at court. "*Henry V*: The Chorus and the Audience," *Shakespeare Survey* 31 (1978): 93–104.

41. Porter, *Speech Acts*, pp. 116–50.

42. S. C. Sen Gupta, in *Shakespeare's Historical Plays* (London: Oxford University Press, 1964), speaks of its "epic spirit" (p. 139). For Charles Barber there is here a "failure" to "qualify adequately its rather simple patriotic-miltitary feeling." "Prince Hal, *Henry V*, and the Tudor Monarchy," in D. W. Jefferson, ed., *The Morality of Art: Essays Presented to G. Wilson Knight by His Colleagues and Friends* (London: Routledge and Kegan Paul, 1969), p. 72.

43. A. P. Rossiter, "Ambivalence: The Dialectic of the Histories," *Angel with Horns and Other Shakespeare Lectures*, ed. Graham Storey (New York: Theatre Arts Books, 1961), pp. 40–64; and in Berman, *Interpretations*, pp. 81–87.

44. Paul Jorgensen, *Shakespeare's Military World* (Berkeley and Los Angeles: University of California Press, 1956), p. 87.

45. Palmer, *Political Characters*, p. 249.

46. Van Doren, *Shakespeare*, in Berman, *Interpretations*, pp. 106–10.

47. Roy W. Battenhouse, "*Henry V* as Heroic Comedy," in Richard Hosley, ed., *Essays on Shakespeare and Elizabethan Drama in Honor of Hardin Craig* (Columbia: University of Missouri Press, 1962), pp. 169–80.

48. Borrowing the phrase from Richard Levin, Dean in "Chronicle and Romance" speaks of the "equivalence" between the main and subplots (p. 23).

49. M. M. Reese, *The Cease of Majesty: A Study of Shakespeare's History Plays* (New York: St. Martin's Press, 1961), in Berman, *Interpretations*, p. 92.

50. C. H. Hobday, "Imagery and Irony in *Henry V*," *Shakespeare Survey* 21 (1968): 111–12.

51. Barton, "King Disguised," p. 117. Or rather, the imitation of the play in *Sir John Oldcastle* shows that Shakespeare had taken the tragical history as far as it could go.

52. Andrew Gurr, "*Henry V* and the Bees' Commonwealth," *Shakespeare Survey* 30 (1977), cautions us, for example, not to bring a too-narrow reading to the companion scenes 1.1 and 1.2 (p. 71).

53. Altieri, "Romance," pp. 223–25.

54. Dean, "Chronicle and Romance," p. 27.

55. Karl P. Wentersdorf, "The Conspiracy of Silence in *Henry V*," *Shakespeare Quarterly* 27 (1976): 279.

56. Ornstein, *Kingdom for a Stage*, pp. 175–202.

57. Norman Rabkin, "Rabbits, Ducks, and *Henry V*," *Shakespeare Quarterly* 28 (1977): 279–96.

58. On the language of the play, and particularly the successful language employed by Hal, see Peter B. Erickson, "'The Fault / My Father Made': The Anxious Pursuit of Heroic Fame in Shakespeare's *Henry V*," *Modern Language Studies* 10 (1979–80): 10–25.

59. Carol Marks Sickerman, "'King Hal': The Integrity of Shakespeare's Portrait," *Texas Studies in Language and Literature* 21 (1979): 503–21. For a negative view of Hal's linguistic achievements see John C. Bromley, *The Shakespearean Kings* (Boulder: University of Colorado Press, 1971), who argues that Hal's speech reflects his own "native duplicity" (p. 92). And Frank Walsh Bronlow, *Two Shakespearean Sequences: "Henry VI" to "Richard II" and "Pericles" to "Timon of Athens"* (Pittsburgh: University of Pittsburgh Press, 1977), who concludes that Hal "talks too much" (p. 42).

60. On this shift in comic "Casts" see Helen J. Schwartz, "The Comic Scenes in *Henry V*," *Hebrew University Studies in Literature* 4 (1976): 18–26.

61. Joseph M. Lenz, "The Politics of Honor: The Oath in *Henry V*," *Journal of English and Germanic Philology* 80 (1981): 1–12.

62. Paul A. Jorgensen, "A Formative Shakespearean Legacy: Elizabethan Views of God, Fortune, and War," *PMLA* 90 (1975): 227–28.

63. C. G. Thayer, "Shakespeare's Second Tetralogy: An Underground Report," *Ohio University Review* 9 (1967): 15.

64. I echo here the general thesis of Calderwood, *Metadrama*, pp. 162–81.

65. Brownell Salomon in "Thematic Contraries and the Dramaturgy of *Henry V*," *Shakespeare Quarterly* 31 (1980), calls Act 5 a "diptych" where the dual emblems portray devouring self-love (Pistol's humiliation) and a betrothal in which the public marriage of Hal and Katherine confirms the "triumph of public ethos" (p. 355). Barton, "The King Disguised," observes that in Pistol Shakespeare lays Marlovian language to rest (pp. 99–100).

66. Norman Council, *When Honour's at Stake: Ideas of Honour in Shakespeare's Plays* (New York: Barnes and Noble, 1973), calls Falstaff the "true and perfect image of life," Hotspur the "true and perfect image of honour" (p. 42), and sees Hal as one who doesn't value honor in itself but rather uses it as a means to success (p. 50).

67. In *The Meaning of Shakespeare*, vol. 1 (Chicago, Ill.: University of Chicago Press, 1961), Harold C. Goddard sees all of Act 5, and particularly the wooing scene, as a second Agincourt, won by "force" (p. 265). Karen Hermassi, *Polity and Theater in Historical Perspective* (Berkeley and Los Angeles: University of California Press, 1977), also stresses the mood here of "pure domination" (p. 114).

68. See Marilyn L. Williamson, "The Courtship of Katherine and the Second Tetralogy," *Criticism* 17 (1975): 334.

69. R. A. Foakes, "Poetic Language and Dramatic Significance in Shakespeare," in Philip Edwards, Inga-Stina Ewbank, and G. K. Hunter, eds., *Shakespeare's Styles: Essays in Honour of Kenneth Muir* (Cambridge: At the University Press, 1980), pp. 79–93, particularly p. 91.

70. Geoffrey Bullough, *Narrative and Dramatic Sources of Shakespeare*, vol. 2 (New York: Columbia University Press, 1962), quoted in Berman, *Interpretations*, p. 28.

71. R. J. Dorius, "A Little More Than a Little," *Shakespeare Quarterly* 11 (1960): 13–26.

72. Robert B. Pierce in *Shakespeare's History Plays: The Family and the State* (Columbus: Ohio State University Press, 1971), speaks of the private and political wooing here as "the public language of the family" (p. 235), and equates it with Hal's own desire for companionship. Pierce also draws an interesting parallel between Hal's wooing of Katherine and Richard's wooing of Anne (p. 232).

73. Leonard Barkan observes that at the end "order is restored to the body politic and health to the body natural." *Nature's Work of Art: The Human Body as Image of the World* (New Haven, Conn.: Yale University Press, 1975), p. 113. Una Ellis-Fermor, "Shakespeare's Politic Plays," *The Frontiers of Drama* (London: Methuen and Co., Ltd., 1945), quoted in Berman, *Interpretations*, comments that for the moment Shakespeare still believes in the ordered state but that in the character of Claudius he recoils from the same ideal public figure he had once celebrated in Hal (pp. 56–58).

74. Charles Williams, "*Henry V*," from Anne Ridler, ed., *Shakespearean Criticism 1919–1935* (London: Oxford University Press, 1936), quoted in Berman, *Interpretations*, p. 35.

75. Ornstein, *Kingdom for a Stage*, p. 202. In *Shakespeare and the Energies of Drama* (Princeton, N.J.: Princeton University Press, 1972), Michael Goldman defines the "achievement" of the play as "its ability to project the glory of the ruler in a way that is true too—indeed depends upon—the price of his role" (p. 70). Goldman also has some incisive comments about the parallel between the Chorus's interaction with the audience and Hal's rousing of his country. Goldman's assessment of the play's "realistic achievement" is echoed by Michael Manheim in "New Thoughts to Deck Our Kings," *The Weak King Dilemma in the Shakespearean History Play* (Syracuse, N.Y.: Syracuse University Press, 1973), pp. 167–82.

See also:

1. Linda Bamber, *Comic Women, Tragic Men: A Study of Gender and Genre in Shakespeare* (Stanford, Calif.: Stanford University Press, 1982), p. 167.

2. Lawrence Danson, "*Henry V*: King, Chorus, and Critics," *Shakespeare Quarterly* 34 (1983): 27–43.

3. Andrew and Gina MacDonald, "*Henry V*: A Shakespearean Definition of Politic Reign," *Studies in Humanities* 9 (1982): 32–37.

4. C. G. Thayer, *Shakespearean Politics: Government and Misgovernment in the Great Histories* (Athens, Ohio, and London: Ohio University Press, 1983), pp. 143–68.

Chapter 8. *The Merchant of Venice*

1. Grant Midgley calls Antonio an "unconscious homosexual" (125); as Shylock is to Venetian society, so is Antonio to the world of love and marriage. "*The Merchant of Venice*: A Reconsideration," *Essays in Criticism* 10 (1960): 119–33. For Monica J. Hamill his love for Bassanio represents "possessiveness" (237). "Poetry, Law, and the Pursuit of Perfection: Portia's Role in *The Merchant of Venice*," *Studies in English Literature* 18 (1978): 229–43. See also R. Chris Hassel, "Antonio and the Ironic Festivity of *The Merchant of Venice*," *Shakespeare Studies* 6 (1972): 67–74. For William J. Martz, Antonio's homosexuality is akin to a death-wish. *The Place of "The Merchant of Venice" in Shakespeare's Universe of Comedy* (New

York: Revisionist Press, 1976). M. G. Deshpande responds to the general argument above, and to Midgley's in particular, in "Loneliness in *The Merchant of Venice*," *Essays in Criticism* 11 (1961): 368–69.

2. The term is from Thomas Fujimara's "Mode and Structure in *The Merchant of Venice*," *PMLA* 81 (1967): 511. Ralph Berry speaks of the "unease" pervading the opening scene, in *Shakespeare's Comedies: Explorations in Form* (Princeton, N.J.: Princeton University Press, 1972), p. 113.

3. A. D. Moody, in *Shakespeare: "The Merchant of Venice"* (London: Edward Arnold, Ltd., 1964), finds the Venetians' worldliness a substitute for religion; they live in a fool's paradise to be equated with "our ordinary varnished reality." Reprinted in Sylvan Barnet, ed., *Twentieth Century Interpretations of "The Merchant of Venice"* (Englewood Cliffs, N.J.: Prentice-Hall, 1970), pp. 100–108.

4. In his excellent full-length study of the play Lawrence Danson comments on the "array of false teachers and abusers of language" (114), and on how Shylock uses language as he uses money, "carefully, and as a weapon" (139). *The Harmonies of "The Merchant of Venice"* (New Haven, Conn.: Yale University Press, 1978).

5. James Smith finds the Venetians becoming reckless as they approach Belmont, not practical or realistic enough, and caught in their own "limpidities" (p. 68), whereas Shylock is the disciplined man in their undisciplined world (p. 61). *Shakespearian and Other Essays*, ed. Edward M. Wilson (Cambridge: At the University Press, 1974), pp. 43–68.

6. For Joan Ozark Holmer the purpose of the ring episode is to educate Bassanio's too-prodigal nature (p. 68). "Loving Wisely and the Casket Test: Symbolic and Structural Unity in *The Merchant of Venice*," *Shakespeare Studies* 11 (1978): 53–76. Elizabeth S. Sklar links Bassanio with Jason's crass opportunism in "Bassanio's Golden Fleece," *Texas Studies in Language and Literature* 18 (1976): 500–509. But for Raymond B. Waddington, Bassanio's rashness is a sign of faith in God's providence. "Blind Gods: Fortune, Justice, and Cupid in *The Merchant of Venice*," *English Literary History* 44 (1977): 458–577.

7. For longer assessments of Shylock's character see John W. Draper, *Stratford to Dogberry: Studies in Shakespeare's Earlier Plays* (Freeport, N.Y.: Books for Libraries Press, 1961), pp. 137–42 and 143–50; and Toby Lelyveld, *Shylock and the Stage* (Cleveland, Ohio: The Press of Western Reserve University, 1960).

8. See Sigurd Buckhardt, *Shakespearean Meanings* (Princeton, N.J.: Princeton University Press, 1968), p. 214.

9. James Edward Siemon observes that Shylock inhabits a different "psychological world" (p. 441) in "The Canker Within: Some Observations on the Role of the Villain in Three Shakespearean Comedies," *Shakespeare Quarterly* 23 (1972): 435–43. John Hazel Smith argues it is Jessica's flight that proves the stimulus for Shylock's revenge, that earlier in the play, particularly at the signing of the contract, he has no consciously evil intentions. "Shylock: Devil Incarnation or 'Poor Man . . . Wronged?,' " *Journal of English and Germanic Philology* 60 (1961): 1–21. Milton Birnbaum, objecting to what he takes as Sylvan Barnet's notion of Bassanio's moral superiority, argues for Shylock's "buried humanity" (1130) in "The Case of *The Merchant of Venice* Reopened," *PMLA* 87 (1972): 1129–30.

10. John P. Sisk, identifying Shylock as the Renaissance "new man," links him with the Greeks in *Troilus and Cressida*. "Bondage and Release in *The Merchant of Venice*," *Shakespeare Quarterly* 20 (1969): 217–23.

11. René Girard argues that the play is paradoxical and hence able to sustain antithetical readings of both Shylock and the Venetians. " 'To Entrap the Wisest':

A Reading of *The Merchant of Venice*," *Literature and Society: Selected Papers from the English Institute, 1978*, ed. Edward W. Said (Baltimore, Md., and London: Johns Hopkins University Press, 1980), pp. 100–119.

12. For Warren D. Smith the "Hath not" speech is philosophically irrelevant (pp. 198–99). "Shakespeare's Shylock," *Shakespeare Quarterly* 15 (1964): 193–99. Michael J. C. Echeruo, arguing that Shakespeare's audience is preconditioned to hate Shylock, labels the speech "a genuine but irrelevant protest, an evasion of the major issues in dispute" (p. 11). "Shylock and the 'Conditioned Imagination': A Reinterpretation," *Shakespeare Quarterly* 22 (1971): 3–15.

13. See Ruth M. Levitsky, "Shylock as Unregenerate Man," *Shakespeare Quarterly* 28 (1977): 58–64.

14. For arguments that the two worlds of the play are not so separate or distinct see W. H. Auden, *The Dyer's Hand and Other Essays* (New York: Random House, Inc., 1962), pp. 232–35; Herbert Bronstein, "Shakespeare, the Jews, and *The Merchant of Venice*," *Shakespeare Quarterly* 20 (1969): 3–10; Burckhardt, *Shakespearean Meanings*, pp. 206–36.

15. In his *The Economics of the Imagination* (Amherst: University of Massachusetts Press, 1980), Kurt Heinzelman asks "how does one balance the economic and the non-economic significance of 'value'?" In *The Merchant of Venice* "we may witness how each 'merchant' in the Realpolitik of this play gains only those winnings which he is able to imagine, and how each is finally sentenced by the economics of his own language." See his "Afterword," pp. 276–82. John Russell Brown talks of the "two usuries" (one positive, one negative) in "Love's Wealth and the Judgement of *The Merchant of Venice*," *Shakespeare and His Comedies* (London: Methuen and Co., 1964), pp. 45–81. See also E. Pearlman, "Shakespeare, Freud, and the Two Usuries, or, Money's a Meddler," *English Literary Renaissance* 2 (1972): 217–36; and Max Plowman, "Money and *The Merchant*," reprinted in *Shakespeare's Comedies: An Anthology of Modern Criticism*, ed. Lawrence Lerner (Baltimore, Md.: Penguin Books, 1967), pp. 125–27.

16. J. Middleton Murry in "Shakespeare's Method: *The Merchant of Venice*," *Shakespeare* (London: Jonathan Cape, Ltd., 1936), pp. 188–211, finds the morality of the Venetians no better than Shylock's. Donald A. Stauffer holds that in Shylock "Shakespeare's conception of suspended or divided moral judgment walks and speaks" (p. 65). *Shakespeare's World of Images* (New York: W. W. Norton and Co., 1949), pp. 59–66.

17. But see Madeline Doran, who contends that Shylock pulls against the direction of the plot. *Endeavors of Art: A Study of Form in Elizabethan Drama* (Madison: University of Wisconsin Press, 1963), pp. 362–63.

18. For J. W. Lever, Shylock here renounces prescribed Jewish behavior and faces Antonio as a man. "Shylock, Portia, and the Values of Shakespearean Comedy," *Shakespeare Quarterly* 3 (1957): 383–86.

19. On the Laban episode see Marc Shell, "The Wether and the Ewe: Verbal Usury in *The Merchant of Venice*," *Kenyon Review*, N.S. 1 (1979): 65–92. Also the commentary by John Russell Brown in the Arden Shakespeare edition of the play (London: Methuen and Co., 1955), p. 26.

20. In essence, Shylock's roots here are in the play itself, rather than in theological controversies. See a similar argument by Alan C. Dessen, "The Elizabethan Stage Jew and Christian Example: Gerontus, Barabbas, and Shylock," *Modern Language Quarterly* 35 (1974): 231–45.

21. For a good analysis of the opening scene see Robert F. Willson, Jr., "The Sinking of Antonio, I.i. of *The Merchant of Venice*," *Shakespeare-Jahrbuch* (Heidelberg) 112 (1976): 7–14.

22. Sylvan Barnet observes that for Shylock the "present is always unsatisfactory," that the issue of the play is "to know one's destiny at the right time," in "Prodigality and Time in *The Merchant of Venice*," *PMLA* 87 (1972): 26–30. On the larger issue of time in terms of the historical movement from Judaism to Christianity, René E. Fortin comments that neither religion would be complete until a bond is established between the two, that the scene where Jessica flees her father and throws down his money bags shows that Christianity itself is not fulfilled until it can blend, rather than flout tradition. "Launcelot and the Uses of Allegory in *The Merchant of Venice*," *Studies in English Literature* 14 (1974): 259–70. See the response by Birnbaum, n. 9 above.

23. Barbara K. Lewalski, "Biblical Allusion and Allegory in *The Merchant of Venice*," *Shakespeare Quarterly* 13 (1962): 327–43.

24. Herbert S. Donow contrasts Portia's filial devotion and Jessica's ingratitude in "Shakespeare's Caskets: Unity in *The Merchant of Venice*," *English Literary History* 40 (1973): 339–51.

25. Alice N. Benston speaks of the play's three fathers—Portia's, Shylock, and Antonio as father-figure to Bassanio—in "Portia, the Law, and the Tripartite Structure of *The Merchant of Venice*," *Shakespeare Quarterly* 30 (1979): 367–85. Unlike Antonio, however, Portia, though restrained by her father, knows and can deal with the cause of her sadness.

26. See ibid. on Antonio as father to Bassanio.

27. For a positive assessment of Jessica see Camille Slights, "In Defence of Jessica: The Runaway Daughter in *The Merchant of Venice*," *Shakespeare Quarterly* 31 (1980): 357–68. On Launcelot leaving Shylock see John F. Hennedy, "Launcelot Gobbo and Shylock's Forced Conversion," *Texas Studies in Language and Literature* 15 (1973): 405–10.

28. On the allegory of movement in the play see Nevill Coghill, "The Basis of Shakespearian Comedy," in *Shakespeare Criticism 1935–60*, ed. Anne Ridler (London: Oxford University Press, 1963), pp. 213–20; and J. A. Bryant, *Hippolyta's View: Some Christian Aspects of Shakespeare's Plays* (Lexington: University of Kentucky Press, 1961), pp. 33–51.

29. See Lever, "Values of Shakespearean Comedy," p. 385.

30. On hazarding in the play, Russell Astley, "Through a Looking Glass, Darkly: Judging Hazards in *The Merchant of Venice*," *Ariel E* 10 (1979): 17–34.

31. On the play's bonds and contracts see Robert Hapgood, "Portia and *The Merchant of Venice*: The Gentle Bond," *Modern Language Quarterly* 28 (1967): 19–32; and Waddington, "Blind Gods," pp. 464–67.

32. Albert Wertheim contrasts Portia's and Shylock's abilities to see clearly and to read the full "text" in "The Treatment of Shylock and Thematic Integrity in *The Merchant of Venice*," *Shakespeare Studies* 6 (1972): 75–87.

33. Lewalski, "Biblical Allusion," finds the caskets offering a choice between spiritual life or death, pp. 327–43.

34. William Empson observes that "fancy can only hide lead, and lead must be enough for the maintenance of fancy," in *Seven Types of Ambiguity*, reprinted in Lerner, *An Anthology*, p. 128.

35. Walter F. Eggers, Jr., in "Love and Likeness in *The Merchant of Venice*," *Shapespeare Quarterly* 28 (1977): 327–33, points out that Aragon and Morocco are more socially "like" Portia than the impoverished Bassanio, but that "real identity, the basis of love, underlies apparent likeness" (p. 332).

36. In his stimulating comments on the casket scenes, Kirby Farrell, in *Shakespeare's Creation: The Language of Magic and Play* (Amherst: University of Massachusetts Press, 1975), observes that for Bassanio what "defies expression

alone has meaning" (147), that while the other suitors cling to formulas, Bassanio has the advantage of having no status and hence is full of play or imagination.

37. William Babula establishes a hierarchy of love in the play, moving from Gratiano/Nerissa to Lorenzo/Jessica to Bassanio/Portia; as one goes up the scale love itself becomes less physically limited (p. 33). "Shylock's Dramatic Function," *Dalhousie Review* 53 (1973): 30–38.

38. For C. L. Barber, Shylock is the play's "accounting machanism," opposed to Bassanio who is able to venture and to invest imaginatively. Shylock moves from being a limited artist who controls to being the controlled in the trial scene. "The Merchant and the Jew of Venice: Wealth's Communion and an Intruder," *Shakespeare's Festive Comedy* (Princeton, N.J.: Princeton University Press, 1959), pp. 166–91.

39. For Marianne L. Novy, Portia embodies "otherness," a full sense of love based on the financial, sexual, and verbal. "Giving, Taking, and the Role of Portia in *The Merchant of Venice*," *Philological Quarterly* 58 (1979): 137–54.

40. But for a negative view of Portia see Harry Berger, Jr., "Marriage and Mercifixion in *The Merchant of Venice*: The Casket Scene Revisited," *Shakespeare Quarterly* 32 (1981): 155–62. For Berger, Portia, once released from her father, tries to control both herself and Bassanio; she knows "the power of the charity that wounds" (161) in giving Bassanio the ring. An aggressive woman, she fights to establish herself in the male society of Venice.

41. For a "legal" redoing of Act 4 see Mark Edwin Andrews, *Law Versus Equity in "The Merchant of Venice": A Legalization of Act IV, Scene 1, with Forward, Judicial Precedents, and Notes* (Boulder: University of Colorado Press, 1965).

42. John L. Palmer in *Comic Characters of Shakespeare* (London: Macmillan and Co., Ltd., 1947) calls Shylock's "a mind so intensely concentrated upon itself, so constricted in its operation" (p. 71).

43. See Ralph Nash, "Shylock's Wolfish Spirit," *Shakespeare Quarterly* 10 (1959): 125–28; and Norman Nathan, "Shylock, Jacob and God's Judgment," *Shakespeare Quarterly* 1 (1950): 255–59, where he argues that Shylock expects "to get his pound of flesh through God's intervention" (p. 257).

44. J. A. Bryant speaks of Shylock's "preoccupation with self" (p. 610) in "*The Merchant of Venice* and the Common Flaw," *Sewanee Review* 81 (1973): 606–22.

45. Still, H. B. Charlton finds Shylock "a towering figure" at the trial, and argues that as a creation of the drama he is inevitably humanized. *Shakespearian Comedy* (New York: The Macmillan Co., 1938), pp. 123–60. For D. M. Cohen, in "The Jew and Shylock," *Shakespeare Quarterly* 31 (1980): 53–63, Shakespeare only endows Shylock with humanity at the end (p. 63).

46. For Hamill, "Pursuit of Perfection," Portia is a poet-lawmaker practicing the ideal within the limits of "law, destiny, and human imperfection" (p. 241). To Stanley J. Kozikowski, in "The Allegory of Love and Fortune: The Lottery in *The Merchant of Venice*," *Renascence* 32 (1980): 105–15, Portia represents "Fortune's ambivalence" (p. 107), giving the seekers what they really, albeit unconsciously want (p. 113).

47. Danson in *The Harmonies* observes that, in contrast, Shylock's histrionic mastery degenerates as we move from scene 3 to the trial (p. 157).

48. W. Nicholas Knight comments that Portia insists "upon an extremely rigorous reading of the letter of the law in order to achieve her humane purpose" (p. 62), in "Equity and Mercy in English Law and Drama," *Comparative Drama* 6 (1972): 51–67. E. F. J. Tucker finds that the law's letter and its spirit are mutual in "The Letter and the Law in *The Merchant of Venice*," *Shakespeare Survey* 29 (1976): 93–101.

49. And see Maxime MacKay, "*The Merchant of Venice*: a Reflection of the Early Conflicts Between Courts of Law and Courts of Equity," *Shakespeare Quarterly* 15 (1964): 371–75.

50. R. F. Hill comments that in the play love is viewed in a "comprehensive light" but still remains "as an unequivocal good" in "*The Merchant of Venice* and the Pattern of Romantic Comedy," *Shakespeare Studies* 28 (1975): 77, 79.

51. Derek Traversi observes that in Act 5 "we return, a little uneasily, to the world of poetry and artifice" (p. 42). *William Shakespeare: The Early Comedies* (London: Longmans, Green and Co., 1969).

52. Yet for Allan Bloom, Belmont is a utopia that, by definition, does not exist. "Shakespeare on Jew and Christian: an Interpretation of *The Merchant of Venice*," *Social Research* 30 (1963): 1–22. For John R. Cooper, Belmont represents old values, the ideal, whereas Shakespeare's realism is confined to Venice. "Shylock's Humanity," *Shakespeare Quarterly* 21 (1970): 117–24.

53. Bernard Grebanier would have Shylock both ways, not the comic character fashioned by E. E. Stoll, nor the tragic or melodramatic figure that many actors prefer. *The Truth about Shylock* (New York: Random House, 1962). And see E. E. Stoll, *Shakespeare Studies, Historical and Comparative in Method* (New York: Frederick Ungar Publishing Co., 1960), pp. 255–336. For James Siemon, Shylock's "emotional force remains untouched at the end of Act IV" (p. 207). "*The Merchant of Venice*: Act V as Ritual Reiteration," *Studies in Philology* 67 (1970): 201–9.

54. For G. Wilson Knight, however, the worlds of Venice and Belmont remain separate; in his *Principles of Shakespearian Production* (London: Faber and Faber, 1936), pp. 135–40, he argues that the contrast should be emphasized by multilevel sets.

55. Richard Henze observes that Antonio trusts too much in fortune, Shylock in the law, with both relying too much on fate, without having an escape clause; as audience, we must have a "faith in predictability" (p. 299). "'Which is the Merchant here? And which the Jew?,'" *Criticism* 16 (1974): 287–300.

56. Bertrand Evans classifies the ring-lesson as an example of complementary awareness and unawareness. *Shakespeare's Comedies* (Oxford: Clarendon Press, 1960), p. 67.

57. Farrell in *Shakespeare's Creation* points out that here "music facilitates metamorphosis" (p. 159). In "Ways of Knowing in *The Merchant of Venice*," *Shakespeare Quarterly* 30 (1979): 89–93, Maurice Hunt calls the music "a background for knowing," and concludes that the "more background music approaches the ideal, the more one's knowledge of value approaches perfection" (p. 91).

58. John S. Coolidge presents a less qualified reading of the events and dialogue of the final scene: "the dawning of the day which brings the play to its happy ending is like the proclamations of the New Testament" (p. 262), the scene itself establishing the "pattern of Christian eschatological hope" (p. 263). "Law and Love in *The Merchant of Venice*," *Shakespeare Quarterly* 27 (1976): 243–63.

59. Critics have made much of Antonio's supposed reticence in this final scene, of this bachelor amidst three married couples. For Jan Lawson Hinely in "Bond Priorities in *The Merchant of Venice*," *Studies in English Literature* 20 (1980): 217–39, Lear is Antonio's "emotional successor" (p. 238). For Allan Holaday, Antonio suffers from pride, and while he and Shylock have both missed salvation, in the final scene man's imperfections are accepted. "Antonio and the Allegory of Salvation," *Shakespeare Studies* 4 (1969): 109–18. Lawrence W. Hyman, in "The Rival Lovers in *The Merchant of Venice*," *Shakespeare Quarterly* 21 (1970): 109–16, sees the news of the return of Antonio's fleet as removing the

236 SHAKESPEARE'S THEATER OF PRESENCE

last sacrifice that Antonio makes for Bassanio (p. 115). Leonard Tennenhouse argues that when Antonio volunteers himself as bond for Bassanio's good intentions, he yields to Portia and releases Bassanio of the charge of adultery; Portia in return "pays" him by restoring his fortunes. "The Counterfeit Order of *The Merchant of Venice*," *Representing Shakespeare: New Psychological Essays*, ed. Murray M. Schwartz and Coppélia Kahn (Baltimore, Md.: Johns Hopkins University Press, 1980), pp. 54–69.

60. On the ring's significance see Marilyn L. Williamson, "The Ring Episode in *The Merchant of Venice*," *South Atlantic Quarterly* 71 (1972): 587–94, where for her the ring represents how much "we invest the meaning of a relationship in an object" (590). And the eloquent comments by Danson in *The Harmonies*: "the letter is again fulfilled in the spirit, as comic faith is confirmed by the flesh and the golden ring" (p. 195).

See also:

1. Walter Cohen, "*The Merchant of Venice* and the Possibilities of Historical Criticism," *English Literary History* 49 (1982): 765–89.
2. Jane Donawerth, *Shakespeare and the Sixteenth-Century Study of Language* (Urbana: University of Illinois Press, 1984), pp. 189–218.
3. Bruce Erlich, "Queenly Shadows: On Mediation in Two Comedies," *Shakespeare Survey* 35 (1982): 65–77.
4. Lisa Jardine, *Still Harping on Daughters: Women and Drama in the Age of Shakespeare* (Totowa, N.J.: Barnes and Noble, 1983), p. 61.
5. William Chester Jordan, "Approaches to the Court Scene in the Bond Story: Equity and Mercy or Reason and Nature," *Shakespeare Quarterly* 33 (1982): 49–59.
6. Cynthia Lewis, "Antonio and Alienation in *The Merchant of Venice*," *South Atlantic Review* 48 (1983): 19–31.
7. Joseph Westlund, *Shakespeare's Reparative Comedies: A Psychoanalytical View of the Middle Plays* (Chicago: University of Chicago Press, 1984), pp. 17–35.

Chapter 9. *King Lear*

1. Maynard Mack, *"King Lear" in Our Time* (Berkeley and Los Angeles: University of California Press, 1965), p. 41.
A Note on the text of *King Lear*: Even though there is now much discussion, much excitement, and not a little controversy about the true text of *King Lear*, I have decided to stay with the conflated text chosen by G. Blakemore Evans in *The Riverside Shakespeare*. Based on the Folio, that text admits roughly 288 lines or part-lines (including 4.3) found only in the first two Quartos. Professor Evans points out in his "Note on the Text" (p. 1295) that "over a hundred individual readings from Q1 (and very rarely from Q2) have been drawn upon to supplement or correct the F1 text." Yet I agree with Stanley Wells in his introduction to *The Division of the Kingdoms: Shakespeare's Two Versions of "King Lear,"* Gary Taylor and Michael Warren, eds. (Oxford: Clarendon Press, 1983), that "future criticism must acknowledge the existence of two authoritative texts" (p. 18). In my "Recent Studies in Elizabethan and Jacobean Drama" (listed in the "Note" to this section on Notes and Pertinent Sources) I speak at greater length about this issue, before concluding that "I like the argument of *The Division*" (p. 477). The

issue, of course, is still up for debate. Should we recognize two fairly distinct plays as existing in the Quarto and Folio—or what Mr. Wells calls "a pair of legitimate—though not identical—twins" (p. 20)? If the Folio does represent Shakespeare's own revisions in light of what he learned about the play in production, should we prefer that version? Or if the Folio shows a hand other than Shakespeare's, should we choose the Quarto? In talking about *Lear* should we use both texts in our analysis, not just of specific moments but in our overall reading of *Lear*? The "mood" or meaning of the larger play is surely influenced by such large differences as the Folio's deletion of the mock trial, its diminution of the Kent's role, or changes in the Fool's status. In his recent and most excellent book *Speechless Dialect: Shakespeare's Open Silences* (Berkeley and Los Angeles: University of California Press, 1985), Philip C. McGuire shows fellow scholars, as well as directors and actors, just what options each text allows in the play's closing moments (pp. 97–121). As I speculate in the *SEL* review, what would be our experience one day seeing a performance based exclusively on the Quarto text, and the next day one based on the Folio? However, given the current debate on the issue, and the fact that the *Riverside*'s conflated text *is* Shakespeare's (unless there are traces of some other hand in the Folio), I play the conservative here: I use the *Riverside* elsewhere in this book, and therefore remain consistent in the tantalizing case of *Lear*. To be sure, the "plays" existing in Quarto and Folio, though different, are not antithetical. More to the purpose of this present book in which I practice performance criticism, the conflated *Lear* is the play that has thrilled audience now for many years, and *is* a text that can be performed and therefore commented on. If some day the "truth" (if there is *a* truth) about *Lear* is known, then I must ask the present reader to qualify, as he or she thinks best, what I say in this book about *Lear*. As a scholar and a director, I am no less ready to abandon my own stance here.

2. A. C. Bradley, *Shakespearean Tragedy* (London: Macmillan and Co., Ltd., 1932), pp. 243–330. Jan Knott, *Shakespeare Our Contemporary* (New York: Doubleday and Co., Inc., 1964), pp. 87–124. And see discussion of Tate in Mack, *Our Time*, pp. 8–13.

3. Arnold Isenberg, "Cordelia Absent," *Shakespeare Quarterly* 2 (1951): 185, 194.

4. Emily W. Leider, "Plainness of Style in *King Lear*," *Shakespeare Quarterly* 21 (1970): 52.

5. S. L. Bethell, *Shakespeare and the Popular Dramatic Tradition* (London: Staples Press, 1944), p. 54.

6. Roy Battenhouse, *Shakespearean Tragedy: Its Art and Christian Premises* (Bloomington: Indiana University Press, 1969), p. 291.

7. Paul N. Siegel, *Shakespearean Tragedy and the Elizabethan Compromise* (New York: New York University Press, 1957), p. 180.

8. Thomas P. Roche, "'Nothing Almost Sees Miracles': Tragic Knowledge in *King Lear*," in *On "King Lear*," ed. Lawrence Danson (Princeton, N.J.: Princeton University Press, 1981), p. 162.

9. R. G. Hunter, *Shakespeare and the Mystery of God's Judgments* (Athens: University of Georgia Press, 1976), p. 191.

10. Nancy R. Lindheim, "*King Lear* as Pastoral Tragedy," in *Some Facets of "King Lear": Essays in Prismatic Criticism*, ed. Rosalie L. Colie and F. T. Flahiff (Toronto: University of Toronto Press, 1974), p. 173.

11. Lawrence Danson, "*King Lear* and the Two Abysses," in *On "King Lear*," p. 128.

    12. Nicholas Brooke, "The Ending of *King Lear*," in *Shakespeare 1564–1964: A Collection of Modern Essays by Various Hands*, ed. Edward A. Bloom (Providence, R.I.: Brown University Press, 1964), p. 87.
    13. Levin L. Schücking, "Character and Action: *King Lear*," *Problems in Shakespeare's Plays: A Guide to the Better Understanding of the Dramatist* (London: George G. Harrap and Co., Ltd., 1922), pp. 176–90.
    14. Julian Markels, *Pillars of the World: "Antony and Cleopatra" in Shakespeare's Development* (Columbus: Ohio State University Press, 1968), pp. 108–9.
    15. Thomas McFarland, *Tragic Meanings in Shakespeare* (New York: Random House, 1966), pp. 127–71.
    16. Arthur F. Kinney, "*Lear*," *Massachusetts Review* 17 (1976): 710.
    17. Winifred Nowottny, "Shakespeare's Tragedies," in *Shakespeare's World*, ed. James Sutherland and Joel Hurstfield (New York: St. Martin's Press, 1964), p. 70.
    18. Devon Leigh Hodges, "Cut Adrift and 'Cut to the Brains': The Anatomized World of *King Lear*," *English Literary Renaissance* 11 (1981): 210.
    19. Wyndham Lewis, *The Lion and the Fox: The Role of the Hero in the Plays of Shakespeare* (New York: Harper and Brothers Publishers, 1966), p. 180.
    20. Norman Rabkin, *Shakespeare and the Problem of Meaning* (Chicago: University of Chicago Press, 1981), p. 34.
    21. Katherine Stockholder, "The Multiple Genres of *King Lear*: Breaking the Archetypes," *Bucknell Review* 16 (1968): 40–63.
    22. James Black, "*King Lear*: Art Upside Down," *Shakespeare Studies* 33 (1980): 42.
    23. Wylie Sypher, *Structures of Experience in Shakespeare* (New York: Seabury Press, 1976), p. 158.
    24. Eliseo Vivas, "Tragedy and the Broader Consciousness," *Southern Review* 7 (1971): 847.
    25. John F. Danby, *Shakespeare's Doctrine of Nature: A Study of "King Lear"* (London: Faber and Faber, 1951), p. 204.
    26. William Matchett, "Some Dramatic Techniques in *King Lear*," in *Shakespeare: The Theatrical Dimension*, ed. Philip McGuire and David A. Samuelson (New York: AMS Press, 1979), pp. 185–208.
    27. Susan Snyder, *The Comic Matrix of Shakespeare's Tragedies* (Princeton, N.J.: Princeton University Press, 1979), pp. 137–79.
    28. Theodore S. Spencer, *Shakespeare and the Nature of Man* (New York: Macmillan Co., 1942), pp. 141–42.
    29. Stephen Booth, "On the Greatness of *King Lear*," in *Twentieth-Century Interpretations of "King Lear*," ed. Janet Adelman (Englewood Cliffs, N.J.: Prentice-Hall, 1978), p. 102.
    30. Jeffrey G. Sobosan, "One Hand Clapping . . .: A Study of the Paradoxical in *Lear* and Kierkegaard," *Revue Théologique et Philosophique* 30 (1974): 53.
    31. Bridget Gellert Lyons, "The Subplot as Simplification in *King Lear*," in Colie and Flahiff, *Some Facets*, p. 28.
    32. Margaret Webster, *Shakespeare without Tears* (New York: McGraw-Hill Book Co., 1942), pp. 156–80. But for a defense of the play's fitness for the stage see Harley Granville-Barker, *Prefaces to Shakespeare* (Princeton, N.J.: Princeton University Press, 1946), 1:261–334.
    33. D. G. James, *The Dream of Learning: An Essay on "The Advancement of Learning," "Hamlet," and "King Lear"* (Oxford: Clarendon Press, 1951), p. 79.
    34. Paul J. Alpers, "*King Lear* and the Theory of 'Sight Pattern,'" in *In Defense of Reading: A Reader's Approach to Literary Criticism*, ed. Reuben A. Brower and Richard Poirier (New York: E. P. Dutton and Co., Inc., 1962), p. 145.

35. C. L. Barber, "On Christianity and the Family: Tragedy of the Sacred," in Adelman, *Interpretations*, p. 119.

36. Clifford Leech, "The Incredible in Jacobean Tragedy," *Rice University Studies* 60 (1974): 121.

37. Lawrence Raab, "'And We Were Left Darkling': Notes on *King Lear*," *American Scholar* 36 (1966–67): 650.

38. Robert Egan, *Drama Within Drama: Shakespeare's Sense of His Art in "King Lear," "The Winter's Tale," and "The Tempest"* (New York: Columbia University Press, 1975), p. 43.

39. S. L. Goldberg, *An Essay on "King Lear"* (Cambridge: At The University Press, 1974), pp. 134, 181.

40. Norman N. Holland, *The Shakespearean Imagination* (New York: Macmillan Co., 1964), pp. 233–60.

41. Joyce Carol Oates, *Contraries: Essays* (New York: Oxford University Press, 1981), pp. 65, 61.

42. Barbara Everett, "The New *King Lear*," *Critical Quarterly* 2 (1960): 335.

43. Howard Felperin, *Shakespearean Representation* (Princeton, N.J.: Princeton University Press, 1977), p. 104.

44. Richard D. Fly, *Shakespeare's Mediated World* (Amherst: University of Massachusetts Press, 1976), p. 115.

45. John Reibetanz, *The Lear World: A Study of "King Lear" in Its Dramatic Context* (Toronto and Buffalo: University of Toronto Press, 1977), p. 120.

46. John Lawlor, *The Tragic Sense in Shakespeare* (London: Chatto and Windus, 1966), p. 160.

47. Laurence Michel, "Shakespearean Tragedy: Critique of Humanism from the Inside," *Massachusetts Review* 2 (1960–61): 645.

48. Martha Andersen, "'Ripeness is All': Sententiae and Commonplaces in *King Lear*," in Colie and Flahiff, *Some Facets*, pp. 164–65.

49. Egan, *Drama Within Drama*, pp. 16–17.

50. Fly, *Mediated World*, p. 115.

51. James L. Calderwood calls this realization "theatricide" in *To Be and Not To Be: Negation and Metadrama in "Hamlet"* (New York: Columbia University Press, 1983), pp. 140–43, 166–75.

52. On this issue of the characters' efforts to interpret the world of *Lear* see Morris Weitz, "The Coinage of Man: *King Lear* and Camus's *L'Etranger*," *Modern Language Review* 66 (1971): 31–39: L. C. Knights, "*King Lear* as Metaphor," in *Myth and Symbol: Critical Approaches and Applications*, ed. Northrop Frye, L. C. Knights et al. (Lincoln: University of Nebraska Press, 1963), pp. 21–38; Richard B. Sewall, *The Vision of Tragedy* (New Haven, Conn.: Yale University Press, 1959), pp. 68–79; Herbert Weisinger, "The Myth and Ritual Approach to Shakespeare," *Centennial Review* 1 (1957): 142–60; and Sobosan, "One Hand Clapping," pp. 47–53.

53. On the play's various trials see Dorothy C. Hockey, "The Trial Pattern in *King Lear*," *Shakespeare Quarterly* 10 (1959): 389–95.

54. This is the position of Harry Berger, Jr., in "*King Lear*: The Lear Family Romance," *Centennial Review* 23 (1979): 348–76.

55. On the play's open-ended nature see John Rosenberg, "King Lear and His Comforters," *Essays in Criticism* 16 (1966): 135–46.

56. On the play's language see Norman Atwood, "Cordelia and Kent: Their Fateful Choice of Style," *Language and Style* 9 (1976): 42–54; Sigurd Burckhardt, *Shakespearean Meanings* (Princeton, N.J.: Princeton University Press, 1968), pp. 237–59; Daniel Seltzer, "*King Lear* in the Theater," in Danson, *On "King Lear*,"

pp. 163–85; Helen Dry, "Words in *King Lear*," *Thoth* 13 (1973): 11–17; Inga-Stina Ewbank, "'More Pregnantly than Words': Some Uses and Limitations of Visual Symbolism," *Shakespeare Survey* 24 (1971): 13–18; Robert F. Fleissner, "The 'Nothing' Element in *King Lear*," *Shakespeare Quarterly* 13 (1962): 67–70; Richmond Y. Hathorn, "Lear's Equations," *Centennial Review* 4 (1960): 51–69. And, of course, the most extensive study of the play's language and metaphor, Robert B. Heilman's classic, *This Great Stage: Image and Structure in "King Lear"* (Baton Rouge: Louisiana State University Press, 1948).

57. Madeline Doran comments that "Lear's voice" dominates the play. "Command, Question, and Assertion in *King Lear*," in *Shakespeare's Art: Seven Essays*, The Tupper Lectures on Shakespeare (Chicago: University of Chicago Press, for The George Washington University, 1973), p. 53.

58. See Hugh MacLean, "Disguise in *King Lear*: Kent and Edgar," *Shakespeare Quarterly* 11 (1960): 49–54.

59. On this movement away from words, toward silence, see Barbara Everett, "The New *King Lear*," pp. 325–39; Esther Merle Jackson, "*King Lear*: The Grammar of Tragedy," *Shakespeare Quarterly* 17 (1966): 25–40; D. G. James, "Keats and *King Lear*," *Shakespeare Survey* 13 (1960): 58–68; Emily Leider, "Plainness of Style," in Colie and Flahiff, *Some Facets*, pp. 45–53; Jill Levenson, "What the Silence Said: Still Points in *King Lear*," in *Proceedings of the World Shakespeare Congress*, ed. Clifford Leech and J. M. R. Margeson (Toronto: University of Toronto Press, 1971), pp. 215–29; Hugh Norman MacLean, "Episode, Scene, Speech, and Word: The Madness of Lear," in *Critics and Criticism*, ed. R. S. Crane (Chicago: University of Chicago Press, 1952), pp. 595–615; Rosenberg, "King Lear and His Comforters," pp. 135–46; J. L. Simmons, "Shakespearean Rhetoric and Realism," *Georgia Review* 24 (1970): 453–71; J. K. Walton, "Lear's Last Speech," *Shakespeare Survey* 13 (1960): 11–19.

60. I take the term from Calderwood, *To Be and Not To Be*, pp. 80–84.

61. See Murray Krieger's critique of Derrida, where he doesn't so much refute as absorb the argument for absence. *Theory of Criticism: A Tradition and Its System* (Baltimore, Md: Johns Hopkins University Press, 1976), pp. 207–45.

62. On this visual dimension see Alvin B. Kernan, "Formalism and Realism in Elizabethan Drama: The Miracles in *King Lear*," *Renaissance Drama* 9 (1966): 59–66; Richard Fly, *Mediated World*, pp. 85–115; Kenneth Muir, "Madness in *King Lear*," *Shakespeare Survey* 13 (1060): 30–50.

63. Paul A. Jorgensen, "Much Ado about *Nothing*," *Shakespeare Quarterly* 5 (1954): 287–95. Also the very provocative article by David Willbern, "Shakespeare's Nothing," in *Representing Shakespeare*, ed. Murray M. Schwartz and Coppélia Kahn (Baltimore, Md.: The Johns Hopkins University Press, 1980), pp. 244–63.

64. Thomas P. Roche, Jr., speculates on the line "Nothing almost see miracles / But misery" in "Two Abysses," in Danson, *On "King Lear,"* p. 162 especially.

65. See Harry Levin's "The Heights and Depths: A Scene from *King Lear*," in *More Talking of Shakespeare* (Freeport, N.Y.: Books for Libraries Press, 1970), p. 99.

66. Krieger, *Theory of Criticism*, p. 207.

67. Alpers, "'Sight Pattern,'" in Brower and Poirier, *In Defense*, pp. 133–51.

68. On the metadramatic dimension of the play see Fly, *Mediated World*, pp. 85–115; Egan, *Drama Within Drama*, pp. 16–55; and Thomas F. Van Laan, *Role-Playing in Shakespeare* (Toronto: University of Toronto Press, 1978), 168–222.

69. For a good historical survey and discussion of the negative attitude

toward the theater see Jonas A. Barish, *The Antitheatrical Prejudice* (Berkeley and Los Angeles: University of California Press, 1981).

70. See nn. 33–50 above.

71. See William R. Elton's *"King Lear" and the Gods* (San Marino, Calif.: The Huntington Library, 1966), pp. 249–53.

72. See Sheldon P. Zitner, "The Fool's Prophecy," *Shakespeare Quarterly* 18 (1968): 76–80.

73. Dean Frye, "The Context of Lear's Unbuttoning," *English Literary History* 32 (1965): 29.

74. I use this term in the chapter "*Hamlet*: The Double Edge of Aesthetics," in *When The Theater Turns to Itself: The Aesthetic Metaphor in Shakespeare* (Lewisburg, Pa.: Bucknell University Press, 1981), pp. 152–76.

75. On Lear's limited trial see Egan, *Drama Within Drama*, pp. 43–44.

76. I discuss such theatrical reference in *Godot* in *Beckett's Theaters: Interpretations for Performance* (Lewisburg, Pa.: Bucknell University Press, 1984), pp. 32–43.

77. Thomas B. Stroup accounts for the ways in which Shakespeare achieves this large canvas in *Microcosmos: the Shape of the Elizabethan Play* (Lexington: University of Kentucky Press, 1965), pp. 81–118 especially.

78. I survey this checkered history and the problems of translating Shakespeare to the film in "The Filmed Shakespeare: From Verbal to Visual," in my edition of *Shakespeare's "More Than Words Can Witness": Essays on Visual and Nonverbal Enactment in the Plays* (Lewisburg, Pa.: Bucknell University Press, 1980), pp. 207–36.

79. See, for example, Philip Hobsbaum's *Theory of Criticism*, "Survival Values" (Bloomington: Indiana University Press, 1970), pp. 143–63.

80. I am indebted to Jack Jorgens's account of the Kozintsev *Lear* in *Shakespeare on Film* (Bloomington and London: Indiana University Press, 1977), pp. 246–50.

81. See Leo Kirschbaum's "celebration" of the character in "Albany," *Shakespeare Survey* 13 (1960): 20–29.

82. On the play's "presence" see MacLean, "Episode, Scene, Speech, and Word," pp. 595–615; and Inga-Stina Ewbank, "'More Pregnantly than Words,'" pp. 13–18. I take the title of this chapter from her perceptive discussion of Edgar's line, "I would not take this from report; it is" (4.6.141–42) on p. 18.

83. In "The Pattern of *Lear*-ending: A Reconsideration," *Literary Criterion* 9 (1969): 35–41, Alur Ram calls the central issue of the play "the hero-experience" (p. 38).

84. On "patience" see John F. Danby, *Poets on Fortune's Hill: Studies in Sidney, Shakespeare, Beaumont and Fletcher* (Port Washington, N.Y.: Kennikat Press, Inc., 1966 reissue), where he speaks of patience not as idleness but as an active state, pp. 108–27; and T. Anthony Perry, *Erotic Spirituality: The Integrative Tradition from Leone Ebreo to John Donne* (University: University of Alabama Press, 1980), "Withdrawal or Service: The Paradox of *King Lear*," pp. 99–115.

85. On the issue of the heart and feeling see Bernard McElroy, *Shakespeare's Mature Tragedies* (Princeton, N.J.: Princeton University Press, 1973), pp. 145–205, particularly his commentary on how feeling generates ethics but also suffering (p. 202); and Ronald Berman, "Sense and Substance in *King Lear*," *Neuphilologische Mitteilungen* 65 (1964): 96–103. Terence Hawkes in "That Shakespeherean Rag" argues that it is Cordelia's heart that is breaking, that Lear asks that her doublet be unbuttoned. In Homan, *Shakespeare's "More Than Words Can Witness,"* pp. 62–76.

86. Helen Gardner uses the term in *"King Lear,"* The John Coffin Memorial Lecture, 1966 (London: Oxford University Press, 1967).

87. Mathilda M. Hills, *Time, Space, and Structure in "King Lear."* Institute for English Language and Literature (Salzburg, Austria: University of Salzburg Press, 1976), p. 178.

88. Hobsbaum, *Theory of Criticism,* p. 160.

89. R. W. Chambers, *"King Lear,"* Glasgow *University Publications* 54 (1940): 20–52.

90. John Holloway, *The Story of Night: Studies in Shakespeare's Major Tragedies* (Lincoln: University of Nebraska Press, 1961), p. 77.

91. Paul V. Kreider, *Repetition in Shakespeare's Plays* (Princeton, N.J.: Princeton University Press, 1941), p. 212.

92. William Willeford, *The Fool and His Scepter: A Study in Clowns and Jesters and Their Audience* (Evanston, Ill.: Northwestern University Press, 1969), p. 225.

93. Terence Hawkes, *Shakespeare and the Reason: A Study of the Tragedies and the Problem Plays* (New York: Humanities Press, 1965), pp. 160–93.

94. Derek Peat, "'And That's True Too': *King Lear* and the Tension of Uncertainty," *Shakespeare Survey* 33 (1980): 49–53.

95. Phyllis Rackin, "Delusion as Perdition in *King Lear,*" *Shakespeare Quarterly* 21 (1970): 33

96. Herbert Howarth, *The Tiger's Heart* (New York: Oxford University Press, 1970), p. 173.

97. Edward Pechter, "On the Blinding of Gloucester," *English Literary History* 45 (1978): 185.

98. W. F. Blisset, "Recognition in *King Lear,*" in Colie and Flahiff, *Some Facets,* p. 115.

99. Michael Goldman, *Shakespeare and the Energies of Drama* (Princeton, N.J.: Princeton University Press, 1972), p. 108.

100. Nancy Lindheim, "Pastoral Tragedy," in Colie and Flahiff, *Some Facets,* p. 181.

101. Berel Long, "Nothing Comes of All: Lear-Dying," *New Literary History* 9 (1978): 557–59.

102. H. A. Mason, *Shakespeare's Tragedies of Love* (New York: Barnes and Noble, Inc., 1970), pp. 202, 226.

103. Hugh L. Hennedy, *"King Lear:* Recognizing the Ending," *Studies in Philology* 71 (1974): 383.

104. Burckhardt, *Shakespearean Meanings,* p. 256.

105. Thomas F. Van Laan, "Acting or Action in *King Lear,*" in Colie and Flahiff, *Some Facets,* pp. 73–74.

106. William Frost, "Shakespeare's Rituals and the Opening of *King Lear,*" *Hudson Review* 10 (1957–58): 584–85.

107. C. F. Tucker Brooke, *Essays on Shakespeare and Other Elizabethans* (New Haven, Conn.: Yale University Press, 1948), pp. 68–70.

108. Northrop Frye, *Fools of Time: Studies in Shakespearean Tragedy* (Toronto: University of Toronto Press), "Little World of Man: The Tragedy of Isolation," pp. 75–101.

109. Madeline Doran, "Command, Question, and Assertion," p. 78.

110. Rosalie L. Colie, *Paradoxical Epidemica,* "Reason in Madness" (Princeton, N.J.: Princeton University Press, 1966), pp. 468–81.

111. Murray Krieger, *A Window to Criticism: Shakespeare's Sonnets and Modern Poetics* (Princeton, N.J.: Princeton University Press, 1964).

112. Sidney Homan, "*The Tempest* and Shakespeare's Last Plays: The Aesthetic Dimensions," *Shakespeare Quarterly* 24 (1973): 75–76.

113. Alfred Harbage, *William Shakespeare: The Complete Works* (Baltimore, Md.: Penguin Books, 1969), p. 1063.

See also:

1. Stephen Booth, *"King Lear," "Macbeth," Indefinition, and Tragedy* (New Haven, Conn.: Yale University Press, 1983).

2. Herbert R. Coursen, Jr., *Christian Ritual and the World of Shakespeare's Tragedies* (Lewisburg, Pa.: Bucknell University Press, 1976), pp. 327–13.

3. Jonathan Dollimore, *Radical Tragedy: Religion, Ideology, and Power in the Drama of Shakespeare and His Contemporaries* (Chicago: University of Chicago Press, 1984).

4. James Driscoll, *Identity in Shakespearean Drama* (Lewisburg, Pa.: Bucknell University Press, 1983).

5. Lillian Feder, *Madness in Literature* (Princeton, N.J.: Princeton University Press, 1980).

6. Philip C. McGuire, *Speechless Dialect: Shakespeare's Open Silences* (Berkeley and Los Angeles: University of California Press, 1985), pp. 97–121.

7. Jean MacIntyre, "Truth, Lies, and Poesie in *King Lear*," *Renaissance and Reformation* 6 (1982): 34–45.

8. A. D. Nuttall, *A New Mimesis: Shakespeare and the Representation of Reality* (London and New York: Methuen, 1983).,

9. Edgar Schell, *Strangers and Pilgrims: From "The Castle of Perseverance" to "King Lear"* (Chicago: University of Chicago Press, 1983).

10. Susan Snyder, "*King Lear* and the Psychology of Dying," *Shakespeare Quarterly* 33 (1982): 449–60.

11. Bert O. States, "Standing on the Extreme Verge in *King Lear* and Other High Places," *Georgia Review* 36 (1982): 417–25.

12. David Sundelson, *Shakespeare's Restorations of the Father* (New Brunswick, N.J.: Rutgers University Press, 1983).

13. Gary Taylor, *To Analyze Delight: A Hedonist Criticism of Shakespeare* (Newark: University of Delaware Press, 1985), pp. 162–236.

14. Mark Taylor, *Shakespeare's Darker Purpose: A Question on Incest* (New York: AMS Press, 1983).

15. William F. Zak, *Sovereign Shame: A Study of "King Lear"* (Lewisburg, Pa.: Bucknell University Press, 1984).

Conclusions. *A Midsummer Night's Dream* and *Othello*

1. William Webbe, *Of English Poetrie*, in *Elizabethan Critical Essays*, ed. G. G. Smith (London: Oxford University Press, 1904), 1:234.

2. See the wonderfully perceptive article on Hermia's dream by Norman Holland, "Hermia's Dream," in *Representing Shakespeare*, ed. Murray Schwartz and Coppélia Kahn (Baltimore and London: The Johns Hopkins University Press, 1980), pp. 1–20.

3. I cannot think of anyone who has more eloquently expressed this notion of theatrical presence, this collaboration during a production among playwright,

actor, and audience, than Thomas R. Whitaker, in talking about our mutual theatrical presence in Tom Stoppard's *Rosencrantz and Guildenstern Are Dead.* See his *Tom Stoppard* (New York: Grove Press, 1983), pp. 62–67. The subtitle of the conclusions is the line of Antipholus of Syracuse in *The Comedy of Errors* (5.1.377). I should also mention here two excellent recent studies on the relation between Shakespeare's spectacle (his visual theater) and the text of his plays: David Bevington, *Action Is Eloquence: Shakespeare's Language of Gesture* (Cambridge, Mass.: Harvard University Press, 1984); and Alan C. Dessen, *Elizabethan Stage Conventions and Modern Interpreters* (Cambridge: At the University Press, 1984).

While this book was in production, I received a copy of Bert States's *Great Reckonings in Little Rooms: On the Phenomenology of Theater* (Berkeley: University of California Press, 1985). In his own way, and marvelously so, he treats the basic subjects of my own work: the function of the audience, the nature of theatrical presence, and the relation between the actor's craft and his or her portrait of a fictive character. If States's book arrived a little too late for my present effort, I know that I will find it a treasure house for the near future.

Index

Numbers preceded by the symbol # refer to items in the *"See also"* sections of the Notes